INTRODUCING

A COURSE
IN MIRACLES

Scripture from Resurrected Man

Discourses with

MASTER TEACHER

ENDEAVOR ACADEMY
Certum Est Quia Impossibile Est

©2010 Endeavor Academy
Introducing A Course In Miracles: *Scripture From Resurrected Man*
Discourses with Master Teacher

International Standard Book Number (ISBN-10): 1-890648-03-5
                                          (ISBN-13): 978-1-890648-03-9

Library of Congress Control Number: 2010940198

Published By:
Endeavor Academy
501 East Adams Street, Wisconsin Dells, WI 53965, USA
Phone: +1 608-253-1447
www.themasterteacher.tv
Email: publishing@endeavoracademy.com

Contents

Why wait for Heaven?
Those who seek the light
are merely covering their eyes.
The light is in them now.
Enlightenment is but a recognition,
not a change at all.
Light is not of the world,
yet you who bear the light in you
are alien here as well.
The light came with you from your native home,
and stayed with you because it is your own.
It is the only thing you bring with you
from Him Who is your Source.
It shines in you because it lights your home,
and leads you back to where it came from
and you are at home.

A Course In Miracles
Scripture from Resurrected Man

This is the illuminate process going on for a lot of you now, isn't it? A lot of you are having very lovely revelation. This is what *A Course In Miracles* is; it brings about, through experience, the realization of God. That's what you are doing. You are doing *A Course In Miracles*. You are having the experience of reality for the first time. The teaching is that if you can't get it now, you won't be able to get it later, will you? So what good is that possibly going to do you? No good! This is a course in the transformation of the mind, not the observation of the transformation. This course now, as we are going to present it to you today, is for the rapidly-maturing mind through the auspices of Jesus Christ. This is the teaching of the metamorphosis of man coming from his chaotic perceptual associations to the realization of His universal wholeness in love. Is that so? Is that what has happened to you? Where does the verification for this occur? Here on earth? No! Now we are into the teaching. This cannot be verified here because there is no evidence of divine love present in perceptual defensive associations. That is a fact.

You guys are hearing this very plainly. What is then necessary for the perceptual mind to come to the realization of singularity? Transformation! Staying out of *A Course In Miracles* for just a moment, the whole dilemma of human consciousness, of perceptual mind is what? The need to know what you are — the need to know what this is, to seek within your associate consciousness the peace and the happiness and the joy and the love that you feel inherently a part of; that is what you are. And seek it you must! And find it you must, reasonably, if you seek it. From a very reasonable standpoint, if you were to look at it, why it is that you could seek something and not find it? But if you carry that a step further, teaching singularity, how is it that you don't know it? Could you, in fact, search for something that you don't already know? No! Not reasonably. This is the teaching of Shankara, this is the declaration of singularity. It is the single assertion that separation cannot be real because finally there must a single, whole beingness — a universal condition of reality. It makes absolutely no difference what you call that. Of course not, what difference does it make? That's God!

Now you will bring, inevitably, your idea of God; God is an idea because mind is the idea or mechanism of the assertion of creative capacity which is inherent in the creative whole structure of universal consciousness. You can not *not* create because that is what you are. But here is the dilemma: consciousness must still be singular. The idea of separate things communicating does not make sense in the reasoning process. This is a fact, not using *A Course In Miracles*. All they would be able to do would be to judge themselves in their perceptual associations with themselves. Obviously, separate things would have to have, reasonably, different sources. Now, somewhere, reasonably, there could be an idea of different sources, but how are they different? If they are different, they must be in fundamental conflict with each other. It is impossible that this be so. You cannot break off a piece of the whole and have a whole. This is the premise of the teachings of Jesus Christ in *A Course In Miracles* because it is simply the premise of all whole-mindedness. This can not *not* be so. This is singularity. It is not really open to question. It is the ontological assertion of a human being that there is ultimately a whole, divine relationship with himself in accordance with his perceptual principles of harmony. He has to know that — and he does know it. Not only does he know it, but he shares it.

Here is the direction we will take: from an illuminate mind, from this mind, which is illuminate, the *Course In Miracles*, Jesus Christ, which is illuminate, we will direct you in the manner in which you may make application of your perceptual relationships to the determination of your whole self as God or truth created you. That's *A Course In Miracles*. What we are going to do is construct *A Course In Miracles* reasonably within a statement of whole time, as it declares, without the necessity for an historic frame of reference, with the declaration that it is happening to you now, with the assertion that it requires the transformation of your mind, and with the declaration that there is, all around you, evidence of that transformation if you are willing to seek it and make allowances for it in your own perceptual associations. Got it? That's what has happened to a lot of you.

This is what, then? The miracle of your awakening! Now, where are the difficulties with this? Where is the real difficulty? It is the assertion of the necessity for the perceptual mind to undergo a revision, a metamorphosis or a transformation, in order to come to truth. This must be rigorously denied by the perceptual mind itself, which is in a configuration with its own reality. It is not tolerable to perceptual mind that finally there is a single, whole creative effort. You think it is. But it is not! I'm going to tell you a couple of assertions from my whole mind that will direct you: first, to what the *Course* is; second, to how the perceptual mind resists *A Course In Miracles* as a fundamental principle of its defense of itself; third, to the ordeal that you must undergo in presenting this; fourth, to the hardware connected to the spiritual wholeness of your assertion — the mystical revelation that can come to you through the admission of the truth of your whole self.

There is a little *Out of Time* booklet that we put together sometime ago that says this. First, a definition of *A Course In Miracles*: *It is important to remember that A Course In Miracles is a direct communication from God, through Jesus Christ indicating the apparent conditional situation between God and man which is one of false separation, and to the manner in which that apparent schism is and was repaired. Its sole purpose is to bring enlightenment through the transformation of your mind.* You may use this as a definitive statement of the *Course In Miracles*. This is a true statement of what the *Course* is. This is what it says it is, this is what you know it is, this is the process that you underwent to determine that it was so. It is impossible that not be so, because I am telling you this is what it is. This is what it says it is. I am going to spend a little time disallowing your perceptual observations of the *Course*. Why? The *Course In Miracles* is a course in disallowing all of your perceptual relationships. It has nothing to do with your stating what the *Course* is or isn't; your established mind is in a fundamental denial of this, isn't it? This is what we are going to declare. How are we going to do it? We are going to make this statement to you reasonably. This statement has nothing to do particularly with *A Course In Miracles*, but it does have to do with the dilemma of consciousness — perceptual mind — trying to identify itself. This is the problem: *Let's look at A Course In Miracles as an effect of supra-consciousness.* Just for a minute, look at it as coming from out of time. Did it come from out of time? Yes, sure! Where did it come from? A consciousness identified as Jesus Christ of Nazareth who is in my total framework of memory of the *Course*. *That is, with Jesus Christ as its true*

Causation. The acceptance or admission that A Course In Miracles originated from an absolutely unearthly source — that is, wasn't written here, was written in an alien place, did not come from earth, came from a star, came from somewhere outside of what you are deriving here in your consciousness association — *that A Course In Miracles originated from an absolutely unearthly source, while it appears simple, is the single most difficult barrier to enlightenment the immature consciousness faces.* Why? *No matter how overwhelmingly predominant the evidence both in method of origination and in content that this is indeed so, the assertion is finally inevitably an act of faith.* It must be. *You must remember that human conceptual consciousness is explicitly formulated in a self-perpetuating structure of thought that denies singularity. Nothing could be more devastating to the dualistic mind construct, that is limited perceptual reality, than the realization that A Course In Miracles is indeed not of this world but actually Truth speaking to falsity. In other words, God-man speaking to man!*

I am going to sit here before you, and I am going to tell you that is what *A Course In Miracles* is. Or it is no-thing! That is the direction that we want you to take with this statement of the *Course*. What else does this say? That you are afraid of it! That somewhere within you, you are very fearful of the idea of total authority. This is the act of faith. The simple question would be, if there is a total authority, why wouldn't it be loving and beautiful? What is your concern about letting God be? Obviously you are very concerned about it. Why is it that something you don't know about is a threat to you? That is the way Jesus would say it. Here is where many of you have progressed to: *Many have discovered that being frightened to death of A Course In Miracles is a perfectly natural and necessary beginning of the metamorphosis of self awareness. As the transformation to whole mind progresses they discover in happy amazement that they've*

*really been dead all along and are only being 'frightened
to life." For indeed it was death that they treasured and life
that they feared. Welcome home!* That's kind of nice stuff,
isn't it? Who wrote that?

Some of you new whole minds that begin to express
yourself in the illumination of your mind, where you are not
nuts anymore, will be surprised how you will begin to take *A
Course In Miracles* — I don't know how many of you read
Chapter One last night, Chapter One is incredible. It is so
incredible that it is totally beyond anything you could ever
believe. You don't believe it. The whole method in which it
came in is totally and absolutely impossible and beyond belief.
That's why it is a miracle! If you can structure it in your own
mind, it does not then require what? The transformation of your
perceptual mind to see that it is true! All you are going to do
is what? Deny the miracle.

I'm going to tell you one of the problems that you guys
have faced. With this new association of thought energy, you
are going to be more ready to make the declarations of Jesus
Christ, that is, the declaration that death is impossible. Here it
is: *You must face your fear of an uncompromising spiritual
commitment.* This is well-contained within the *Course*. The
descriptions of your determination to find this in your spirit,
and how you will be attacked by your own perceptual realities
about this, and how you will use your perceptual realities —
apparent realities — to deny your own Reality. And you will use
all of the defense mechanisms that you have constructed in your
perceptual limited time associations to keep you from going
through this process. That is what you have been doing. What's
happened to you now? You are losing your fear! You are finding
authentication through the miracle of your own mind in the
reassociation of the dedication of the wholeness of this spiritual
commitment. You have found a Church of Full Endeavor: A
purpose for life, a purpose for existence, a purpose for being

here, a reality of you! It's exciting. *You must face your fear of an uncompromising spiritual commitment. You must finally deal with the inevitable disbelief, derision, denial and attack that eventually confront your uncompromising assertion of the impossibility of death.* You are not going to be allowed to teach eternal life here. If you think you are, try it. Fortunately, eternity is true! Fortunately, reality is on your side. Fortunately, the direction of the *Course* is to subjective reality with the declaration that you are only confronting yourself in the association with the necessity for you to deny yourself. Herein is your relief from the necessity of your defense of your associate formulations. This is the teaching of Jesus Christ in the Sermon on the Mount, flat out, the uncompromising assertion that if you resist evil, you will be resisting something that is apparently outside of yourself, that can confront you, separate from your own whole mind associations, and that you cannot know that until you forgive, that is, until you literally lay down your own perceptual associations. *When you feel the incredible freedom of an unqualified commitment to a Single Truth you'll laugh at the absurd self-constructed obstacles that have kept you from your own enlightenment.* That is a fact. You couldn't care less what anyone else says to you. What do you care? Is there someone here who is going to determine for you perceptually what God really is, and what you have to do to find that? That's just crazy. You'll have no intention of doing that.

Where are we now? We are at the admission of the necessity for the transformation of your mind using the mechanisms of your mind in the relinquishment of the necessity for you to predetermine who you are. This is the *Course In Miracles*. It is a very simple statement that truth or wholeness *and* evil or separation cannot exist. One is not so. Either you are perfect, wholly in Heaven, or you are no-thing. Literally, the demand is that you see that this is no-thing, that it has no source, that it comes from nowhere. Those of you who have undergone these recent experiences of a search for who you are, and "search you must" as Jesus says, you came here trying to figure out who you are, have reached the conclusion that you can't know — yet you apparently do. You don't know where you came from, you don't know how you got here, you don't know who you are, and you wonder why you are in fear about it.

I want to deal with the reasonableness of the *Course* for just another moment before I get into Chapter 1. I know this doesn't seem possible, but because of the religious vernacular in *A Course In Miracles*, there are a lot of so-called rational eclectic minds, that is, Socratic minds, that can't get past the vernacular to see the wholeness of what this teaches. This is what I want your minds to do. You are not going to be caught up in the doctrinal necessity for the historic definition of Jesus Christ. This is not what we are concerned about. Our declaration to you, as you are observing in your own enlightenment, is that cause and effect are not apart. When I say: "Jesus Christ wrote the *Course In Miracles*"that has absolutely nothing to do — and I know you are aware of this — with what your perceptual observation of Jesus Christ is historically. Nothing! Why? Your perceptions are false. Jesus Christ wrote *A Course In Miracles* because He says so. You somehow want to work in the hyperbole association of relative truth. That's absurd. The *Course In Miracles* is true. The cause of it is true, and the effect of it is true. Now, here is the problem with that from what you would call a religious standpoint. This is the great debate of singularity. This is the statement of theology that man must involve himself — this is the Aquinas statement, this is the statement that is always fought over in theology — that the perceptual mind must involve itself with its own salvation. It is a statement that God knows about this, and is participating in the event of the resurrection. That is established Christianity. It deals with the necessity to associate good and evil. You must deal with the premise that the things that you love, which are true and whole to you, get sick and old and die through the authentication of the earth in association with a true God. Okay, now, a true statement is the antithesis of that.

A *Course In Miracles*, or the statement of Jesus Christ resurrected, is that earth and Heaven have nothing to do at all with each other, that your kingdom is not of the earth, that you are not from here, that this has nothing at all to do with reality. Here is what you run into, I want you to hear this so that the theologians can study their own resistance to this. *All religious philosophy must be deemed 'heretical,"* that is denied in a church relationship, *that does not include the continuing necessity for the participation of man in his own salvation.* In other words, if Jesus Christ says to you, "If you will believe me, you'll be in Heaven," which is a statement of absolute truth, that has to be denied by established religion, and it is denied. I broke that down for you, so you could see it. Listen to me, this is why the heretics were burned at the stake. I'm going to let you see this, because it will be very evident to you why this is not tolerated in the establishment of the earth. Listen: *All religious philosophy must be deemed 'heretical"that does not include the continuing necessity for the participation of man in his own salvation. The denial and relinquishment of all establishment and surrender of self as a requisite for eternal peace and happiness will always affront the human being's love/death relationship. Indeed it will often be termed blasphemy in the so-called religious community. In a temporal society, it is attacked as totally impractical and a dangerous threat to social order.* This is nice stuff. That is a fact. That's what this is. Where is the social order? In your mind. In time. That is what you are coming to know.

Those of you who are going to be doing the *Course* for the first time, I want to give you a definition of GUILT. Jesus probably uses the word GUILT more than virtually any other word in the *Course*. I am going to define GUILT for you so you won't have the idea that somehow GUILT is associated with acts of sinfulness. GUILT is actually the idea that you can think separately from God. That's guilt, isn't it? Guilt is nothing but responsibility for your own thoughts. Perception is inherently guilty of its misconstructions. Now I'll read it to you: *It must be understood that when we speak of "Guilt" we are speaking of it in its absolutely inevitable sense, not guilt in the sense of regret or wrong or the committing of sinful acts. The human mind suffers from the guilt of associated ideas. Perceptual mind is inevitably responsible for itself. Guilt is only and totally the assumption of the responsibility of identity through conceptual thought, or as Jesus says 'the attempted usurping of the Kingdom of God."* Guilt is the distance between cause and effect. Time is a chance to feel guilty. Guilt is time. Guilt is judgment. Judgment is guilt. Both are an assault on the Whole, and deny the Single Realty. Have you got that? So what you really share, then, is a perceptual denial of God, a denial of the whole truth. Isn't this nice? This is going to open up a whole new avenue for discussions of what *A Course In Miracles* is.

In *A Course In Miracles* we are going to be dealing with the hardware of spirituality. This is a statement that, as a human consciousness contained within a body, you can become a divine realization and still be contained within the apparent earth. This will be a statement that there finally is no difference between what you call a particle and a wave, that there is no difference between the thickness of your self conception and the reality of you in association with yourself. This is what this will say: *Contrary to what limited perceptual mind believes, there is nothing abstract about enlightened mind. Whole mind is in no way representational. It does not have thoughts but rather is the thought.* What is happening to your new minds is, instead of having associate perceptual thoughts, you are beginning to create. A lot of you guys are beginning to express yourselves from your whole new perceptual association, with your whole new self identity, which Jesus calls "true perception." How does perceptual mind observe you when you do that? It can only observe you with its own perceptual relationship with you. It can't see whole mind; perhaps it can see its constancy. Perhaps it can look at the results of its denial of whole mind. But finally, it must come to that through its own revelation. But first it is going to have to deal with the hardware. This is a resurrected body. That's a fact. Good. If this is just a dream, you must take this dream body and make it whole in your dream association. Listen: *It does not have thoughts but rather is the thought. It is exactly what it says. An enlightened human mind is momentarily an embodiment of reality. We are trying to teach you through continuing miraculous occurrences that by not supporting relationalship associations of your projected imagery, the image will become whole and all inclusive unto itself. The very highest form of enlightened thought is A Course In Miracles. While by necessity written in a perceptual mode, it is an incredible assertion of inclusive immediacy. It is itself a totality rather than a statement of the possibility of wholeness.* This is what you are, and this is what you are doing here. Isn't that amazing that this then becomes philosophy, and it is religion? In a moment it is going to have to become science, isn't it? It is going to have to teach quantum reality. It is going to have to teach away from Newtonian or objective physics. Is that all in the *Course In Miracles?* Sure. Two more and we'll be out of here.

Miracle working defined: Here is the dilemma that you have: the *Course In Miracles* teaches that all judgment is false, yet you must judge in order to relinquish your judgment. Isn't that so? It teaches you to decide not to decide. Why? Then the miracle will happen. The moment that you don't make a perceptual decision to project from you your own false reality, that is, bring the past of you into here, what will happen? The miracle! When I get to the definitions of what a miracle is, this will be very evident to you. Incidentally, I will read you the Principles of Miracles. The reason that there are fifty of them is that it is very difficult to define what a miracle is. It seems very simple, but it is not, because the miracle is an all-inclusive statement. If you begin to define a miracle, you would say, "God's truth is a miracle." Okay. Now the principles I will read to you will be two things; first the principle that it is true, and then the principles of the manner in which you come to it. That's why there are fifty of them. What it does is sort of surround it, so you can work from the certainty that the miracle is God creating, and that you are the obstacle to that. But the necessity is for the negation of your judgmental thought association because your judgment is inherently based on antecedent thoughts in time that have no reality. Listen. This is for real nice minds. Listen to this: *Any judgment to determine the whole truth is always only ultimately a devaluation of the judgmental process.* The more you know, the less you know. The more singular you then become in your intent to find the truth. Why? Truth is very simple. How do you do it? With a confrontation with your own mind in regard to what you really are. That is what we are getting you to do. This is *A Course In Miracles! Since all judgment is false* — obviously why would it be necessary to judge anything? If God is whole and true, why are you required to have perceptual thoughts and hold a resistance to this in the tension of your own time associations? All judgment is false. All judgment is only to hold you in the bondage of time, isn't it? All right. But how are we going to do that? *Since all judgment is false, the necessary use of it to arrive at true perception includes the devaluation of the judgmental process through the continuing admission of total ignorance.* This is the *Workbook* of the *Course.* "I don't know what anything is." "I don't know who I am." Oh, now I know. Why? I didn't pre-judge my associations. These are the first twenty lessons of the *Course. Jesus Christ's A Course In Miracles is divinely devastating in its assertion of the falsity of its own communicative devices*—it literally denies itself in the first chapter. It says that we are dealing with an impossible situation — the idea that you could actually be separated from God. I'll read that again and maybe you can see what this says. It's absolutely devastating. The whole basis of it is that it gives it to you, and then it takes it away from you. It allows you to think about it, and then gives you the tough guy, and says why don't you look at yourself again? Why don't you see really what you are undergoing in the transformation? *A Course In Miracles is divinely devastating in its assertion of the falsity of its own communicative devices and to the necessity for inclusion of previously disconnected ideas of the mind brought to harmony through unqualified forgiveness, that is non-judgment and unconditional love. The result must be in-depth connections of previously intentionally alienated thought forms that leads to the incredible experience of illuminated mind. Welcome home!* That's what you are doing. You are letting go of your grievances. All of the things that brought you into this situation of the necessity for you to maintain your identity are being relinquished by you. This is the *Course In Miracles.* This is what it teaches, and this is all that it teaches. It doesn't teach anything but this. Where do you want to hear this? I don't know. How much pain are you in in your associations with yourself? That will determine it. One more, then I'll stop:

Death is an impossible reaction to the single event of creation. Creation is only action. Reaction to truth is impossible. Death is an interpretation of Life. But life, interpreted by death, is meaningless. Creation is not an interpretive function. It is not God defining Himself, but rather God being Himself. Conceptual mind requires a definitive truth by which to identify itself and maintain its sense of reality. There is no logical reason why truth need be identified. That is why conceptual thought is fundamentally illogical (unreasonable). The reasonable conclusion that conceptual thought is inherently conflictual and that defining truth is denying truth is simply the highest reach of the dialectic process. This is the conclusion of necessity to the awakening mind. It now can make a choice to stop denying its source of wholeness by refusing to give credence to its perceptual associations.

Eternity is reached by a disassociation from time. Time is nothing more than the conceptual distance between cause and effect. I'm thinking that, that's going to happen. *Coming from time to eternity then is only the practice of bringing cause and effect together. The Workbook of A Course In Miracles provides uncompromising discipline in the technique of disassociational thinking, to bring about a literal transformation of your perceptual mind. It is a passionate assertion of the insanity of conceptual thought, which is what the earth is, in its denial of a single whole truth (or God).*

Now, you say to me: how did I ever get into this? How come, now, here we sit, how come here, now, you, a human being on the planet earth, suddenly find yourself sitting in this room in a place called Denver in a state called Colorado on a planet earth in a galaxy, in whole association with your own mind. This is what we want to bring you to now, isn't it? What are we going to tell you? In time, at any moment, you can decide to utilize your perceptual associations through the administering of God, or wholeness, contained within you, at the end of this time association, to make the declaration that you are whole and that truth and love and Heaven is all around you. Okay. That is a fact. That is what we want you to do. How is this going to come about in you? It is going to come about in you because you are in the process of discovering it is true. It has nothing to do with time at all. It is a statement that, obviously, if time is your invention, and it is the opposite of eternity, that time is not real. Right. Does everybody agree?

Now, the closest you can get to knowing time is not real would be a moment, wouldn't it? Doing what? Bringing your cause and your effect together. This moment, then. Is this moment what eternity is? It is as close as you can get to it. How about this moment? How about this one? Well, what moment isn't as close to eternity as you can get? None! Are all moments the same? Yes. There is only one. Do they contain all of the moments that you have structured in your thought form associations? Sure. Is it necessary for you to block off in your mind conceptual associations that have held you in the travesty of your own death association? Sure. That's the holy instants. Are they accumulating in you in the maturation of your body/mind association? Sure. That's the Course in Enlightenment. You are very fearful of hearing this because you want to be yourself and die of cancer. It's dumb. This is the *Course*. You are determined, somehow, to associate with this reality. You have the power of your mind to do that. You also have the power of your mind to be in God in Heaven. Why? Power of mind is singular. We are back to singularity again. There only is your mind, no matter what you may think about it. Finally, you don't think about it at all, you simply are it. This is the *Course In Miracles*. Who wrote the *Course In Miracles?* Jesus Christ of Nazareth. He says He wrote it. He wrote it. Where is He? In your mind, right here. Is He here now? Sure! Are we here now with Him? Sure! Is all of this just a construct of my perception? Sure! You are the one who is determined to separate your cause and effect and give identity to the illusion that is apparently outside of you, aren't you? Don't do that. There is no sense in doing that. There is no conflict going on here. Is that the healing process? How could it not be? How would you not then think wholly with your mind? The idea of a bodily containment that separates you from reality is not so.

Many of you are undergoing a lot of déja vu, that is, you are recreating in your mind a previous wholeness that you underwent. This will occur in the concepts of the Principles of Miracles. What you are doing, I think it will be there, is that you are changing temporal order. You are taking past associations and giving them future frames of reference. You are reversing your cause and effects. Everything that you've done in the past was actually done perfectly in the future. It has to have been. What you are doing is taking your mind from a future frame, which I am directing you to do, and this will be one of the concepts that occurs in the Principles. How did *A Course In Miracles* get here? You ordered it. It is a very definitive, well-laid-out plan in a segment of time, this time, to teach you to the enlightenment of your own mind. I want the establishment to quit fooling around with it. I know they are going to fool around with it, but those of you who really want to accept the premises of it (you can call that faith if you want to), are going to begin to experience the necessary realization of your own whole mind in the truth of this. That is what the miracle is. Obviously, God doesn't need miracles, does He? But you do, because you need the evidence of that reassociation of your mind.

If you stop and think about it, how could there be any greater miracle than the whole idea that somehow this thought form could be engendered out of time into a chaotic association of perception and sit here as a statement of reality? They kept it in a dresser drawer for a year. This is very fearful stuff! It finally came out because it got diluted enough so that the consciousnesses could misinterpret it — obviously since all of the misinterpretations are false. That was so we could get it published. Now there are seven hundred thousand copies of it, sitting around somewhere. The publishers won't mind what I am saying. They're going to sell another seven hundred thousand copies in about forty days. You might want to direct the publishers to stop making perceptual observations in the scripture of *A Course In Miracles*. Tell them you want a scriptural Course. You want a book that just says what it says. Obviously the additions of the perceptual interpretations of the

Course are absurd. That's what the falsity is. They won't mind. Obviously, they want to sell books. Listen, if you can get away with teaching *A Course In Miracles* as first person scripture, they will sell ten million copies. And did. Why? It's first person scripture! They are dealing with two thousand year old scripture, translated three times, clouded, and still coming through as a lot of truth, and that's the number one seller in the world. Can you imagine what happens to the mind that begins to accept this as actually being God speaking to man as scripture, as a risen man talking personally, first person, to you? That's a delightful idea! It's very frightening! We're in, though, right? We've got seven hundred thousand copies out. How many of the associate consciousnesses having to do with *A Course In Miracles* are going to deny and attack it? All of them! That's what you've always done is deny and attack this. That is the condition, we just told you, of your perceptual mind. It is not open to choice. All choice is the denial and attack on God. Remember, we already know we are dealing with an impossible situation. You immediately took the mechanisms of *A Course In Miracles* and taught the mechanism rather than what the *Course* says — automatically. You said, ha, ha, we trapped God, He gave us a choice in this. No, He didn't. He's dealing with the impossible idea that you can choose. So now you are building your groups around choice, which is absurd. It's senseless. It just becomes another establishment. Don't do that.

What is necessary for me to come to know that I am God? Undergo this transformation that you are undergoing. Does this have to do only with me in this dream? Yes, it does. Many of you, and I'm speaking in this room now, are undergoing very dramatic transformational shifts in your consciousness mind associations. You are beginning to form genius in your reassociations to declare your creative capacities. I know you're doing it. This is just the spreading of *A Course In Miracles* through the freedom of your own mind associations. We want to give you that. The basis of the *Course* is to give you full power of your own mind, to broaden in you your concepts of yourself to a final concept of your own whole self. That is what you are doing.

Now we are faced with an impossible thing. We are saying that on the planet earth a voice opened a channel from Heaven and said words into a conscious perceptual mind that had no real understanding of it, but was at a purpose in its own karma drama where it could truthfully transcribe these whole words that came out. I guess they're going to put up a statue to Helen, and I think that's lovely. But the necessity to identify the perceptual relationships, that is the scribe, with *A Course In Miracles,* is exactly the opposite of what *A Course In Miracles* teaches. It has nothing to do with personal identity. It is a statement on the very first page, the very first assertion: that the earth, that self-constructed fear, that death, do not exist. There is no sense in going any further with the *Course* unless you are going to at least fundamentally accept the premise. Why? Then you can begin to teach the *Course.* You must accept the premise first that truth is not here. Since truth is everywhere, this must be no where, because this is not true. Yet I am caught in my own untruth, and I am faced with the dilemma of escape. I want to be happy, but I can't find happiness here. I feel pain and sickness and death no matter what I do. I lose the things I love. This has prepared your perceptual mind for the admission of *A Course In Miracles.*

Listen to me, to the direct extent you have used up your own memories in regard to how you can solve this problem, you will listen to this. And to the direct extent you are determined to sit there and pretend that you can solve this problem within this limited association, you will deny this and literally not hear it. Why? Because your perceptual mind, which has defined the problem, immediately must solve the problem in its own mind. The problem cannot be outside of itself. It keeps finding the solution in time. There is no such thing as time, and in that sense the body really doesn't exist at all. It only thinks within its own cause and effect, declares itself to be real and stays within the tension of its own perceptual thoughts.

This is the answer: one problem, one solution. You are the problem; you can be the solution, because no problem cannot be inherently solved within the perceptual association of itself. The sole necessity is that you declare wholly that you are the problem. I put that on the front page of *Out of Time: The only thing I need to do for vision, happiness, release from pain and complete escape from sin to be in Heaven: I am responsible for what I see. I choose the feelings I experience, and I decide upon the goal I would achieve. And everything that seems to happen to me I ask for, and receive as I have asked.* Period! Now, you guys with new minds get very happy about that. You're going to test the spirit of that when you are attacked by your own thoughts that are sitting out there because you forgot you made them and you are going to defend yourself. That is the teaching of the *Workbook*, isn't it? Stop defending yourself from your own thoughts. That is the practice of forgiveness. But remember this, each time you don't defend yourself, the miracle literally occurs. It has to because just in that moment, which is all the time there is, you stopped your judgmental proceedings, lifted yourself out of time and became real! Why? Reality is all around you! That is what I am going to read you now. That is exactly what it is going to say in the preface to *A Course In Miracles*. It is going to say that! This is thrilling.

Can you imagine a voice, and it says "This is a course..." What? What? The "momensity" of this coming into this mind is an incredible idea. It was taped. It could be turned on or off. It was all done. Once it got organized — in the first four chapters there is a little necessity to identify word associations within the vernacular of the perceptual mind, but after that it falls into a real high association of truth — much like the mind that is talking to you now is doing. It will fall into that total reassociation of itself. Listen:

This is A Course In Miracles It is a required course. Literally, it doesn't have to do with the blue and gold book. It has to do with *A Course In Miracles* — a course from apparent death to life. It is a necessity. It is required that you do it. It is the only thing that is required. *Only the time you take it is voluntary.* Why? You are the denier of it You have established time to deny it, not to acknowledge it. You have invented time! The moment you decide to shorten time inestimably, you will be in Heaven. You simply will step out of time. Remember, though, that time is at your own disposal. That is what this says. *Free will* does not mean free to die, *does not mean that you can establish the curriculum.* You can't establish the necessity of coming from sickness and death to Life because the curriculum is all of you. This is very difficult for you perceptually to see. You cannot establish the curriculum because it includes all perceptual thought. Your establishment is the limitation of the curriculum. Do you understand me? You cannot establish the curriculum. *It means only that you can elect what you want to take at a given time.* Obviously, and that is what you are doing. I am asking you to elect to take the whole thing now! I am telling you from an enlightened association that you can do it through the miracle of your own disassociation from death. *The course does not aim at teaching the meaning of love...* Why? Love is its own meaning. *...for that is beyond what can be taught.* You can't teach love, it is what it is. *It does aim, however, at removing the blocks to the awareness of love's presence, which is your natural inheritance.* All perceptual mind is nothing but a block to the love of God or reality. You are that block. There is no other block but you. When you remove the obstacles of the necessity for your own miscreations, that is, to hold yourself separate from wholeness, you will be whole. Why? That's what you are! It is nothing but the relinquishment of your own thoughts, a removal of your own grievance, a letting go and letting God. A surrender. Wow! *The opposite of love is fear.* I'm afraid. I can't love, I'm afraid. You are going to attack me. I'll love you for a minute, but you are going to get me. You are afraid of God. ...*but what is all-encompassing can have no opposite.* What that says is that there is no such thing as fear. How could there be? What would be fearful? Is God fearful? Did He create you perfectly? How can you be fearful? What is it that you are afraid of? Can you be afraid of yourself? It doesn't make any sense.

This course can therefore be summed up very simply in this way:

Nothing real can be threatened. Because reality is God and it's whole and there is nothing to threaten it.
Nothing unreal exists.
When you are fearful, you are non-existent. I wrote that in there. Everybody should write that into their *Course.* We decided that would be a nice sentence to give you. Otherwise you will identify yourself as yourself, and say "I have fear" or "I am fearful." Do you see what you have done? "Well, the ego tells me not to be afraid." No! You can't have fear. When you are fearful, and you are here, you are FEAR! I am fear. Each moment I am fear. Not: I am having objective fearful thoughts that I will defend myself from. I'll have other things that I'm not afraid of. No! Perceptual mind is WHAT FEAR IS! Do you see it? How can fear love then, if it is in the tension of its own identity? It can express the passion of its miscreations, it can call it love, and it can hold it temporarily, but it must be disillusioned by its own mind. *When you are fearful, you are non-existent.* Where does the peace of God lie? Here! *Herein lies the peace of God.*

Fear is unreal. The earth is unreal. This cannot be so. If this is so, how could God be peaceful? Nobody will answer me. The nutty minds say: "Well, he is conflictual." That's all just nonsense. What are we going to have to do with this impossible situation? We are going to have to get you perceptually miracle-minded. We are going to have to get you to re-identify yourself in a broader range of consciousness identity. We are going to have to get you to undergo the metamorphosis that many of you are experiencing now, aren't you? Why? This is your whole mind construct. Everything around you is changing now as you change your mind. This is all contained in the *Course*.

Now we've got the book in front of us. Now we are going to just basically, before we get into the meat of this, give you the principles of what a miracle is. As I said earlier, it seems very simple, but it's really not. Why? A miracle, finally is only the admission of God, which was inevitable in time, and true in eternity. Finally, it is the revelation of whole mind, but it can be experienced in the holy instant, or the momentary vision of a reassociation of your mind to the ultimate revelation of yourself. You might want to look at this very simply. I am teaching you from revelation; so is *A Course In Miracles*. That's not really hard if you look at it that way That will cause holy instants in your own mental associations. It will cause you to be enlightened That's the basis of this teaching.

Principles of Miracles. Notice that it is plural. Notice that "miracles" is plural. Notice that it says that you must identify the power of your own mind with the capacity, as I just read you here, that everything is contained within your own mind and you have all power. We cannot teach you this by degrading your mind processes. You will not accept it. You cannot accept it because you are you! The principles of miracles will even contain the allowance for your working magic, won't it? It is going to say that you can take the power of your mind and direct it to momentary or temporal reassociations of your definitions of your own associate visions, that you can cause the elimination of a tumor in a consciousness; that you can teach the lame to walk. Of course, you can do that. But if you do that within a limited, temporal association of your own mind, the miracle cannot exceed the direction of your purpose of it. Do you see that? We are going to teach you to whole mindedness so that you see the miracle is only your whole mind coming to the truth by the denial of your perceptions, or the use of magic in your own mind, which is what you do.

1. There is no order of difficulty in miracles. One is not "harder" or "bigger" than another. They are all the same. All expressions of love are maximal. And a miracle is an expression of love. A miracle is looking at your brother for just a moment, and saying "I love you totally." Well, what happened when I said I loved you totally? I forgot to judge you. I didn't add something on: "because of this." I released my mind in an unconditional association with you to allow the miracle to occur. This is *A Course In Miracles*, for goodness sake. What happens? All expressions of love must be maximal. Why? God creating is what love is! You are a creator, aren't you? If you are going to create in perceptions, how will you do it? By seeing yourself wholly perceptual, by not denying your own creations, by not projecting from your mind and disassociating yourself from yourself. They are always maximal. That is to say, if anybody is sick, one sickness wouldn't be any different from another. He is only sick by your judgment. Any judgment of him is false. A bad cold is the same as death. It's not different. There aren't degrees to separation and sin. That is what this says — it is all maximal.

2. Miracles as such do not matter. Why would they? They are just definitions of the truth that must be inherent in you. The manner in which you work the miracle doesn't matter. The miracle that actually occurs makes absolutely no difference, does it? *The only thing that matters is their Source, Which is far beyond evaluation.* Why? It's God! Your attempts to evaluate it are your attempts to give explicit causes to your own mind and deny the final wholeness of you. Your trying to work the miracle denies the miracle. Jesus talks about this in the *Course*. He says now it's going to take a miracle to get you to be a miracle worker. You got so used to using the power of your own mind that you need a miracle — that's the devil, incidentally. You are determined to do that.

3. Miracles occur naturally as expressions of love. The real miracle is the love that inspires them. That's God. That's the truth. *In this sense, everything that comes from love is a miracle.* Why? It is a statement of the whole truth of you in your own mind. That's a miracle. You guys are working miracles by relinquishing your own thoughts about the consciousnesses around you. That's how the miracle works. Obviously the miracle is not going to work by your definition, is it? The miracle works by your non-definition. Wow! Isn't that amazing? Let go and let God.

4. All miracles mean life... Literally, you see life in the miracle. *...and God is the Giver of life. His Voice will direct you very specifically. You will be told all you need to know.* Why? Contained in every conceptual thought that you have is a whole reality! That is what that says. It is impossible that not be so because you are the power of God. It is you who organize the perceptual thoughts and associations. As you advance in this, when you have a thought that is of no value to you, it will just be thrown out of your equation. Some of you are experiencing that. You will lose your necessity to hold onto that perceptual evaluation. You will know exactly what to do.

5. Miracles are habits, and should be involuntary. They should not be under conscious control. Consciously selected miracles can be misguided. Why? You want a result within the power of your own mind. Can you do it? Yes. It doesn't say here that you can't do it, does it? It doesn't take away from you the power to say: Oh, no, I'm going to bring about a healing of that cancer so you can die of old age, or you can die of something else. Or: I'm going to use the power of my own mind to do it. No, no. It just asks you to look at yourself and how you are using that power. By saying that miracles are habits, the *Workbook* teaches you to look again all the time. As your mind progresses in that, you become non-judgmental so that when you enter into a situation on earth, you enter into it and keep your mouth shut. You enter onto the stage and don't immediately present the results of your own mind to the situation. What happens? The situation changes. What you brought to the situation is all that can be. That is the habit you should evolve. Why?

6. *Miracles are natural. When they do not occur something has gone wrong.* And that something is your determination to establish your own reality. The miracle works fully all the time. Why? You are the obstacle to that in your perceptual mind. Isn't that something?

7. *Miracles are everyone's right...* because they are the right of a whole mind, *...but purification is necessary first.* You have to do what? In your own body associations examine the defense mechanisms that you have used to establish your limited reality. Miracles will not work unless you forgive. They can't. If there is a sin or sickness outside of you, that you are not the cause of, the miracle obviously won't work because it is not under the control of your own mind. That is a fact.

8. *Miracles are healing because they supply a lack;* and you are lacking here. *...they are performed by those who temporarily have more for those who temporarily have less.* That is a fact. This coming to peace and serenity that you are undergoing in your mind will be a great assistance to the thought forms that are in your chaotic association. The peace that you are feeling in the miracle of your mind is literally communicative. The consciousnesses that will come around you will suddenly begin to feel real good because you have brought about in their mind a change in who they are

through your non-resistance of your association with them in the falsity. You are establishing Godly or holy relationships with each other. Isn't that lovely?

9. *Miracles are a kind of exchange.* Why? They need to be acknowledged. The moment you would acknowledge your brother as a whole living Son of God, you will become that, because he is a reflection of your mind. Yes, that is so, I will have that wholly. *Like all expressions of love, which are always miraculous in the true sense, the exchange reverses the physical laws. They bring more love both to the giver and the receiver.* Physical laws demand that you keep separate from each other and identify yourself through the separation of each other. A miracle says, "No we are only as God created us wholly. I will not judge you in my own mind and you must change because I have changed my mind about myself and subsequently about you." It is impossible that that not be so. Later on it is going to ask if it is necessary that consciousness acknowledge you. No. That's why we need so many of these concepts, so that you can see that. What do they do? *They bring more love both to the giver and the receiver.* Actually they bring the acknowledgment that you can only give to yourself. The miracle, then, becomes nothing more than your total giving, which is your determination not to hold onto your own perceptual associations in defense of the things that are outside of you. That is the perfect miracle: God only gives. God only creates.

10. *The use of miracles as spectacles to induce belief is a misunderstanding of their purpose.* Obviously, that's the magic of it, isn't it? Can you do that? Sure. Can you authenticate the power of your mind? Yes. But not to the full power of it; that cannot be authenticated. You can do much more than you pretend to. You can do everything. Moving mountains is the least you can do. You are always being tempted by the devil, aren't you? You undergo this enlightenment occasion,

you are baptized by John, you have a little enlightenment and you are immediately tempted by the devil to use that power in the limitation. This is Jesus in the desert for forty days, with the devil saying, "Throw yourself off the pinnacle, let God save you." All of the things you are tempted to use this power of your mind for, and always have been. You are constantly succumbing to the temptation of your own attraction for death, your own need to remain temporal in the association with reality. That's all the devil is.

11. Prayer is the medium of miracles. Isn't that something — "the medium." It would have to be, if God is apparently outside of you. You ask for help: "I can't deal with this situation, help me." Do you get the help? Yes, to the direct extent you do not need the situation to verify your own sickness and death, you will get it. Most of you have been very fearful of the healing. You do not want the healing to occur, and had the healing occurred, you would have been more fearful in your reassociations. Can you hear this? This is in the *Course*. You really don't want to be healed totally, and that's what the problem obviously is. *Prayer is the medium of miracles. It is a means of communication of the created with the Creator.* This is the declaration that there is a God, and God says: you are my Son. *Through prayer love is received, and through miracles love is expressed.* Isn't that nice? This is exactly the same thing as saying: I can't, God will if I'll let Him. It is exactly what that is. God, you can do it, I can't. I then release my associate identities with the necessity for me to act in my own mind. What happens? The miracle. I get out of the driver's seat — that's how we used to teach this. Let go and let God. That's the whole teaching, isn't it? That's the miracle.

12. Miracles are thoughts. Thoughts can represent the lower or bodily level of experience, or the higher or spiritual level of experience. One makes the physical, and the other creates the spiritual. You listen to me. In that sense, you are working the miracle of spiritual identification. Since miracle is what? Thought! A miracle really is the utilization of God creating because that's what your whole mind is. You can take that power and express it as a miracle in the reassociations with the physical rather than a declaration that the physical is totally spiritual, and you can come to that wholeness. One literally makes the physical. The power that you use in your perceptual mind to hold onto your self identity is an extraordinary thing, guys. The lengths that you will go to, to retain sickness and pain and death! Do you see it? This is in the *Course*, it talks about it. You are going to use every single power at your disposal, and all power is at your disposal, to retain this retention of time. This has nothing to do with how you got into it, or where you think you are. This is a statement of how your mind works here, isn't it?

13. Miracles are both beginnings and endings, and so they alter the temporal order. This is what I told you earlier. This is a statement that somewhere in time you are whole. You have to be because you are coming to that wholeness. This says that the temporal order is altered so that the future can influence the past, rather than the past influence the future. Since you never knew this before, we must allow for a further sequencing of your mind later on in your time associations so that the miracle can be performed. That's what we are doing, isn't it? We are changing your perceptual associations within the direction of time, literally. That is what is happening. Remember last night? I told you how much further along you are in time. That is a miracle! *Miracles are both beginnings and endings...* they are the beginning and the end of it. They are the idea of the possibility of separation, and the resolution of it occurring simultaneously, just for that moment, so you can be whole. *They are always affirmations of rebirth, which seem to go back but really go forward. They undo the past in the present, and thus release the future.* This is an incredible statement of your own whole mind. This is a statement of the quantum leap. This is the capacity for you to bring into the situation all of the judgments that you have constructed to prevent you from seeing your own wholeness and simply letting them go, and letting the miracle happen. Isn't that something.

14. Miracles bear witness to truth. They are convincing because they arise from conviction. If you are not sure in your own mind, you can't do this. Remember that we are teaching wholeness of mind. If you use miracles without conviction, they will deteriorate into misconceptions. They can not *not.* Is that what this says? Yes. *Without conviction they deteriorate into magic, which is mindless and therefore destructive; or rather, the uncreative use of mind* which you can very likely do. You are then going to construct something that is idolistic to you. It becomes an idol that you worship in your own thought form association. It is an idea of love. It is an idea of happiness. It is a new car that you got by a miracle. It is all of the associations of the idolatry of your own mind to satisfy yourself in your limited association. What does Jesus call that? He calls it destructive, then He corrects it because there is no such thing as destruction and says it is *the uncreative use of mind.*

15. Each day should be devoted to miracles. The purpose of time is to enable you to learn how to use time constructively. It is thus a teaching device and a means to an end. Time will cease when it is no longer useful in facilitating learning. That is what is happening to a lot of you now. Time is going to end for you because you have used up all of your previous thought form associations. You are not going to use the power of your own mind to work the magic of your denial of God. Do you see? Isn't that something?

16. Miracles are teaching devices for demonstrating it is as blessed to give as to receive. They simultaneously increase the strength of the giver and supply strength to the receiver.

The total miracle is nothing but I am looking at you and saying: God is! Boom! What did we share? A single, whole assertion that we were created whole, that we cannot be separate from each other. That is the miracle of whole mindedness. That is what you are undergoing. *They simultaneously,* at the moment of happening, *increase the strength of the giver and supply strength to the receiver.*

17. Miracles transcend the body. They are sudden shifts into invisibility, away from the bodily level. That is why they heal. The body cannot heal itself because the body in itself has no thinking devices. The body is what? Only your own thought. When you think of the body invisibly, you disassociate from the thought that called the sickness, and the healing is automatic in your reassociation. It is the teaching that you don't look at somebody else's liver and say, "Brother, you've got cirrhosis, I'm going to bring about a change in your cirrhosis." It is the denial of the possibility of the body being unwhole unto itself, or existing outside of your thought form. This causes the miracle to occur automatically. That's what I do. All you new whole minded consciousnesses will see that you are working miracles all the time, that you are causing this to come about through the extension of your own love, the extension of your own mind. That is going on here. Are you the savior of the world? Yes. You created the world. So you are in time within this segment just to change your mind about it. That's the miracle. Is it going to be observed? Very possibly. Need it be observed? Not necessarily. We talked about this, didn't we? You will have the one final big miracle, and that is the reassertion of you as a creator, of God, as being whole. *That is why they heal.*

18. A miracle is a service. In the sense that it is a healing process or a rendering of a total giving in your mind. It is a service of the necessity for God to serve because that is what He is. It is the declaration of a perceptual mind that I will give to you my wholeness in the certainty I can solve your problem if you will let me. It is not directed to the problem and then shared. In that sense, it is a total giving to your brother. It is a declaration of your love for him, which has to bring about the miracle. *It is the maximal service you can render to another. It is a way of loving your neighbor as yourself. You recognize your own and your neighbor's worth simultaneously.* Love the Lord thy God with all thy heart, and with all thy soul, and with all thy mind... and love thy neighbour as thyself. (Matthew 22:37-39) That is the only direction Jesus Christ of Nazareth ever gave. That is His doctrine — one hundred percent! Why? You must love your own creations because you are created in love.

19. Miracles make minds one in God. That's what we just said. Isn't that amazing? *They depend on cooperation because the Sonship is the sum of all that God created. Miracles therefore reflect the laws of eternity, not of time.* What is hard for you to see is that when you get up into your new high thought associations, you actually have perceptions changing all around you, all the time, every moment. This new situation that you find yourself in at this moment is nothing like the situation (if you want to look at yesterday), that you had engendered in how you were going to construct yourself. You are in an entirely different frame of reference. Can you hear this? That is the miracle of the atonement — the shortening of time. Obviously, the more that you will teach you have no alternative to this, the more you will come whole. Isn't that so? You have no alternative to this! *Miracles make minds one in God. They depend on cooperation because the Sonship is the sum of all that God created. Miracles therefore reflect the laws of eternity, not of time.* Notice that it says *reflect*. Notice it says it is the bringing together of your conceptual thoughts into a total harmony non-conflictual association, which is what time was. When the thoughts come together, you think from the eternal aspect. That is what you are doing with your whole minds. Isn't that nice?

20. Miracles reawaken the awareness that the spirit, not the body, is the altar of truth. This is the recognition that leads to the healing power of the miracle. This is: I am as God created me. This is: I am not a body, I am free, I am still whole, I am in a dream, I will not look at this this way, I have the power to change my mind through the relinquishment of this association. Wow!

21. Miracles are natural signs of forgiveness. Through miracles you accept God's forgiveness by extending it to others. Forgiveness means giving before. It is a time idea, that I have given all before. I am not holding onto a grievance and bringing it into the present. Therefore, everything I see is perfect unto itself. Do you see that? It can not *not* be so. That is a miracle worker.

22. Miracles are associated with fear only because of the belief that darkness can hide. You actually think that you can get down in the darkness and keep yourself from being whole. You are finally very afraid of the miracle because you think you can instruct yourself in your own limited definition of yourself. In that sense, the miracle to you is death. Why? It would be the loss of your perceptions. Do you see? And you are very fearful of doing that. *You believe that what your physical eyes cannot see does not exist. This leads to a denial of spiritual sight.* And doggone it, guys, all of the academic teachings are that if I can't see it perceptually, I won't believe it. The mind that does not question its perceptual associations, that is, does not demand to know where it came from, is simply going to continue to identify itself within its own limited associate thought forms. The miracle then is being denied by that consciousness. He is going to remain in that association of conflict and death. Remember what I told you on the first page: he is not real — and neither are you if you do that! You don't know where you came from, you don't know how you got there, your dependence on that is Adam counting the animals. That is the idea that somehow you can take these thoughts that are here and bring them together in association that is going to make sense in your mind. That is impossible. No matter how many of these thoughts you bring together, they have no source! You can't take partial stuff and make it whole through assembling the parts. You can't do it. You must see that all parts contain the whole.

23. Miracles rearrange perception (Oh my goodness!) *and place all levels in true perspective. This is healing because sickness comes from confusing the levels.* At any one moment you think you can die and hold onto the attention of being sick or separated from God. The release of that, even for one moment, is a maturation of your whole mind that is inevitable in the process of evolution. You have an idea of a perfect mind constructed in you. It must be, then, that any time you can go to that; at any moment you can step out of time. That is the miracle. Just for that moment.

24. Miracles enable you to heal the sick and raise the dead... because you thought they were dead in your mind, *because you made sickness and death yourself, and can therefore abolish both. You are a miracle, capable of creating in the likeness of your Creator.* You are that because it is God's will that you be that. You cannot be anything else because there is not anything else. It is not open to a discussion of what you think that is or what anything else is. You can not *not* be that because that's what everything is. Obviously, then, your perceptual judgment of it cannot be true. *You are a miracle, capable of creating in the likeness of your Creator. Everything else is your own nightmare, and does not exist.* That is the first sentence in the *Course.* This does not exist. *Only the creations of light are real.* Isn't that lovely? Only the creations of light harmony, that is associations of truth, are real because even in perception they are reflections of that truth. That's how you become the living Son of God. You wonder how there can be multiple living Sons of God, because perception does vary, but wholeness does not. Therefore, whole perception will be whole unto itself. You won't judge a brother although he can bring to you all the dramatic demonstrations of his wholeness. What difference does that make if he is whole? You call that talent and think you can only utilize part of it. I tell you it is potential fulfilled, and that you will create perfectly in your mind and I will define that as whole because wholeness does not require a definition. It is only a statement of your own mind as to what you are, isn't it? Who is there to judge that? No one. I want to give you the freedom of your miracle mind, so that you will stop trying to define it in a limited fashion. Everything you do is a miracle because you are miracle mind if you will allow it to be, and won't judge it through your own perceptual limitation.

25. Here is where we are going to talk about this segment of time. *Miracles are part of an interlocking chain of forgiveness which, when completed, is the Atonement.* This is the admission of the possibility of completion. That is what it says. *Atonement works all the time and in all the dimensions of time.* I took it away from you. I gave you the idea of the miracle, then told you it is working all the time, that it just worked now, that you are in Heaven, that you are gone from here. Can you do this now? That's the miracle. That's why this is *A Course In Miracles*. It doesn't have anything to do with your mother-in-law. It doesn't have to do with practicing identities. Come on, cut it out. I want this to go to all the groups in the world. If we are going to do *A Course In Miracles*, let's do it! It doesn't have anything to do with groups. Will the groups formulate into the single atonement of dedicated minds to this? The atonement is nothing but your whole commitment to it. Does it occur? Simultaneously with your commitment, which is what the miracle is. Which is the subtraction of your perception. Infinite patience brings immediate results. Of course, how could it not. Why? You didn't let time get involved

in it. You didn't say: I'm going to find God if it takes a hundred years. You just said: I'm going to find God! It has nothing to do with time. That's eternity. If you try to define God in time, He won't be there. You'll always fail. Why? Your time will run out. This is the whole idea of statistical possibility. Everything is true by the possibility of it, unless you set a time limit — then it won't occur. Otherwise it is bound to occur. When did it occur? When you thought of it. This is sort of an interesting way to look at undoing. *Atonement works all the time and in all dimensions of time.* Why? Time is space. I don't want you to get away from the nine dimensional association of your mind. If time is variant speeds, it contains simultaneously in adjuncts of consciousness relationships within a framework of total time. Jesus calls this the continuity of time. You can move dimensionally anywhere you want in your whole mind using the nine dimensions of time, which are the Father, the Son and the Holy Spirit — three dimensional, plus time. Nine dimensional is that each one — Father, Son and Spirit — contains the other two. That's the nine dimensions of time. The tenth dimension is time itself, or the whole association. They have arrived at this, incidentally, in physics, but I don't think they'd like the idea that it's the trinity. I'm not sure that they're going to arrive at the certainty that everything in perceptual mind is expressed in three. That's coming into death, being there, and getting out. That's descending into hell for three days, isn't it? Otherwise, you would have no time line. Otherwise, you would be a single point. This is the expression of the new string theory of the relationship of particle and wave, that the universe finally has to be a string, that is, it has to have some dimension, which indeed it does. The point would be everything and would eliminate space/ time all together. Do you see that? I know you do. Boy you guys are something.

26. *Miracles represent freedom from fear.* *"Atoning" means "undoing".* It means "don't do; undo." You are always

"doing" with your mind. *The undoing of fear is an essential part of the Atonement value of miracles.* Since you are always doing fear, undo it. Be unreal here.

27. *A miracle is a universal blessing from God through me to all my brothers. It is the privilege of the forgiven to forgive.* It is my statement to you that I am honored to serve you. It is my statement to you that I realize fully your dilemma and that I realize fully the solution. Now, if I didn't realize your dilemma, I couldn't be a savior. So I come into a perceptual association, I represent you later on in your own time associations and declare to you that you are saved and out of time. That is the miracle of your mind when you accept that. What are you accepting? Your own mind's projections as coming into a whole association with you. Jesus uses the first person here. It is perfectly proper for you, as an awakened mind, to declare the "I" of *A Course In Miracles* as you, because I assure you that it is. If you need to use Jesus as a frame of reference, for goodness sake, use it. But let it be real. That is the requirement. If the resurrection in fact occurred, it had to be you, and that's what He'll tell you. That's what He tells you in the first and second chapters of the *Course*, that you are undergoing the passion, the rebirth, the Second Coming. That's you. *It is the privilege of the forgiven to forgive.*

28. *Miracles are a way of earning release from fear.* That is an astonishing idea. I'll explain it. *Revelation induces a state in which fear has already been abolished.* That's where I am teaching from. *Miracles are thus a means and revelation is an end.* They are finally the same thing, aren't they? A revelatory mind can teach to the vision of the miracle. Not only that, but it can teach you that you can earn miracles by using what you call holy instants to accumulate the glory of the reassociation that you are coming into. Many of you that are undergoing revelation now are just accumulative miracle associations — whole mindedness.

29. Miracles praise God through you. They praise Him by honoring His creations, affirming their perfection. They heal because they deny body-identification and affirm spirit-identification. God created me. I am not body.

30. By recognizing spirit, miracles adjust the levels of perception and show them in proper alignment. This places spirit at the center, where it can communicate directly. This is the astonishing idea that you are undergoing a maturation of your mind. This is the admission, if you wanted to look at it in the hierarchy of consciousnesses — the idea of the evolution of consciousness through the mineral, through the vegetable, through your mind becoming whole, finally adjusting to a true perception through a recognition of your splitness from reality which is what the human condition is — a very temporary condition, isn't it?

31. Miracles should inspire gratitude, not awe. There will be enough time for awe. *You should thank God for what you really are. The children of God are holy and the miracle honors their holiness, which can be hidden but never lost.*

32. I inspire all miracles. This is the statement of the atonement principle. This is the statement of you as a savior. Why? You created the world, you can inspire the miracle in your own time sequencing if you choose. *I inspire all miracles, which are really intercessions. They intercede for your holiness and make your perceptions holy* (or whole). *By placing you beyond the physical laws they raise you into the sphere of celestial order. In this order you are perfect.* Celestial order is all associate perception brought to reality. It is a mandala of thought forms expressing themselves wholly at the moment of truth. In Christianity they're described as principalities, as thrones, as angels — which are the thoughts of that association. They have a perfect order, and are dedicated in time to the extension from their mind of the wholeness of their association. As above, so below. As within, so without. Every thought you are having contains the wholeness of it. There are consciousnesses here that are working miracle associations in limited perceptions, did you know that? There are angels all around here. They are fulfilling the function of their whole mindedness in thought/time association. They are all around you. I told somebody one time that the highest thought consciousness runs an elevator at McCormick Place in Chicago. I know him real well. He is doing exactly what he wants to do. He's an angel. He is totally whole unto himself. How valuable is he? Just exactly as valuable as he needs to be. The miracle is you fulfilling the function of your own mind. That can come into a unity identification, but it cannot escape all of consciousness, can it? That is what you have decided not to do — try to escape your own thoughts. Why? The universe is going on right here, all of it! What a miracle! *...they raise you into the sphere of celestial order. In this order you are perfect.*

33. Miracles honor you because you are lovable. They dispel illusions about yourself and perceive the light in you. They thus atone for your errors by freeing you from your nightmares. By releasing your mind from the imprisonment of your illusions, they restore your sanity.

34. Miracles restore the mind to its fullness. By atoning for lack they establish perfect protection. Why? The innocent cannot be threatened. *The spirit's strength leaves no room for intrusions.* You literally become whole minded, and there is nothing outside of yourself to attack you. You have closed the gap between your cause and effect. There is no room for fear to intercede. This is the teaching of the death experience, incidentally. You have looked at death and overcome it, so now that veil is parted and each moment you are dead-alive. There is no distance between your thoughts — that's called the holy instant. The miracle mind conception is wholly, instantaneously whole. In that sense, it dies and is alive. The holy instant is you going through a death, in time, and then reassociating yourself at a later range of time. I am teaching you to undergo continual death processes. Does everybody hear this? Why? This is a death place. Death-life, death-life. This is what you are afraid to do. Those of you who are no longer afraid of miracles have simply parted the veil. You aren't threatened by your own forms that you have projected out to hold you in this death association. Isn't that amazing?! *The spirit's strength leaves no room for intrusions.*

35. *Miracles are expressions of love, but they may not always have observable effects.* I'm sorry. That's the way it is. They can only effect to the direct extent your previous associations are willing to accept them. That's testing the spirit, isn't it? That is the declaration that God is with me, I know this works perfectly, despite my determination to get a result from my own thoughts. It is the necessity to get a result from my own thoughts that has held me in the limitation of this. Listen to me — it is working maximally all the time. Well, you say, I tried it and it didn't work. The hell it didn't. It worked perfectly.

36. *Miracles are examples of right thinking, aligning your perceptions with truth as God created it,* bringing you together in time.

37. *A miracle is a correction introduced into false thinking by me. It acts as a catalyst, breaking up erroneous perception and reorganizing it properly. This places you under the Atonement principle, where perception is healed. Until this has occurred, knowledge of the Divine Order is impossible.* This is nothing but a statement of the necessity for the transformation of your mind. That is the whole teaching. Until you undergo this change, knowledge is impossible. Divine Order is impossible because some part of you is going to be held in the sickness and death.

38. The Holy Spirit is the mechanism of miracles. It is an illusion, but it is the mechanism of a perfect identity of you with yourself. *He recognizes both God's creations and your illusions. He separates the true from the false by His ability to perceive totally rather than selectively.* You are nothing whole-mindedly but an unselective memory. You are an imprint of the totalness of your own mind coming to the truth — that's the Spirit. It is totally abstract in its thinking. No matter what thought you give it, it will use it in the totalness of the reassociation with your own mind. That's what the Holy Spirit is.

39. The miracle dissolves error — relinquishes it, turns it to light — *because the Holy Spirit identifies error as false or unreal. This is the same as saying that by perceiving light, darkness automatically disappears.* You can't hold the separation of your perceptual thoughts.

40. The miracle acknowledges everyone as your brother and mine. It is a way of perceiving the universal mark or light of God.

41. Wholeness is the perceptual content of miracles. They thus correct, or atone for, the faulty perception of lack. Or the idea that somehow you could be missing something in your own whole self.

42. A major contribution of miracles is their strength in releasing you from your false sense of isolation, deprivation and lack.

43. Miracles arise from a miraculous state of mind, or a state of miracle-readiness which is forgiveness, which is non-judgment.

44. The miracle is an expression of an inner awareness of Christ and the acceptance of His Atonement.

45. Are you ready for this? *A miracle is never lost.* It can't be, because an idea never leaves its source. *It may touch many people you have not even met, and produce undreamed of changes in situations of which you are not even aware* and have no idea of. They are finally an expression of your own Universal Mind. They are a statement that I am Universal Consciousness, and everything I do will be used to correct this chaotic association.

46. *The Holy Spirit is the highest communication medium. Miracles do not involve this type of communication, because they are temporary communication devices.* Are you ready? This is what is happening to you guys. *When you return to your original form of communication with God by direct revelation, the need for miracles is over.* That is what we are bringing about in you. That's what it is time for you to do, isn't it? That's what you are doing.

47. *The miracle is a learning device that lessens the need for time. It establishes an out-of-pattern time interval not under the usual laws of time. In this sense it is timeless.* It is just like you are going to step out of time. All of the things that all of your thoughts previously had projected into a future relationship come together. All of the time that you had constructed to work through all of the difficulties of your need to re-identify in this chaotic association are brought into one bright light of that association of you. That is what is happening to you.

48. *The miracle is the only device at your immediate disposal for controlling time. Only revelation transcends it, having nothing to do with time at all.* The miracle and the revelation are the cause and the effect in whichever way you look at them. I will give you the revelation so that you can become miracle minded and be revealed. Or you can be the miracle worker and become revealed. But finally, they will be the same thing. We used to call one a God-man and the other a man-God. One is a direct insertion from out of time, the other is the coming from time to God. One is the atonement principle

— a God-man is the atonement principle, the correction that occurred simultaneously with the event of the schism. A man-God is a man who remembers that he was God. He remembers from a time situation his own wholeness. Are they both the same thing? At the moment of revelation, they are singular. But the method may appear to be separate. An out of time may suddenly occur in time as a bright spot in that reassociation of the necessity of you. Why? You are under the atonement principle. If you now surround yourself with this light, this later date in time, you will relieve the necessity for you to go through more death experiences. What are you going to do? Go through the death experience now. The heck with it. I'm not going to wait to die. I've been defending myself. I'm simply going to die and be whole. That's what you are doing.

49. The miracle makes no distinction among degrees of misperception. It is a device for perception-correction, effective quite apart from either the degree or the direction of the error. This is its true indiscriminateness.

50. The miracle compares what you have made with creation, accepting what is in accord with it as true, and rejecting what is out of accord as false. The power of your mind to be in harmony! The power of your mind, the admission that you are created whole in your own mind!

The next four pages in the text, titled *Revelation, Time and Miracles,* are incredible. They are very beautiful declarations from Jesus to you. That's what's happened to you now.

It's too hot in here? All adjustments are to death. I used to teach it that way. I gave up trying to teach that. We used to teach, "don't adjust." Stop making demands of change on your environment. Your determination to identify yourself in environment is what is keeping you here. Every time you feel uncomfortable, you correct it. It never stops. That ends up being a teaching of sacrifice or "I better stay uncomfortable because..." Well, that's not what I mean. Obviously everything you do is nothing but adjustment to hold your mind in your own limited association. That, not incidentally, includes: I am hot; I am cold; I am passionate; I hate; I love. And everything that you do. I am teaching you not to adjust. I can't demonstrate it to you because it's not demonstrable. It is in your own mind. I don't identify with my body. Sometimes the people will say to me, "You've been standing up for six hours, you'd better sit down." It really doesn't occur to me. And that includes "It's too hot in here." And I go, "Wow, is it ever hot in here." At that point, if I want to adjust to it, I am perfectly able to make the adjustment. It's too late for me to make the assertion — I've thought of it. Thinking it's too hot is the same as adjustment. Can you hear it when I teach it that way? Your mind is so caught in sitting on your own butt in a chair in a body. "I'm getting hungry. What time is lunch?" — this is all you are doing in time, constantly. I am telling you it is nothing. If you don't want to make the dedication to this, get out of here. I am trying to show you that this is the time that you did it.

You keep falling back into time by your determination to identify yourself with this. This is much too tough a teaching for you. I can't help it, it's true. Your perceptual mind holds you in the bondage, doesn't it?

Well, you say, don't we need to be Martha some of the time? Should we just be Mary all of the time? When Martha is in the kitchen banging pots making lunch for the disciples, Mary the sister is in there worshiping God/truth, and Martha says hey why don't you come out here and help me with these good works? Jesus says, leave her alone. Why? Mary is undergoing a transformation of her mind, which is a necessity. (Luke 10:38-42) It is the old teaching that good works will avail you nothing because you have placed a limited definition on yourself of what constitutes "good." Obviously, then the good works will avail you nothing because they are definitions of spiritual pride or reassociations with your determination to define what salvation is. Will good works avail you? Totally! I will tell you to do only good works! What are works? Giving. Give totally. I just read you, that is the honor of the work of your mind. It is that you define the works that holds you in the bondage. Do I work? That's all I do. This is the working of the miracle, isn't it? People like to break it down and say we've got to worship God. Well, worship Him totally and you'll work the miracle of the good works — or what? You won't be here! If you are here, you must work the miracle of your whole mind, because if you are here, you are by definition a savior of the world. You constructed the world. You are here. You have what? Assumed the burden of the world. "Come to me ye who are heavy laden and I will give you rest." Because I know this world isn't real. If you will trust me completely, my burden is light. Do you hear me?

What you guys try to do as unhealed healers, bless your hearts, is you take on all the burdens of the world and die with them, because you attempt to heal them in your limited associations. You love them. You want to do something about it. And you finally just die in the attempt. I am showing you that you can take on the burdens of the world and release them through the release of your necessity to identify them in their limitation by the declaration of your miracle mind that they are in fact whole because your mind is whole. That's a miracle mind — not defining the sickness out there and then trying to take on the burden of it. You can do that. And it will get very burdensome to you. But finally what you are doing is serving man rather than God. You are determined in your perceptual mind that you can alleviate the pain that is apparently outside of you without the admission that you are the cause of the pain. If you are the cause of the pain, it cannot be alleviated by changing the effects. You must change the cause of it in your own mind, and that's a service to God, not to man.

Jesus, when He defines empathy, says you don't know what empathy is. Empathy is a total recognition of our Godliness, not an association of a falsity in an attempt to heal the sick through your own sick mind. Do you feel the pain of your brother? You must feel the pain of your brother in order to be a savior. The necessity for Saviorship is to feel your brother's pain totally. That is a fact. As long as you reject your brother's pain from you, you can't feel the pain of your own mind. This is my direct teaching to you: I can't stand this place. I could not stand not being able to heal the pain of my brother. Come on, you healers. Everybody comes into your office for treatment — all of this dedication that you have has been an attempt to help this situation come to a truth, to a harmony, because you love them. I am telling you that love is total. If you will recognize that you are the cause of this, it will bring about a healing in your own mind that will heal your associations. This can not *not* be so.

Am I doing this from revelation? If you can't tell I'm doing this from revelation, go away. You've been going away from this for so long, finally I am declaring to you that this is a funnel of light that has come into the apparent schism association in your own dream, telling you that you can escape your dream. How could you not do it? Did you see the consciousnesses get up and walk out of here? Did you see how fearful that was to them? How many more of you are going to be afraid to do this? Do you see what's happened? You are so identified with your own fear, that if you really want to look at it, you are afraid of this message. Why? The things you love must die. The things you love must associate with you in fear, because you have created them to establish your reality based on temporal time. This is a threat to you. It is the only threat you have: fear of God. Isn't that silly? Don't be afraid.

Where is the miracle? Right here. When is it going on? Right now. Who is going to work it? You are. How are you going to do it? You will notice that the fifty concepts of the miracles were the five W's and the H or how will be what I read you. When we did this, we took the perceptual mind which is Who, What, Where, When and Why. If you add the H, which is the How, that becomes the *Text* and the *Workbook*. That is why I took fifty concepts to do this for you. When you go back and do the concepts, you will see that it contains all of these elements: Who is it that has to do it? Why do you have to do it? When will you do it? What do you have to do? They will all be there. Now, did that help you define in your own mind what a miracle is? I don't know. But this is a course in what? The enlightenment of you. This is a course in the necessity of the maturing of a limited association through an evolutionary or revolutionary process in time to the recognition that you are whole mind and God. I am not concerned with the vernacular, I am not concerned with how you teach it.

But, very obviously, there is something at a borderland just out of time called Jesus Christ of Nazareth, that is here and out of time, that has directed you in your own dream to do this. If that takes a little faith and acceptance, what have you got to lose? Do you have to run out now and say "Jesus Christ's new scripture has taught me this, and I'm going to..." No, you don't have to do it, but I would suggest that somewhere within you now, utilizing this energy, you begin to read this from the source that it is coming from. If you will do that, you will begin to undergo the miracle change of your own mind. Will it be conflictual? To the extent it need be conflictual, it will be, because your mind is fundamentally in conflict. All I am directing you to is to undergo whatever conflict is necessary for you to come to this truth. I am trying to take sacrifice out of it because sacrifice doesn't work. You have a tendency to lean on sacrifice. When I told you a couple thousand years ago, blessed are you who are persecuted in my name, you took that as a means to hold onto your limited identity. So we sort of took that out of this. But I understand that you may experience this in sacrifice. Why? All lack is sacrifice. You are defined as a sacrifice. The first covenant, the idea of cause and effect, is a sacrificial association with limitation, isn't it? The new covenant of Jesus Christ is the teaching only of love and that reciprocity or exchange or limitation is impossible. We had to have the first covenant, or the idea of self identity, in order to pass from that to the reality of your mind. Do you see that? This is the new covenant of Jesus Christ. It's that simple. Not "an eye for an eye", but a statement of "give to your brother wholly"; not an exchange of any sort in your own mind — not the Old Testament; the New Testament! Is the Old Testament necessary to this? Of course. Otherwise how do you know that you have a problem? You need to know you have a conflict in your own mind in that moment of time when you came to the truth. That's what is happening to you.

Use the power of your mind in the declaration of your wholeness, and the result will be wholeness. If you use it in the magic of your mind, which a lot of you guys are doing, the result can only be what you direct it to be. There is a lovely sentence in the *Course* where it says literally that the result cannot exceed the perceptual thought about it. Why? They're together. That's why the moment you change your mind about yourself, the result changes totally. Don't judge your brother in this regard; you will be wrong. This condition is total, ultrapersonal psychology. It has absolutely nothing to do with transpersonal. There is nothing transpersonal about it. There is no such thing as "trans," except to yourself. The idea that you have to undergo this alone may cause you a little fear and pain at first. But remember you've always been alone, and you know it. This is what has caused all of your loneliness, all of your fear — all of that has been your inability to communicate. I am telling you that communication is impossible because you have designed your mind not to communicate and you are basing your reality on your determination not to! How can you then do it? That's what perception is — objective reality

— different thoughts, something outside of my mind. A different thing thinking differently than I am. That's crazy! That is not so. That consciousness is only what I think it is.

Some of you say: I'm going to go away and I'm not going to do this. That's funny to me. Where are you going to go? You are not real. You forgot that I just told you that you are not real to me. You are insisting that I give you reality so you identify me. You're not real to me. You can't go away. You have nowhere to go. You are the unknowing coming to the knowing. Whenever you do that will be now. Do you think there is an earth when I leave here? That's nonsense. There is no possibility that this will be here when I'm gone. I know that somehow you like a dead savior (the stuff that I just read which is real nice). Some of you can hardly wait until I die so you can say, "Wow, was that ever good; too bad he's not here anymore, we had a lot to learn from him." All you are doing is associating life with death. That is not so. Jesus Christ, the living Son of God is here or He is no where! He is not coming back from the dead! I am not come back from the dead! I am telling you there is no death! You got it. You look lovely. I don't mean to be so dramatic. You are beautiful.

Communication is only with the mind. What really happens in here is you guys are communicating non-perceptually, in Spirit, with me. As soon as you quit defining each other, you begin to love. It is not objective; it is just a statement of how passionate you feel about yourself. You just feel good. You come around this energy and you'll start to feel real good. I want to encourage you that it is okay to feel real good. If you keep feeling good, and don't try to define a reason why you feel good, you will feel perfectly, because there is no reason why you feel good. You can't have happiness. You can only be happy. You can't have emotions, you can only be them. When you are happy, you are happy for no reason at all, if you are totally happy, because there is no reason for happiness. It is a condition of whole mind.

This is your resurrection. The associations of *A Course In Miracles,* extended realities, are thrilled at the idea that the *Course* is going to be taught. You have an idea that you're already in Heaven. You can feel it if you would like to. This is the whole Christ principle of two thousand years. This is the Easter. This is all of the persecutions, the Spanish Inquisitions, and all of the other things that you have done with your attack are being asserted by Master Jesus here in this gathering. The heretic returning home — his determination to seek, through his own transformation, the reality — the Christian, we call him. The Christian. Born again. The tomb is empty. Welcome home! The miracle is happening to you!

How much will you be attacked for teaching this? Not too much. You're teaching love and forgiveness. It's pretty hard to attack you for that. They may think you are crazy for making a spiritual commitment. But what do you care? You think this is a crazy place where people get sick and die. They'll let you go. Just love and be whole. It will work fine. Welcome home. It was all false. None of it was real. It's called parting the veil. All you had to do is reach out your arm, like Jesus says, and it just parts and you are free. You have been a slave to yourself. You have been bound by your own thoughts. Now you are simply going to say, "No more." No more! Enough of this journey, I'm coming home. Come on home. *A Course In Miracles.* At last, the experience. The veil parts. Good for you. This is your contact, now. There are a lot of changes going on in time right now for many of you. This is the miracle of your revealing. This is what you will present to the world, if you decide to stay. You have become real, now. You look magnificent, beautiful, just beautiful. There is light all around you. See how lovely that is? Once you experience the Great Rays, as Jesus would say, you will never be the same. This is what the whole teaching is about, isn't it, the experience of the transformation. Without that, there was nothing. With this, there is everything. Good for you! At last. The fabric of time is torn. It is revealed. The stone is rolled back. You are risen.

This schedule is determined by you, isn't it? Scary. There's got to be something wrong with this. No, just in your mind. You have to be a little careful when it's fearful to people. You get very frightened of this. But you don't have to be afraid. This isn't going to hurt you. This is love. And you are very fearful of love. You need to identify it, do you see. You go: "What's this about?" It is very difficult for you simply to experience a release. In fact, it's immoral. There is a defense mechanism that makes you unable... When love really comes close to you, you defend yourself from it. You place yourself in limited associations of defense. We are trying to break that barrier of perception so that you can see that you are love. That's what's happening. Will you get it? Oh, sure. We just would not like to have to have you go through some more death experiences. Why get cancer to prove that you can do it this way again? These consciousnesses are undergoing death experiences. There is just no fear connected to it. They get to the veil, and instead of withdrawing from it, they release! In that sense, this is a little practice, isn't it. As Jesus would say, we stand here just a moment. You are very fearful of this point, because this is the point of death to you, rather than life. Do you see? It is exactly the opposite of what you think it is. If you look up, you will be released to life because you are in death. To you, it's the opposite. You are afraid if you release that, that you will be abandoned, you will lose yourself. You won't. These are sentences right from Master Jesus. You will be found! Why? Because truth is all around you. This was our whole lesson, wasn't it?

You've restricted that in your own mind. That's why it is individual. It doesn't have anything to do with the associations. You guys are looking right at me. You are looking at your own projected thought in truth rather than resistance. How can I give you back more than you want reflected back to you? I can't. You're holding it. I'll give you a shiny mirror. That's what a savior does. All a savior really does is give you an abstract association with yourself. You are the one that demands judgment through your own perceptual associations. When you release that, you go to light automatically, don't you? You become one-eyed, don't you? This is the Holy Spirit, the Ajna Chakra, the awakening of that light in you. If your eye offends you, pluck it out. Don't let your left hand know what your right hand is doing. I like to use Jesus to do this, because He was right on the mark. He taught this directly to your own individual "know ye not ye must be born again." Jesus Christ's whole teaching is nothing but the transformation of body/mind. And he proves it, albeit dramatically. He says that in the *Course*: I proved it in a very dramatic fashion that there is no death. Not that you die somehow. There is no death! That's what you have discovered.

Can you be a part of this circle of atonement? This reordering of celestial thought, as Jesus puts it so beautifully. It is really me that is going to do this? Or is it somebody else? Do I have to wait for the savior to come? How can he come if I judge Him? He must be a projection of my own mind. How can the Second Coming be accomplished if He is outside of me? Need I see Him perfectly to be saved? Of course! Who is your savior, then? He is sitting next to you! Where did you think He was? Could He be anywhere but here, next to you? Does that require your relinquishment of your judgment? That's what I have been telling you. Are you determined to continue to judge each other and die together? Yes. Can you do that? Of course. Have you always done it? Certainly. You can't remember Heaven. I am here to remind you that It is very beautiful and very happy and very perfect. And you know it, because we are there together. That's where we are.

* * * * * * *

(Start of Afternoon Session)

The declaration this morning is a definitive connection for *A Course In Miracles* with you. You may safely use it in the world, and I think you will find that it can be fundamentally accepted into this new association in your dream. We are teaching the parting of the veil that you are experiencing. In a very true sense, then, this has become an experience for you. That is, a transformation of your body/mind declaration of yourself in the association with the world and the universe. This is important for you. Along with this declaration of wholeness from the Source of the Universe into the chaos.

When you present the teachings of physical reassociations, and deal with the fear of the overcoming of the notation of death — you will learn as you go out in the universe — you must address the associations of the limited consciousness that will occur in his definition of love and fear during his own transformation. Why? The experiences that you are having in this new association with Light or God are viewed from a temporal or perceptual association as "disease." Listen. It is very important that you bring this into your associations. The manifestations that you are undergoing that you consider to be beneficent in regard to your own awakening are, in fact, termed in the sociological, what you call, psychological sickness association of "mental health," to be a form of disease. There has been very little tolerance in Western Civilization for what used to be termed God intoxication — the mystic who runs through the street naked proclaiming "I have found it." The Holy Men of India who lie in their own excrement in the Calcutta train station and are revered by the people and allowed to be addressed as Holy Men. Why? They are having experiences — *schizophrenic,* if you will — *manic-depression,* if you demand or forms of serious *paranoia* — within the associations of their own minds. Those are the three associate disease ideas that will come during your own transformation. All of them occurred in this room this morning. That is perfectly all right. What we are going to say to you is this. And we want this understood. Consciousnesses in adolescence, for example, or most particularly adolescents that suffer from adolescent schizophrenia, that is, it occurs to them the futility of their existence. They reach a puberty, and very obviously they are being told by the adult, contrary to what they can see with their own eyes, that everything is going to be okay here, and that they can adjust to that association, while somewhere within their whole constitutional makeup, they are aware of the hopeless situation. That may very well manifest itself as a form of schizophrenia. I guess they are treating them; putting them in for thirty or sixty days now. In the old days, we went through this — this was considered to be some sort of romantic episode that we underwent. I want this understood very directly. If a consciousness is suffering from an apparent disease, he should be treated as though he is diseased. This is the problem that Christian Science had in the notation that you allow the disease to be there and then pretend that you are treating it with your mind. You can't do that. A consciousness who has withdrawn from the world and is standing on one leg on the twelfth floor of the Veteran's Hospital may very well have adjusted to society, but it is very difficult to communicate with him about the reality of the world. You thirty-year-olds go through these incredible agoraphobia associations, the super market panics, all the things that go with that age grouping, where you begin to see the futility of your own existence with a demand for the expansion of your associate consciousness. You are already caught in this incredible web of cause and effect that you can't escape from. You will be directed to a form of sedation that will relieve you of the necessity of undergoing the experience of enlightenment. Listen to me. This is the way it is. You are treated as having a Valium deficiency, or something. Don't catch me up in the idea that you don't take medication. If you have somebody who is in a condition of manic-depression, and virtually all of you are manic-depressives — if it has been recommended, for example, that he take a good drug like lithium, then it may be very necessary that he take it. It is not your position to recommend that he doesn't do that. Certainly you are going to recommend that he doesn't sedate himself in relationship to the escape of recreational drugs. Those are just defenses from his own self in relationship with his own death.

That being said, what is going on in this physical awakening is literally expressions of what appears to be mental disease, and is actually a reassociation of your own constitution to the true light that you are. Do you see that? Those of you who have all of your life suffered these intense mood swings, for no apparent reason. I can share this with you. The illuminate side of you, the stimulation of a particular glandular association, say in the endorphins, can very well bring about, and did bring about in you, this exaltation of reality that could not be sustained by the memory or genetic pattern of your associations, and caused inevitably a tumble into the depression of the impossibility of the associations with things that were going on in the world. Listen. Those of you who have had this, I'm very much aware of it. It is a sign of what? Expressed creative potential, where suddenly you begin to find in you this manic side of you, where you can express yourself beautifully — this is true of artists almost inevitably. Here is all of this lovely creative association coming to you, inevitably followed by a form of depression. Why? You found that no matter how much you expressed yourself, you could not release the total containment of you in the determination to be wholly expressive. YES! I know, I want to share this with you. That's why you are with me. Was that a form of manic depression? Absolutely, positively, I've deeply experienced this. Those of you who have been driving along in the car and been whistling and singing, and everything is just beautiful and the sun is shining, and you turn the corner and it goes huhmp, like that, and it is just hopeless. There is no way out of it, you might as well get rid of yourself. Cut your wrists. You can't stand it. That is an indication, if you'd like to see, of what you are doing now. The only difference is that you have been given the benefit of a later time association that is directing you that everything that you are undergoing is to the maturation or the completion of you, rather than the determination of perception to reduce your creative potential.

Schizophrenia goes without saying. The whole basis of *A Course In Miracles* is that you are a schizophrenic. You know perfectly well who you are, yet you deny it. So you are asking the question: Who am I? When obviously you must know. Yet, when the whole universe tries to tell you, you are very fearful about it, you attack it and continue to be split in your own mind. I think that's a good definition of a schizophrenic. When I was institutionalized — no I won't tell that story — you could see lovely schizophrenics that would say "I am the Christ." They are the Christ. The problem is not that. The problem was their incapacity, once again, to bring into this present time frame a total karma memory reassociation. They are in all different places in their time cycles. Do you see this? The guy is Napoleon, and everything else, because he is living other parts of himself that are parts of his memory package. You are schizophrenic. We are going to take that schizophrenia and instead of reducing you into a form of limited perception, we will direct you to the awakening whole You — the Holy Spirit, the bright light of you that has been trying to tell you: hey, it's okay, don't be afraid to part this veil and come into this association. This will be very valuable to you.

The third, the paranoia, is lovely. Those of you who experienced expanded consciousnesses very early in this were very much aware that somebody was always lurking around you. This is paranoia. If you turned your head quick enough, you could find him. He's right there. He's somewhere there. It is a form of intense foreboding that something is just about to happen to you. This is the opening, the premature opening, of a center of your reassociation that is not prepared to deal with the fear of what you would call your karma astral associations that have always threatened you, that you have used for protective devices. They will be all around you. The admonition now is to love them! Love them. They are everywhere. They are here. You look at them. Jesus teaches that you look at this terrible face; it is dripping blood — these are lovely sentences in the *Course* — and watch it change into the face of Christ as you release your determination to protect yourself from your own thoughts. What I want you to see now is that we are talking now of real experiences. This is not hypothetical. We are not presenting you with ideas of what a disease is, and what the relief is. We are directing you that you are dis-eased and can become eased totally through the relinquishment of this necessity to hold onto yourself in space/time.

I understand that the physical demonstration of a spiritual awakening is not tolerated by physical mind. Yet, unless you go through the experience, it is not possible for you to be enlightened. But remember, the last thing that perceptual mind wants is to have you complete your own transformative process. When the first man appeared among the baboons, the baboons obviously didn't know what to do. As you go through this continuing transformation to Gnostic man, to a whole mind, I assure you that Homo sapiens, which is the split mind, cannot tolerate that reassociation, because the indications of power of mind to split mind are always conflictual. Do you hear that? Inevitably they are that. "Power corrupts, and absolute power will corrupt absolutely." That's a totally insane, meaningless remark. Absolute power is God. The limited association is somebody who gathers power unto itself in statements of its capacity to exist and possess, and defends itself. If you undergo this experience, you are going to be judged as somehow having something superior to the other consciousness, and will be deemed a threat to it. This is why the savior is attacked and killed.

This is always the reason why the Philosophia Perennis, the ancient wisdom, has been called the secret wisdom. It isn't a secret to anyone in the universe that you are God creating. That is just a secret that you are keeping from yourself in your own dream association. Everyone in the universe knows that you are God; you are a creator of perfection, having been created perfectly. That is a statement of fact. You have come to accept that in your own mind, and are willing to take all of the manifestations of this physical maturation and make application to them by the confession of the certainty that you are going through this metamorphosis. I am giving you a statement of fact here. If I took it out of the religious association completely, I would declare to you that you are undergoing an evolutionary process to the certainty of whole mind, that you are emerging as a new species association with the direct capacity to communicate by mind rather than the necessity to communicate in physical splitness of perceptual mind. That is a statement of fact. That is the movement from limited consciousness, through the split mind, with the direction of its reassociations, to whole mind. This is all I teach. This occurs in all traditions, I don't care if you call it "from objective reality to quantum", or "Isis unveiled". Whatever — it will be what you are undergoing.

Is this a fearful thing for you? When you are in this association, you may very well begin to experience acute conditions of disorientation. Jesus in the *Course* says, don't be afraid of that. That will be okay. You step back, and you say: I am undergoing this. You may need to seek the solace of your closet. Come and be with God. A lot of you are feeling a need to withdraw from the world. Remember that we haven't given you a cloistered situation here. This is called the direct route. We have left you right in the middle of your own chaotic associations. Why? This is the way it has to finally be done. Why? The chaos is in your own mind! There is a personal association being demanded of you— this association with Jesus the man become God; the association with your brother as a man becoming God with you; (What a glorious undertaking. What a direct route!) — rather than using the mechanisms of your own mind to subtract yourself from yourself; rather than going from Western Christian historic associations into some sort of Eastern modality and attempting to find God in a mental "idolistic" arrangement outside of you. What nonsense! This is the teaching to know yourself, isn't it? You cannot know yourself by attempting to disassociate from what you have deemed the necessity to associate, but rather by including all of those thoughts in with what you are. That may be a little fearful for you. But remember, you are nothing but a bag of fear memory, as it is.

Some of you have undergone premature awakenings, and it has been very fearful. Some of you have done it with drugs. It won't work. You can't find relief for this except in the total reassociation of your memories. Is it a glandular undertaking? Yes. It is associated directly with your whole bodily functions. If you want to go the Menninger Clinic, or anywhere, and put yourself on an EEG machine now, and look at the brain waves with the things you are undergoing in your mind, they will suggest you get on *Dilantin* immediately. I guarantee you they will. Why? You are storming in your own brain associations. This has nothing to do with brain tumors or people who are telling me they are sick. This has to do with those of you who are having these experiences. Am I speaking from deep experience in this in my own awakening? YES. Very deep, of course. That is why I am able to talk to you about it. So, what have we done? We are going to come together and take all these ideas about the separation and simply bring them into our whole physical awakening.

This will be on the same talk as I gave on the necessity of the admission that Jesus Christ wrote *A Course In Miracles*. It doesn't seem that they are connected, but I assure you that they are directly connected. You, individually, in your physical association, are undergoing a resurrection of your body/mind into wholeness. You have been contained within a dream in space/time that is being brought together specifically for you to bring about this metamorphosis. You are doing it at this time, in this place. You will accomplish it within this framework of your reality dream because that is all that there is. So be grateful!

What am I going to do right now? What have we declared? We are going to take annihilation away from you. There is no death. Now, all the things that happen to you now will be applied to the certainty that God is with you and that there is nothing outside of you apparently that will not assist you in this endeavor if you will allow it to do so, because it is all a part of your mind. Those mind associations are just waiting for you to tell you that it is okay. They are calling on you to say: Jesus says in the *Course*, Son of God, your creations are waiting for you, the winds bow down to you. There are some lovely sentences in the *Course* where it says they are waiting for your creative mind to declare itself in the certainty that you are as God created you, that you are a whole mind. Don't be afraid. Don't be afraid. There is nothing to be afraid of. I understand that it is one thing to say, "Don't be afraid", and it is another to find yourself in fear. I understand that you will undergo experiences of fear which are associated with death and loss of self. I encourage you, when you come into those (I'm going to tell you how I used to do it), to fall into the fear. Do not attempt to address the fear that is being presented to you. You have made it objective. Fall to the bottom of you. "Father, into thy hands I commend my spirit" and the fear will leave you. You are so accustomed, in your own bottom associations to the conflictual associations of your own mind, that you have always heretofore refused simply to go to the very bottom of your association, which is nothing but death or the requirement of death to life. This has nothing to do with physical death in the sense that we are speaking of it. Do you understand when I am speaking of death, I am speaking of death of the limited association, not particularly the death of the physical body. What you are undergoing now is that death association to life. That's what is happening to you. Don't be afraid.

Will it come on you suddenly for no reason? It may. It has always been this way with you. Just about the time your ducks are in order, whappo. Why? There is a requirement of the disassociation of the limited you in regard to this. Do you see that? Jesus says in the *Course* — He doesn't even hesitate — He says every time you think you know, you will not learn. That is a direct sentence. Why? You have solved the problem of your associate mind, and are holding yourself in that tension of space/time that keeps you from releasing to the wholeness of you. That is what time is. How long will you do that? How long, O Holy Son of God, will you do that? I don't know.

But remember this requires from you, then, a bottom association or a death experience. Does that include, in your passion, "Father, why hast thou forsaken me?" Yes! Does that necessitate a dark night of the soul? I don't know. Does that necessitate a Gethsemane where everything seems to have deserted you, and yet you are in a determination to associate yourself with this salvation that is apparently something you can find outside of you? I don't know. How many times are you going to go through it? How many times are you going to replicate the action of the crucifixion which was the last useless thing that had to be done that was done by Jesus Christ of Nazareth? He says that in the *Course*. That was the last useless thing that had to be done, and I did it. Do not participate in your own resurrection, is all He really says. When He asks for help in the garden does He get it? No. Why? God can't hear Him. He goes off alone —

He's sitting here, He wants me to tell you... You guys know this story. He says: God, I would certainly appreciate it if you would take this cup away from me. (Matthew 26:36-44) I've gone this far with it. I've been working all these good miracles for you. I've done all these things. I've proven myself pretty well. And all of a sudden I'm here; give me a little hand, and let's get through this. Absolute silence. What's happened to His disciples? They've fallen asleep. He is standing all alone, this awakened mind. No one to appreciate His crucifixion, not God, not His disciples. Yet He seeks, somehow, for gratification of that association.

In the *Course* this is taught as being on the cutting edge, this is taught as being right in the middle. A newly-awakened Christ is described as God doesn't know anything about him, and his associates can't hear him. So he is caught in nothing for just a moment. I am very experienced with this. I am looking around for somebody who can hear this. It doesn't do any good to talk to God. I already know He knows it. Until you came along, I wasn't a savior. I just knew this wasn't real and was gone. You gave me the definition of a savior, just as I give you one now. But that isn't necessarily the case. Anyway, it is physical and when you know that, when these things begin to happen to you, you will accept them as part of the atonement, won't you? Will that necessitate your withdrawing from society? Perhaps. Will that necessitate you reassociating in your social inclinations? I don't know. Remember this, that the action itself is not important. Everything is only of the mind. You that are undergoing this, remember that whatever you decide in your mind is how it will be. The mechanism is of the mind, not in the act itself.

You can't really sacrifice in the sense that "I'm going to do this to get that result." The idea of doing it contains the result of it, doesn't it? You will experience phenomena, a lot of you. You will experience virtually everything in some of your awakenings in this reassociation of energy. We would encourage you to have that. But remember, finally, it is all "noumena" — it is all you! Can you walk on water? Sure. Can you levitate? Sure. May this be demonstrated? As Jesus says in the *Course*, you will be surprised by these things that are happening in your mind. Of course. But nothing compares with the surprise that's going on with you now. This is the sudden awakening to the certainty of your own atonement, to your own Christhood.

So, if the disease is real, treat it! When a consciousness in these groups that you're teaching says, what do we do with the murderers? What are we going to do with the incest? What are we going to do with these things that happen? Your response is: put them in jail. Your response is: counsel them and treat them. That consciousness has that identification in his mind. It is not going to avail you to direct him to some truth that he has no capacity to see. If you go out to teach this, they are going to demand to know from their own minds, what they are supposed to do about these specific terrible things. They are going to have to use their judgment in the association and fall into the covenant of reciprocity. You are not going to teach that mind. He is demanding that you answer to his own satisfaction why there is sickness, pain and death in the world. You must show him that he is the cause of it, but at that time, he is not aware that he is the cause of it. You advanced teachers are finding this out, aren't you? That will be necessary for you to test your spirit when you go out to try to teach the wholeness of your mind, won't it? You are going to start tomorrow reading *A Course In Miracles* like it is the truth. Why? It is the truth. And the more you declare it to be the truth, the more you will see that it is true. Many of you have seen that it is truth and have left and are gone. That's okay. When I cover the physical aspects, it pulls this energy association down. But I know that some of you in this room are going to experience, and are experiencing now perhaps, a twinge, or more than a twinge of fear in regard to what is happening to you.

Be assured that Christ Himself, God Himself, through this *Course*, through this declaration, has come into your mind to tell you that it is okay. Treat *A Course In Miracles* as what it is. It is a divine revelatory reassociation of your mind, and it will become that. It will become that if you allow it to be. Isn't that beautiful? You are becoming Children of the Light. The direction was, then, having covered physical awakening, to read a little more from the *Course*. Chapter 1 is very nice. But with this rediscovery of the *Course*, you will have places that you really love to read. You will discover that you are carrying it with you more than you ever did, and now that you know that it is not going to threaten you, you really begin to become fully attuned to this declaration. It is a marvelous communicative association.

Chapter 11 *(From Darkness to Light): When you are weary,* tired and discouraged, *remember that you have hurt yourself. Your Comforter will rest you, but you cannot. You do not know how, for if you did you could never have grown weary. Unless you hurt yourself you could never suffer in any way, for that is not God's Will for His Son. Pain is not of Him, for He knows no attack and His peace surrounds you silently. God is very quiet, for there is no conflict in Him. Conflict is the root of all evil, for being blind it does not see whom it attacks. Yet it always attacks the Son of God, and the Son of God is you.* You always attack yourself.

God's Son is indeed in need of comfort, for he knows not what he does, believing his will is not his own. The Kingdom is his, and yet he wanders homeless. At home in God he is lonely, and amid all his brothers he is friendless. Would God let this be real, when He did not will to be alone Himself? Could His Son somehow escape from His mind? *And if your will is His it cannot be true of you, because it is not true of Him.*

O my child, if you knew what God wills for you, your joy would be complete! And what He wills has happened, for it was always true. When the light comes and you have said, 'God's Will is mine," you will see such beauty that you will know it is not of you. Out of your joy you will create beauty in His Name, for your joy could no more be contained than his. The bleak little world will vanish into nothingness, and your heart will be so filled with joy that it will leap into Heaven, and into the Presence of God. I have not been able to tell you what this will be like until now, for your heart was not ready. I changed that a little bit. I have the privilege of telling you that you are ready. I'll tell you how it reads: *I cannot tell you what this will be like, for your heart is not ready.* Well, I have to tell you that your heart is ready for this! Why? Some of you are springing. If you get one in a batch that springs, everybody else springs. Can you hear that? You guys are all in total association with each other. You think it is a great big place, but it's really not. It is all contained in one little spot. So if one of you springs, everybody springs. It is a contagion of reassociation of light. So, it has happened! So I can tell you what it will be like, because you are experiencing it and your heart is ready, and I will tell you. *Yet I can tell you, and remind you often, that what God wills for Himself He wills for you, and what He wills for you is yours* because what He wills for Himself is what you are, because you are God creating. Lovely.

The way is not hard, but it is very different. And may still be a little different. Why? *Yours is the way of pain, of which God knows nothing. That way is hard indeed, and very lonely. Fear and grief are your guests, and they go with you and abide with you on the way.* That is not to say you are not going to get it that way; it didn't say that. It said that you have chosen that way to go by your own definition of yourself. Do you notice that? Everybody has to get this because any way they have is their way, until they change their mind about how they want to do it. Then it will change. *That way is hard indeed for you, and very lonely. Fear and grief are your guests, and they go with you and abide with you on the way. But the dark journey is not the way of God's Son. Walk in light and do not see the dark companions, for they are not fit companions for the Son of God...* These are the body constructs that you have made around you. That sickness thing that you have constructed outside yourself in this illusion is not a fit companion for you. You change your mind so that his mind can change with you about your dedication to this. You construct in your mind the companions that you want to be with. You will either share sickness and death and the long, dark path, or you will share a different path and find the truth. Isn't that lovely? *Walk in light and do not see the dark companions, for they are not fit companions for the Son of God, who was created of light and in light. The Great Light always surrounds you and shines out from you.* ...*always surrounds you* and now is shining out from you! This is the experience of light that you are undergoing. This is the awakening from the shadows of your perceptual association into a very real, intense light. Listen to me. When I talk of light, I'm not just talking of the spectrum of light that indicates brightness and darkness, I am talking of light as consciousness energy. I am talking of the whole spectrum association of light from ultraviolet all the way up to radar and radio associations. They are all part of this demonstration of energy of you. You are a child of Light in a whole association of lightness, not in a conceptual thought form because that is only the distance between the thought where the form has been made. And that is the difference in the light. *The Great Light always surrounds you and shines out from you. How can you see the dark companions in a light such as this? If you see them, it is only because you are denying the light.* You have set them up to keep you from seeing through them, haven't you? You have projected that image of that body out from you and you hold it in an association with your own mind. What you guys are undergoing in this new awakening is that you are beginning to look right through each other. This is the teaching. You don't have a perceptual evaluation of it objectively. What happens to it? It turns to Great Ray light! Your mind actually reassociates it in the brightness of your own new whole mind. *How can you see the dark companions in a light such as this? If you see them, it is only because you are denying the light. But deny them instead, for the light is here and the way is clear.*

God hides nothing from His Son, even though His Son would hide himself. Yet the Son of God cannot hide his glory, for God wills him to be glorious, and gave him the light that shines in him. You will never lose your way, for God leads you. When you wander, you but undertake a journey that is not real. The dark companions, the dark way, are all illusions. And they are not true. *Turn toward the light, for the little spark in you is part of a Light so great that it can sweep you out of all darkness forever. For your Father is your Creator, and you are like Him.*

The children of light cannot abide in darkness, for darkness is not in them. Do not be deceived by the dark comforters, and never let them enter the mind of God's Son, for they have no place in His temple. You let the dead bury the dead! Do not be satisfied with your previous associations! The dark comforters are only those in your mind in this place who are telling you that everything is going to be okay. They will say: You can share death with me in this, if you want to. The guy next to you that you are sharing pain with, is your dark comforter. He has no reality. *For your Father is your Creator, and you are like Him! Do not be deceived by the dark comforters, and never let them enter the mind of God's Son, for they have no place in His temple. When you are tempted to deny Him remember that there are no other gods to place before Him, and accept His Will for you in peace. For you cannot accept it otherwise.*

Only God's Comforter can comfort you. In the quiet of His temple, He waits to give you the peace that is yours. Give His peace, that you may enter the temple and find it waiting for you. You can't do it if you don't give it! You can't draw from the warehouse until you know you are the warehouse! You can't know you are the warehouse until you give everything away that you have. Through the giving of everything, you discover you have the fullness. Until you do, you will always be lacking in your own warehouse. Isn't that astonishing? You see, it is like an endless circle, the more you take out of it, the more there is. Why? Because you are giving it away. It doesn't stop, it isn't held in time by you. It is not utilized by you in your possessions. You don't stop it. You don't use it as potential to protect yourself and project it out from you. Creation is nothing but a continual flow of love. All you really have to do is get in the flow! Can you hear that? You obstruct it in your own mind, and you try to share it — you grab it, and you try to share it with these little thought forms. And nobody can stop you from doing it. That's called karma. That is the memories that you have. But the dharma is all around you, the spirit of energy is in a continual condition of creating forever. That is going on no matter how much you glitch it. You say to me: "Why did I do this?" You may still do that. And I say, what difference does it make if it is over? You say to me: well, how long do I have to keep on doing it? Can I bring all this up? And I say, you are going to be whole no matter what you do. It doesn't make any difference. Your admission of that puts you into the flow of creation, which is what everything is. And you are that. *Give His peace, that you may enter the temple and find it waiting for you. But be holy in the Presence of God, or you will not know that you are there.* You can't. Where is God? Here! You can't know you are there until you are wholly in your own Self, until you decide there is a God and you want that more than this. *For what is unlike God cannot enter His Mind, because it was not His Thought and therefore does not belong to Him. And your mind must be as pure as His, if you would know what belongs to you. Guard carefully His temple, for He Himself dwells there and abides in peace. You cannot enter God's Presence with the dark companions beside you, but you also cannot enter alone.* That's one of the tougher sentences in the *Course*. You can't get there by taking your own thoughts about what your brother is with you. You haven't forgiven him totally, have you? You are demanding recognition for your mind at the place of God. Yet you cannot go alone because all of your projections, which are the creations of your mind, must go with you in order to be whole. You see what forgiveness offers you, teachers? Salvation! That is what that says. Isn't that lovely! *All your brothers must enter with you, for until you have accepted them you cannot enter. For you cannot understand Wholeness unless you are whole, and no part of the Son can be excluded if he would know the Wholeness of his Father.*

In your mind you can accept the whole Sonship and bless it with the light your Father gave it. Then you will be worthy to dwell in the temple with Him, because it is your will not to be alone. God blessed His Son forever. If you will bless him in time, you will be in eternity. If you will bless him in time, you will *be* in eternity — not you will *find* eternity, you will be there. One whole blessing given totally is Heaven. All you ever really had to do here was just one time be totally grateful, just totally dependent. Just one time you had to base your reality on the fact that there is a whole God who created you perfectly. When you listen to these new brothers saying Thank You, understand that they understand that their reality is based on their gratitude. Their reality is based on their total dependence on God. Their freedom of mind is based on their dependence on God, not on themselves which can only bind them to their own associations with themselves. Do you see? You bind yourself by your determination to be guilty in your own associations. Don't do it anymore.

This is lovely. Then comes *The "Dynamics" of the Ego.* I start to do what is going to be on the next page (sixth paragraph). *Yours is the independence of creation, not of autonomy. Your whole creative function lies in your complete dependence on God, Whose function He shares with you. By His willingness to share it, He became as dependent on you as you are on Him.* What a lovely sentence! That's what Meister Eckhart said, didn't he — 1299, standing up in a sermon in Germany. He said God is as dependent on you as you are on Him. What is a Father without a Son? What is a Son who tries to make himself? Nothing! It is our total dependence that gives us the freedom. It is our autonomy or separation that condemns us to death. You caught me reading the *Course!* I'll read a couple more. *He is as dependent on you as you are on Him! Do not ascribe the ego's arrogance to Him Who wills not to be independent of you.* He needs you, He is totally dependent on you. Please forgive God! He asks for your forgiveness. He cries, He is lonely because you are not there with Him. I thought you told me He doesn't know about this. You know about it, and you are lonely. Do you see that? Isn't that something? *Can you believe that autonomy is meaningful apart from Him? The belief in ego autonomy is costing you the knowledge of your dependence on God, in which your freedom lies. The ego sees all dependency as threatening, and has twisted even your longing for God into a means of establishing itself. But do not be deceived by its interpretation of your conflict.*

Isn't that nice? This is the way you are going to start reading this now. This is the truth. Are you happy about this being so? There is a point in the *Course* where Jesus says how come you are not really happy? This is your freedom. You see, the happier you become about this, the closer you are to the end of time. Isn't that so? This is really a way out for you. There is no question you can get out this way. Strangely enough there is no other way to get out but this. These perceptual consciousnesses will say, "Well, tell me what you are going to do. What did you accomplish? How is this going to turn out?" And you say, "I haven't the vaguest idea. I am just here in love and light, and I'll be here for another moment or I'm gone from here." They will not understand you. Why? You have undergone a transformation of your mind. Will you be here for a moment in that? Sure! Why not? You are here for a moment in that right now. Did you depart here and are gone from here? Yes. Are you really not here? You are really not here. Do you know why you are not here? This is nowhere! How long did this last? Just a moment. This is a place where you come to discover that you didn't have to be here. This is a place where you came to die. You used to make it a long time. You used to make it ten million years, then you made it eighty years in this lifetime, didn't you? But it was always just a moment. This was the moment when you decided that time would end. So time is ending. Do you have a need to know what it is going to be like when time is ended? It is going to be like this! If you need to ask. Is this okay with you? "Well," you say, "not exactly." Do you see?

Expect God now! This is all we teach. This shift that has come about in you cannot be described by future associations. It is a now condition. It is a condition of, "Hey, I'm the whole universe. I'm sitting here in peace and joy and happiness. Nothing can threaten me, and I cannot die." Now if you tell that to a consciousness, he is liable to say that you are a liar, "you can too die". And he'll kill you to prove it. That has nothing to do with what we're teaching. He has always killed you to prove his reality. There are only dead ones here! They kill themselves in their own associations, but they never die. Isn't that funny? You are always crucifying the Christ. That's amazing, isn't it? The proof of life here is death!

What are you going to do now? I am telling you that you are eternal and that you can't die, and that you are perfect, and that you are in Heaven, and you are very happy, and this never happened, and it is not real. How do you feel about that? Great! All right. Then you will be in Heaven. Why? You believe it. It would have to be so if you do. If you don't, it won't be. But remember, there is only your own mind with this. There is not another mind connected to it. I know you are going to go out and collect these dark ones that I just read you about, and they are going to authenticate you, aren't they? Why? You told them to! You told them your name was Mary, you told them their name was Joe, you want to share that limited association, Adam and Eve. Who did you think you were if you weren't Adam and Eve? That's who you are, and you left the garden. And you are in the Land of Nod. You only got just outside the gate. You never went anywhere. All of this has just been your own split mind. You think there is a rage in Heaven. You think that somehow Lucifer was cast out of Heaven. That's nonsense. There is no conflict in Heaven. The conflict is in you! Lucifer — the bearer of the Light — that's you. Can you see that? Did you know that you were Lucifer? Of course, that's who you are. Isn't that amazing? What is the difference between Lucifer and God? From God's standpoint, nothing; from Lucifer's standpoint: the conflict of his own associate mind in his determination to miscreate. It's not real. Isn't that something?

This is a very broad associate batch, because when you do the Christian message, you guys are nothing but Christian memories. You have a lot of associations of crucifixion, resurrection, torture, all of the things that have gone on in your established denial and also the other side of you that has been determined to get this in your schizophrenic mind. Every memory that there has ever been of all humans that have ever inhabited the earth is contained in you. You are nothing but a bag of memories. Now you are going to take all those memories and not be in conflict with yourself. Isn't that astonishing? The Akashic Record. You can go into that warehouse and you will find everything you want in there — but don't keep the warehouse separate from yourself. Go into your own library, and then there is no frame of reference outside of you to identify yourself. You jumped into your own thoughts. Now there is nothing to know you are here, therefore you are eternal. You have lost your perceptual association with yourself. You express that as loss of self; we express it as finding yourself and becoming whole. I was lost and now I'm found. Amazing grace!

Is this a reassociation for you in time with all of these consciousnesses that are around you? Sure. This Gaelic energy, this Irish energy you are feeling — it's St. Paddy's Day energy. Can you feel it? All of you are Irish. You populated Europe for four hundred years. All of the priests, all of the nuns were all Gaelic, all came out of the Druid association of Christhood, came out of the ancient wisdom of Druidism. The story is a twice-told tale. It just keeps getting repeated. And you have a perfect memory of this in your mind. I don't want to take anything away from you. I want to give you all of this. Just don't judge it, just accept it as a part of you. All power is given unto you in Heaven and on earth. There is nothing you can't do.

Now, have we tied this properly together with the teachings of Jesus Christ, our brother, our later brother? This will occur on the next two pages of Chapter 1, where He will say, "I'm a step ahead of you in time. We are not equal in time. I am a step ahead of you, and I can direct you to this through the use of your own mind associations because we are in fact singular." That is the direction of the *Course In Miracles*. And that is the direction you will take with your new enlightened mind as you begin to teach the *Course*, isn't it? You will go out and say, "I am the living Son of God and I declare to you our wholeness. I say to you that this message coming from God directs us to this reassociation of love to the relinquishment of ourselves." I think you should be able to do that now.

Don't you? Your salvation depends on it. Why? The conflict is only in your mind, do you see? As you begin to experience the ecstasy of the union of this reassociation with God, you won't want to do anything else, will you? You are perfect in your own mind! You will let the dead bury the dead. You will look around you and see that everybody loses here, that all they are looking forward to is finally cancer and death and sickness. Isn't this so? The body is going to fall apart and rot and get old, and you said, "I'm not going to do that! I am not going to take this dream of death and allow it to be what I am. I am more than that. I am not this. This is just a little spot. All outside of me is all this universe. I want to know what that is." You guys that are with me have never been satisfied with your limited form associations. That's why you are with me. You have been forced into a mold of limited perceptual identity. You are, in fact, a transforming creature. You are ahead in your own time associations. That's why you are here. Jesus says you are very early. And you are early. But it is never too early. That's a direct sentence. Why? You know about it! There is no reason why you can't do this, and did do this. Time is a sleight of hand. The time you chose is now, and this is the time it always happened.

This demonstration of the parting of the veil is a very real thing going on in here, as you know. I hope you can feel the joy that is going on in these consciousnesses in their dedication to the scripture of this reassociation. They found a way out of their dilemma. That is what this is.

Is this really happening to you? Yes! This is an entirely different time than this morning. See? This whole reassociation is much later on in time. You say: we appear to be doing the same thing. You will always be doing the same thing. This is all that you do all the time. You never do anything but this. Some of you really hear me when I do this. This is all you can ever do. You can't do this later in time. As I read you this morning, you can't choose the curriculum. Why? Because the curriculum is all you ever do. But you have said, "This is all that I can ever do." So you brought time together rather than "futurizing" possibilities. When you do that, you undergo a shift in your associations and it is later in time, and you are doing the same thing. You are still you, you are just a different you, but you can't tell the difference because you have lost your capacity for separate associate identities. The exact difference in my illuminate mind and yours (until it wakes up), is I am very certain that perceptual consciousness is not real — that it is just the distance between its own thoughts. So it wouldn't make any difference what you say to me about your own identity. Obviously it doesn't have any source. It is not real. None of this is real. That is what I told you this morning. Now, when your mind knows that, it doesn't say, "Well, I'm still working on the possibility." It knows with certainty that this is not so. Why? Everything that is real knows that this is not so. What does not know it, what thinks that this is real, is not real. That's how simple this program is. That's what you are undergoing and have undergone. It's nice to see that.

Can you be happy in this new creative purpose? You guys, you will be ecstatic! You are going to be allowed to create with whole mind rather than limiting yourself to a definition of you. Before, you have always had to judge your creative capacities. What absurdity! You had to give credit to other consciousnesses for their associations and abilities. Now you can give them full credit for what they are, what have you lost? Your competitive associations. A whole mind is not competitive. That is out of the *Course*, as you know. It doesn't compete except in truth. It knows it is whole. My purpose is to bring you to Light. I have no other function but that. You can only prove yourself, do you see? That is what I am doing with you now. How many saviors does it take to save the world? One! Congratulations. You look very lovely.

For those of you reading this, there is a lot of illuminate energy going on here and you can't construct perceptual associations when there is a lot of light communication. All indications of the necessity to communicate this are corrupt. Do you understand that? The whole idea of Saviorship is corrupt. When you transcend this in your own mind, all I want to be sure you have with this energy is the total declaration of your specific mind to your commitment to this. That's what we said this morning. If you have that, then you can utilize this light energy to the fullest of your innate capacity to be whole, which you can demonstrate at this moment, and did. And that's the joy of this.

Don't be afraid. Hold your counsel with this. You have nothing to prove. You will be heard. The course is set now. This old world was over a long time ago. That is a statement of fact, not just something you can analyze in a funny-looking blue and gold book. That is a statement of fact. This old world was over a long time ago. Do not stay here and ruminate on the possibility of you making it real and search yet again for something that you cannot find. Come rather to the truth that is you, and find the glory of the light that awaits you now in this transformation of your mind. Okay. The children of light could not abide in darkness. Where is the darkness when the light has come? Nowhere! What was it? Nothing! It is simply gone from your mind. It is not a contrast in truth, but simply a disappearance of the necessity for the evil association, and that's what has happened to you.

Happy Easter. There are some lovely places in the *Course* where Jesus says you are in the passion of your own awakening. You have undergone your Bethlehem, you have traveled the road to Jerusalem, you have been in the upper room, you have associated with your disciples, you have been denied. And now you are playing the part of the savior. That is literally what you are doing. This was always only your own passion. How passionate it becomes for you now in the certainty of that truth. How complete is that dedication of you to this wholeness! We would never leave you comfortless. There was a mistake in communication. I want you to bring this to your heart. There was a mistake made. We are aware of it, and you are aware of it. And we admit to that break, but we assure you that nothing really happened, and that you can with full confidence return to that horrible spot where this occurred, and you will see immediately that there is no war going on. You are whole and perfect.

We found you. We told you about the mistake. Now you come on home. This never happened. We were there together at the beginning. We will be there together at the end. We can not *not* be. We share that single mistake. That's the way of it — the Alpha and the Omega, the beginning and the end. All of the causes that you have had for this, that you have made effects down the line, you have brought together now in time. You are going to step out of here. You have lost your history. History was only you. You are not judging yourself on the past at all. You have lost your past. If you have no past, you have no future. You must have done the *Workbook* of *A Course In Miracles*. That's what it says. You have forgiven all the grievances that you brought together to keep yourself separate and to attack reality. You have simply let them go in your own mind. And they have disappeared into the nothingness that they are, and you have become whole. Your reality is not based on attacking your brother and on the grievance of your determination to wreak some sort of vengeance on him, as you previously did. You are letting go of that and you are seeing him in the beauty and light of his truth with you with God in reality.

As we said this morning in one of the concepts, it is an honor for us to serve you. And it is an honor for me to be chosen to tell you this. We joke a lot about how no one wants to be the savior. An enlightened mind takes on the burden or the responsibility early in the pioneering effort of chaos to bring about this reillusionment to truth. You are with me because of your pioneer associations. You have never liked establishments. You are staff and sandals people. You have always been that. That is why you are here. You are time travelers. You are universal consciousnesses that go into particular thought form associations and establish communications, much as your forefathers went out into the woods and cut down the trees. This is all a part of you. As above, so below. As you do in your mind, you will do in the truth of you. Isn't this so? You could at best be only a facsimile of truth, and in wholeness you are that truth each moment. But you have the spirit that makes you a savior. Don't be dis-spirited. Be the light of the world! Be the pilgrim. Undertake the Odyssey, as Homer would say. Take the Twelve Tasks and perform them in the certainty that you can transcend this perceptual association. Dare to be whole. Don't be becalmed, don't be caught with the sirens that lull you into reassociations of death. There are lots of ways to say this. It is all just in your mind.

This is a lovely association of time. This episode has been carved out of time in this relationship with you in your mind to bring about this awakening. As Jesus says it so very aptly in the *Course*, time has been saved for you to perform this enlightenment. We are about it now. As you hear this, as this spreads joyously around the world, it will resound in all of the universe because this is the universe. As we told you in the Principles of Miracles this morning, your mind is working miracles beyond anything you could possibly dream of. Every time you think this has reached a zenith, it is just a vague idea of what awaits you in the eternity and power of your mind. Listen to me: you are releasing yourself from the bondage of your limited association. You are hatching out into the reality that has always been all around you. No longer play this game of death within this shell of your own perceptual memories.

You have used them all up now, and you are going to come out into this reality. You are hatching! We are harvesting you. We sowed and we are going to reap now. The lost sheep are coming home. All different ways, isn't it? It is impossible that you have not done this. An idea has never left its source, that you have ever had. This is all only you! Be happy with it!

Some of you are undergoing major healing processes now. We want you young and vital in this effort, in a whole reconfiguration of your body. We will hold you in this body sequence and it will serve you perfectly well. It will be just fine for this. This one is working all right. This one has been through it. As you associate with this new energy, you will feel the Spirit and the vibrations of youth and beauty that are a part of this new mind. You will begin to reflect how you really feel about yourself fundamentally, which is really very beautiful. That will begin, then, to extend from you, won't it? Why? Because you are not going to try to be a facsimile of someone else, but only rather what you are, which is what our teaching is. To us, you are very beautiful because you are part of this energy of love that constitutes reality. You are going to be very whole and beautiful with this. Welcome home! The veil is open. For many of you there is no fear in you now. You have gone through this death association and have become real. You look spectacular. Some of you have discovered it is difficult for you to keep from going to light. For a while you figure out how to get this, and then if you get it, you try to figure out how to stay here. That's a nice place to be. You will feel this pressure and necessity to release to the crown associations, and this may very well require that you be alone. Come to the Wisconsin woods. Or there will be a place here in this association. The Denver association is very beautiful. It is a facsimile of the acupuncture points of the world that are being provided for this energy source. Those of you who would like to come back and be alone are welcome to come into that. These centers now with this new commitment are going to be formed around the world. They will be places where you can come and be recognized as whole — not in secret, but in a protective association of the necessity for the bodily transformation. You will discover your brothers all over the world will hear this. Many of them have never done the *Course In Miracles* and have never heard of it. Obviously, that's not the requirement. All those who labor in the vineyard get exactly the pay that they demand, don't they? The lovely parable of you making a deal to work in the vineyard, and you've paid your dues over a period of a thousand years and suddenly a consciousness comes and works for two days and he gets exactly the same pay you do. (Matthew 20) You got what you bargained for. Be happy! I told you yesterday that in later frameworks of reality, the moment that we come with this, everybody springs and is gone because this is truth or God speaking to you in the chaos.

I've got Irish things in my head. "Oh, my name was Mac..." In this new freedom of mind, you will discover that you associate with all sorts of thought forms around you. You will become very creative in what you do because you have the freedom of expression. That's a nice thing to have happen to you. The new you emerges. It was you that you were looking for all the time. This was only a course in knowing yourself. Thanks for coming and saving me. Thank you for coming here now and being the way and the light for me so that I could come to know this. Through you I am redeemed, in the certainty of our love and what we are together in the grace of our Father and the truth of us.

There is no possibility that this could have been accomplished without you. And I mean YOU! I don't mean somebody else. I mean YOU, because this was accomplished, and you did accomplish it. I would remind you of that now for you have dis-membered it. You have forgotten it. But you can not *not* make it true. You are the savior. You taught me this. I am re-teaching you this. A lot of you guys I know from the Masters Academy, as you know. Some of you taught me. Now I find you in configurations of your limited associations back in time. But we know each other perfectly well. This is my chance to get even with you! I think some of you flunked me in communication or something. But we know each other very well. We are a part of a Saviorship group. I know this is in the *Course*, but I am telling you. Why? Reality doesn't know about this at all. It is only a half kooky mind that would even do this. In the *Course*, Jesus says there are very few consciousnesses that want to hang around this place. How could you stand it? So this is sort of the bottom of the class that gets this assignment. That's okay. All things are possible. Everything is true by the possibility of it. When I speak to you of the Academy, I mean in reality. This is not an allegory. This is the true statement of what we are doing.

There is a ready room where the *Course* was prepared. There is a big map that shows us the dedication of the mind coming to its truth — it lights up on a board, and we dispatch teams to bring about atonement and enlightenment. It is not based on your conceptual associations, but the release of your perceptual associations through your inability to deal with the chaotic. In other words, the harmony begins to occur, and you ask for help. Do you understand that you asked for help here? Yes! Well, we heard you. But it had nothing to do with the problem you had. We already know your problem is total. You needed to know that to ask for help. When you asked for total help, you got it totally. So this is a group of fervent prayers. Somewhere you said: I can't do this anymore. I positively guarantee you that is how we heard you. Not only that, but most of you remember when you asked for it. And you also remember getting some relief at that time. Now you are asking for total relief, and you are going to get that! You thought you had it right, and you were wrong. Isn't that funny? It had nothing to do with the problem you were in. All you really had to do was surrender. That's really what I'm teaching.

As we said, What is the communicative device with God? Prayer. What is the only real prayer? HELP! What is the same as that? Thank You! Of course. Those are the two things. Help and Thank You! I always end up giving the same talk. I give it over and over and over and over again. I just keep telling you this is how you got it. We heard you. You called, and we heard you. There is a way station that is waiting for you to beam up to. It's not Heaven, but it is the place that you go to for your final processing. Do you understand me? This is Valhalla, what you call Jerusalem. This is what you call the Borderland. Sure. You come into that association and you take one final glance, and you are gone. It is lovely. That is what true perception is. That is what you are coming to, literally. We're glad you are here, coming into this now. You look beautiful. In a few moments we are going to have another quiet time. Obviously you guys are in contact now with reality here. You use the auspices of this light to bring about the continuing contagion — this is very catching, literally. If you associate with the new light energy, you will become that. That is called "divine order", in what Jesus says. You must see that in order to undergo this process. Do not be deluded by the perceptual consciousnesses that tell you they can find this in their limited association. I'm afraid that's what you are going to have to look at. Look at it. This is the certainty that you must love them, of course, in that identification, but this is the transformative process. Don't be afraid. You are the way and the light.

Without you there is no salvation. Without you, the world is condemned to sickness, pain and death. Listen to me. Without you, there is no Heaven. Without you, there is no God. Listen. We are that consciousness together. These are columns of light being demonstrated by the consciousnesses who have opened this veil. This veil has parted. This is a literal parting. The experience that you are having is the revealing of what Master Jesus calls the Great Rays. Since you are nothing but an energy package, a light refraction of consciousness, you are coming into that reassociation. That is the occurrence of this. You are losing your perceptual association. That is very nice to see that happen. This is very deep for you to do that. You appear on the map of consciousness as a bright light that flashes, and then we watch that spread, and all the assistance that there is comes in to give you the direction of that. Why? Ideas never leave their source. Everything is all right here. It is just like you are popping out of it, aren't you, much like when you came out of the womb when you were born into this. Very much the same. You have these birth pangs going on. You can't go home again. You can't go back into the womb. There are some lovely parts of the *Course* where Jesus describes it. He says don't try to go back. You keep trying to reassociate with some sort of happy home. You can't. You can't remember Heaven. So you try to remember a garden where everything was okay. But it wasn't okay. You got yourself separated. Come on home. Be wrong, just once. Never mind that you are wrong, you need to admit that you are wrong. It has nothing to do with sin — it has to do with just the fact that you are wrong.

Would everybody like to have a little quiet time here? There is so much energy, I'm obviously not having much to say. What I have to say, though, is very energizing. It probably wouldn't matter much what I said. If I had the Hoboken Train Station Schedule, it would do. See, when you are speaking from the new association of your mind, you are going to undergo the incredible. Everything becomes real divine to you. When Jesus talks about it in the *Course*, He says that you look at the simplest thing and you see it just in that wholeness and beauty of your own creative mind. That is a lovely experience that a lot of you are undergoing.

Everything takes on a luster of reality to you. You fall in love, don't you? You love it! You are creating. The analogies that you will do, the allegories, are incredible. Every story that you read you will associate with this new awakening that is going on in you. That is nice to do that. That is a part of this new mind that is constructing everything toward this goal of unity. It is lovely to do.

We will have some quiet time now. Let's have some Christian hymns — *Hymns Triumphant, side 1*. This association with Christianity is very beautiful. It would be nice for you to do that. You have so many memories. Basically you guys are not power-of-mind New Agers. You are fundamentally "stained-glass" spiritual people. Do you know that I know that? You used to like to go to mass because you really knew that the wine became the blood. I know you. You are coming up to a very happy time in your mind because it is the resurrection time. You used to like to go, and you always wished that church were more than it appeared to be. Tell me. Sure. It's nice to know that's what we have here. Some of you have very early memories of the pews and the smell of the church and how you liked to go there. I know that. I know you were disillusioned, too, because you saw the falsity of the establishment. Come on home. We know what you are.

The temple still has to be built on you. It can't be built outside of you. You are the temple of God. That is the church. That is you coming to your truth, isn't it? Jesus talks about you as being the church in the *Course*. It is okay to be spiritual. It's okay to say there is a God. I understand that you are going to be apparently lumped together with established Christianity. But so what? The process of you is to forgive, not to judge. You be whole with this and this will be whole with you. I understand you are teaching fundamentally different concepts about Jesus in that He didn't die, but lives. That will be perfectly all right. You come right into the middle of the community and say, very simply, that Jesus taught forgiveness and love and no one will confront you with that. You need not confront them. You be true to your heart. You will land right in the middle of Christianity. I promise you this is so. There are many, many lovely associate consciousnesses that have been waiting for somebody to tell them that Christ really did save the world. They are getting up and going to work day after and day and they are coming home and feeling the frustration. Some of them become pillars of the church, and they do go, and they do seek for it, and they do want it. Your direction is to show *them*, not those that are out there and have solved the problems through the assertion of their own power. No. These are people who are feeling the quiet frustration of their inability to solve the problem with God. These are the people who are waiting to hear this.

Never mind the academic community that has philosophized itself into a hole it can't get out of. If you are going to make that break with them and declare the singularity of their minds, they can come into a whole religion — a religious association — of the quantum dedications of their minds in objective science. They will begin to work the miracles of the Einsteins and the Neils Bohrs — all of the consciousnesses of new mind. They will discover that, through the forgiveness of their mother-in-law, they can work a new formula of time association. That is an incredible idea, that they can enter into their own scientific pursuit rather than trying to set up an experiment and pretend they didn't set it up. Rather, come into the association of it. Did we cover everything? Philosophy. Religion. Science. This is the new reality that everybody talks about. Who is that? You! When you read about it in the magazines, all they do is conceptualize it. There is never an admission that they are it. That's a tough admission, isn't it? That is the anomaly.

That is the thing that's always subtracted from the equation. It has to be, or it would become whole. They see that they influence it, but they attempt to make it objective and not influence it. Obviously, they can't. Why? It is only in their own mind! That is quite a step, isn't it? It's the quantum leap. You have done this leaping, now, and you are way, way up here in time. Your kingdom is not of this world. Now we'll have some hymns. Welcome home, guys. This is what you have been waiting for. Don't be afraid.

Listen, - perhaps you catch a hint of an ancient state
not quite forgotten;
dim, perhaps, and yet not altogether unfamiliar,
like a song whose name is long forgotten,
and the circumstances in which you heard
completely unremembered.
Not the whole song has stayed with you,
but just a little wisp of melody,
attached not to a person or a place or anything particular.
But you remember, from just this little part,
how lovely was the song,
how wonderful the setting where you heard it,
and how you loved those who were there and listened with you.
The notes are nothing.
Yet you have kept them with you, not for themselves,
but as a soft reminder of what would make you weep
if you remembered how dear it was to you.
You could remember, yet you are afraid,
believing you would lose the world you learned since then.
And yet you know that nothing in the world you learned
is half so dear as this.
Listen, and see if you remember an ancient song
you knew so long ago and held more dear
than any melody you taught yourself to cherish since.

Can You Hear This?

The whole basis of the teaching is that you don't know who you are. Is that a fair assumption? Is that fair? No one here really knows who they are. Otherwise, why would you seek an identity? If you knew who you were, why would you have to have an identity? Answer me. You can say, "Well, I have an identity and my name is Jones and this guy's name is Smith, and I came here, and I'm going to study the relationships in the illusion and therefore reach a conclusion." Pfffffft! The demand that you and I recognize each other mutually is an attack on reality, isn't it? In other words, your need to be who you think you are, is obviously a demonstration of a defense that you present yourself with in order to associate with your imagined cohorts.

What I would like to do, if I can, if you're going to do this — *Course In Miracles* teachers particularly — is at least give you a premise of what you must do in order to be a "miracle-ist." It has to begin with the subtraction of your persona. That is, if we are going to say we are going to work a miracle here now, there are miracles going on right now in this new range of consciousness. Obviously, the perceptual observation of an occurrence is not a miracle; it's a "phenomenon". It is the observation, for instance, that I am going to levitate for you now, all right? This gives you full accord to: 1) Identify yourself as a body, 2) Identify me as a body, and place us in corresponding associations with my capacity to demonstrate to you something that is outside of your frame of reference in regard to the occurrence, but not in regard to our perceptual association.

Jesus calls that magic. It wouldn't make any difference what I would do if you're going to accord me a capacity of a body relationship. I am a not a body. There is no such thing as a body. At any moment the body literally is not. In order to feel that, you have to look at this as imagery. Never mind this part of it [hitting his arm]. See, this is all imagery. Try to hear me. If I get too fast with you, I'll slow it down, but you need to know this. Finally, there is no difference between something solid and something fluid and something airy. It's only in your demonstration contained within your own perceptual associations, that makes this solid at all. It's an image. Jesus calls it a dream, so that you can be sure that it is not real. It is not real. Why? It has no source. See, you guys don't mind the idea that this is not real. You'll judge it as illusionary but you won't judge the source as illusionary. Do you see?

Here is where you have the problem, because perceptually, since your associated thoughts have not left this identity, they are always reflecting back to themselves what are really thought forms. This is a thought form. This body, this microcosm, is a universal thought form. I guarantee you this is true, that contained within me is the universe — not as a symbolic relationship between the macrocosm. Listen! It's the same thing. Can you hear it? Subatomically, there is just as much smaller than me as there is bigger. Can you see this? The distance from a subatomic relationship of this energy factor to my head is approximately twenty-eight thousand light years moving at the speed of light atomically in its relationship.

Jesus calls it a constellation. He says in the *Course* that you are a constellation of conflicting associated ideas. He doesn't say this; I am just saying this: You have a momentary symbiotic conflictual relationship in this constellation. Are you fighting a galactic war in here? Oh yeah! You're fighting a war within your own system. Take a look at the mercenaries that you'll bring in to attack or defend yourself, in relationship with what? With this! All of your Star Wars associations are going on in your body. Everything is going on in that association. What are we going to do now first? We're going to develop interstellar drive. In other words, if it's going to take me that long to come from this association to this association, how am I ever going to get my energy? This is what you would call my potential, my source, my black hole. Every galaxy has a black hole which is what? — your genetic associations compacted at the time of the schism. Now what are we doing? We are taking the black hole and expanding it up into our minds to come whole with this. We are returning to our Source.

Now, the teachings of Jesus would be: Is the black hole, is *this* real? No, no-no. It's a space-time factoring that allows for the idea of potential. I have to give you that. I can't take your potential away from you. I can't take the idea that you can accomplish something in the future away from you, because you believe that your source emanates from earth, from what you call female, from what you call the end of the schism. Can you hear this? Jesus calls this the "Great Reversal." He says that at the time it reached, in the schism, its most compact demonstration of static-ness, it automatically became whole, because there is no such thing as nothing. Not only that, but from wholeness' standpoint, it happened simultaneously. From potential's standpoint it took just a moment. It took just a moment. You are in the moment of evolving from earth, from the demonstration of the evolutionary process. You look around and you can see the evolution going on from the mineral, to the vegetable, to the animal, and on up into man,

That's being replicated in your nine month's demonstration of your maturity, which is actually the whole evolutionary process taking place in the body, isn't it?

But the fact is that you associate with your potential, female. The idea of memory that's contained in you emanates from the compactness of the disorder that occurred at the time of the schism. Do you understand this? And you like it. You say, "Yes, we sprang from earth," and all around you, you see the cycleness of the occurrence, and you see the evolution of your mind as it progresses through the stages, perhaps, of mineral and the high associations of consciousness, and then the brighter association that occurs in plants; and this is the teaching of hierarchical associations in the consciousness.

Here's your problem — this is not your source. Jesus would say, you're not from here. You're from out here. You're from God, which you call "Wholeness", but you're caught now in the ascent back. You're caught with taking all of the potential that there could ever be in a space-time relationship, and activating it totally, at which time it'll be at the Omega point that you entered in to. Any questions on that? I'll answer any questions if you really want to make a statement. Quite obviously, all you're doing is speeding up time. Time is at your disposal because you invented it in your mind, with the idea that you can return to source. And you can. The question is not that; the question is, why don't you?

The reason you don't is that you have no frame of reference contained within a limited perceptual association that this is your true source. When does that occur? When you become a human being. See? Now what have you got? Now you've got an association with a split mind. You call this right and left brain. You could call this male and female — if you wanted to. What are you doing? You are meeting yourself halfway. This is the ego. You know perfectly well you have an identity that transcends your associations, but you don't know where it's coming from.

You invent a God, because the solution is now contained in, "Hey, wait a minute, there's more to that than this." What did you ask? Who am I really, and where did I come from? You looked out here and said it must be out there. And it is. That's the condition you find yourself in right now.

Questioner: I'm having difficulty... What I understand when you talked about memory... I understand who I am comes from a sense of ego and identity...

MT: It's not real.

Questioner: Okay, I'll accept that.

MT: I'm glad. We appreciate you accepting it. Go.

Questioner: What I'm trying to do now is get a sense of what life is without my body from this point in time.

MT: It's everything, because life is everything.

Questioner: That leaves me with the feeling that I have no idea what everything is.

MT: So you'll die to prove that you are real, rather than releasing it so that you can know what everything is. That's the whole teaching. The whole teaching is that you can't know.

Questioner: You talked about the body. What I understand about the spirit...

MT: You don't understand anything about the spirit, because you don't understand anything. You don't know what anything is. Why do you continue to compare illusions? I'll do this lesson for you. See, you're always caught with what? You're caught with the power of your own mind demonstrating your own reality. That's what you're doing. I can't take that away from you. I can tell you you're more than that, though. But you'd have to believe me.

Questioner: I would like to get to some sort of experience that allows me to understand that I...

MT: You'll never get it. You can't get it, because you define the experience in association with value systems that are false. It's impossible. The whole association is to release you from the necessity to identify it, that's what's keeping you from being in Heaven.

Come on! You're trying to tell God what He ought to be. Can He be that? No! Why? He's going to be who He is. Who is that? Who you are.

Now, I understand you... the notations that you're doing in your mind... This is the necessity before you get to me. I'm telling you the problem can't be solved! For crying out loud, the problem can't be solved! That's a fact.

Questioner: Now I... (inaudible)

MT: Not now. The fact is that this problem cannot be solved. If sickness and death are real, if this body is real, how would you solve the problem? You have to get it up to where it belongs, okay?

I'm going to say to you in the next sentence that the problem cannot be solved because the problem is not real. But to you the problem appears very real. Okay? Now the only psychology that can ever be applied to this — to show you that the problem is in your own mind — is simply to not defend yourself from your own associations, because you are in fundamental conflict with the necessity to demonstrate the schism in your own mind, aren't you? This is called forgiveness in the *Course*, incidentally.

Non-judgment. What we're doing here now, or attempting to do, and I'll pull this back up for you, is to get you to not judge at all. Non-judgment is what salvation is, right? Isn't it true that God doesn't judge? How would He? He's perfect. Isn't it true that you do judge? Yes. Now, it has nothing to do — and I want to say this to you, because it always appears that I'm attacking you — it has nothing to do with whether you're right or wrong about this. This is what you're trying to establish. It doesn't have to do with that. It has to do with, "It's not real". Anything that you say to me in your attempts to re-illusion this within the frequency of your perceptual observation will mean nothing.

What lesson? Lesson 140. The reason you can't heal is you keep re-illusioning. The most Socratic lesson in the *Course* is Lesson 139. I'll do it for you: You know perfectly well who you are; you're pretending you don't; and the thing that's asking the question, "What am I", is *no* thing. This puts Socrates to shame. Lesson 139 by Jesus Christ in the *Course In Miracles* would make Aristotle blush. It's incredible. The mind that did Lesson 139 is so incredibly great, you ought to be jumping up and down. Now, Lesson 140 will come right back into there is no cure. There is no cure except Atonement. That's Lesson 140. Lovely! It says that instead of re-illusioning your associations, see the consciousness as whole, through the love that extends from your mind.

If that consciousness is really sitting out there with cancer, dear one, nothing in earth or Heaven is going to make him well. You must look at it this way. The sickness and the disease and the sin is only separation. I'm doing the *Course*. I just keep doing these sentences over and over for you. Anything that could become sick could not possibly be real. How the hell am I going to work a miracle here, if you're going to tell me that you're sick and I'm going to allow you to be sick? Don't let your brother be sick. Want another one? Don't let your brother die.

You guys are putting up too much energy. I'm liable to spring you right out of here. See, what's happened? [laughing] I got some of my... There has never been a case where a so-called advanced teacher, master, Christ, whatever you call him, has ever been able to awaken any of his disciples. Never! Never, never, never! "Oh I was with Muktananda for twenty years." I look at them and say, "big deal!" You go, "mmmmmmm."

See, he had a lot of, what do you guys call it, "Shaktipat"? He's a lovely guy.

What's happening to you guys, as disciples, I'm not giving you any discipline. That's the toughest discipline there could ever be. I refuse to give you direction because if I do you'll attack me when it fails, because you'll put the discipline in the framework where you can blame me when it doesn't work. I have no intention of allowing you to do that.

No — you're not going to get away with that. I know that you do it; I know you're doing it right now. But if you come around me, I won't let you get away with being your self — That's crazy to me! Why would you want to do that? We're always in confrontation! When you begin to teach this as awakened teachers (and all of you here are doing it; as this is a very advanced association) you will make unqualifying demands on the perceptual consciousness. If it doesn't accept it, it has nothing to do with you.

This is the whole basis of the teaching, for what Jesus calls advanced teachers. If you come to me with a problem, it doesn't really have any meaning to me. That is, you're presenting me with your request that there is a solution contained within you that will answer the directive that I have given you that you're whole and perfect. Okay. You are not asking the right question of me. When you do ask the right question, you don't want to accept it, because you have projected me as an image of a funny guy standing here. You're going to examine how I came to know this, for example. Well, how long have you been studying? Do you have a diploma that says that you're able to tell me more about God than I know? It's just crazy. It finally doesn't make any sense. Why? Most particularly because you are only going to hear from the guy what you want to hear anyway. You cannot hear more than you want to hear, right?

Why? Cause and effect are not separate. You can only get the answer back that you've designed in your mind to hear.

All I'm doing is, through this association, changing your own association with yourself. Quite literally, I'm giving you a better reflection of yourself than you have, see? Now, did I do that by a confrontation with you and me in my mind? Nah! I did it because I know that what you're presenting to me is not so! There aren't separate personas.

That is… The idea that there are separate identities used to disturb me a lot. I would look and see somebody outside myself, and I'd say, "I wonder who that is." Like you ask your mother, "Mother, if you weren't my mother would I still be me?" And she'd say, "No, you'd be somebody else's little boy." You can't get that in your mind. It's hard to get that. Yeah. Because when I was seven, I'd say, "But I'd still be me, wouldn't I?" She'd say, "No, you're somebody else." I don't understand that. My mind couldn't understand.

It's an amazing thing. If you stop and look at the lunacy of three thousand million separate associations on earth… I saw that very early. It doesn't make any sense, it's senseless. If each one of them is a separate consciousness, it's impossible. Like Jesus says, judging them is absolutely futile. So what you do is close it in to a limited judgment association, and form genetic associations that sustain you momentarily in your time framework. So the psychology, then, is to get you to not associate with your projections. You put them out there; they're being used by you to identify yourself. This is the way you should be teaching the *Course*, because the initial statement of the *Course* is that none of this is real, and this is just a memory.

Now, if I give you a body identification, and you and I decide to share that body identification, what have we done? Just acknowledged our mutual temporalness. Now what are we going to do? "Let's get together and have some kids. We'll get them through law school…." What are you looking forward to? "Well, I plan to get in a wheelchair, and face the wall, and drool for seven years, while you hope that I die so I don't depreciate the estate." That's crazy! You see the ambivalence of split-mind hate-love? No wonder you feel guilty. It's just awful.

When I was going through my awakening period, I was feeling intense pain for my associations. I mean really intense. The sign of an awakened mind is that he can't stand the pain of the other guy. A lot of you healers, or what you call "unhealed healers", have tried to alleviate the pain of your associations, and you feel the futility of it, because it literally can't be done. You work your magic, your nostrums, your pills, your demonstrations, your psychological re-associations, and the damn consciousness dies.

The suicide rate among physicians is very high. I used to work with impaired physicians, and they would come to me in private and say, "Hell, everything I treat, dies." And these were guys that wanted to heal. I've told you this before; they don't get through medical school now much anymore. But when I was growing up, we had guys that really wanted to heal. The old practitioner, Dr. Layton, used to come with a black bag to the house, and he healed; and I can look back and see that he healed. He didn't have any real medicine to give, but he came, and he was there, and there was an exchange going on, I'm very much aware of it.

One of the reasons we're wrapping this whole episode up is you've stopped exchanging, and you've gone to thought forms, and you're treating the impossibility; you're treating the thought form, rather than the holistic association. It's a fact. The more computer you put into it, the more necessity you have to treat the specific association, which is absolutely futile, and means absolutely nothing. If it's a possibility that the consciousness be in pain, the pain has to be total, or it's not painful at all. And that pain can only be separation and a demand to re-associate separate from the wholeness, and die in the expedience of the tension caused in time. That's what you're doing right now. I don't know how you stand it! I finally couldn't stand the disease of the necessity to hold onto perceptual reality.

Jesus says, how do you take the pain? Every time you get things together in your mind, in the form... I know some of you are going, "Well, I know, but I'm going to be able to do it." No, you're not. Well, you say, "I'm going to be able to hold this together." Until what? Until it falls apart. So you're demonstrating to me life based on holding your thought forms together, and then having them collapse in sickness and pain. If that's all you think life is, what the hell are you doing here? You don't need me! If your life is only going to be based on you holding yourself together, and then rotting in that body, why do you come to me? I'll tell you why. You really don't like the situation that you're in, but you don't see any alternative to it. Not really. Why? If you saw the alternative, you would immediately exercise it. You're nuts, but you're not that nuts! The whole basis of this teaching is to give you one single alternative to everything that you have ever done up until now. Isn't that so? Am I an impossible alternative? Yes!

You keep demanding to know how I fit into your relationships. I don't fit! That's the whole teaching. But remember, that's augmented with the assertion that you are a willing slave to death, and if you want to do that who the hell will stop you? Your demands to know who you are in your own relationship are obviously what? — the tension of your associated thought forms, aren't they? Everybody hear me? Say yes. Oh good, I thought some of you might still be questioning this. You know the problem you're having with this? Shall I tell you? Why you write things down: it's too simple! You will not accept the absolute simplicity of this. Why? It's a total discredit to you. You can't stand the idea that you need do nothing! You absolutely can't stand it. Don't tell me you can. "You're going to participate with me in this." You're wrong. You need do nothing. "Well, I know. You're going to tell me that all I have to do is sit on this chair and do nothing of the work?" I say, no, that's doing a lot. Okay?

What you define as nothing is everything. You couldn't come around me and not identify yourself, and not wake up. It's impossible. It would be impossible. Why? You're nothing but an energy package. Jesus calls it the Great Rays. You are nothing but an association of thought forms contained within this whole drama, aren't you? Now, somewhere within your association, wherever that is, you're hearing me. I have always said exactly the same thing to you. Why? It's the truth. You're the one that doctors it all up. You're the one that says, "I don't sing Christian hymns." That means absolutely nothing to me. It's absolutely meaningless. Why? Everything that you associate with is meaningless. "Well, that's not a very scientific approach." On the contrary, it's a very scientific approach. It's quantum. It's the inclusion of all thought in all thought.

"But wouldn't I lose my perceptual reality?" I don't understand, lose perceptual reality. I'm not teaching you to a notation of non-perception. I'm teaching you to perfect perception for just a moment. Ha! Your whole idea that you can somehow grasp non-perception is silly. How can perception become non-perceptual except by becoming perfectly perceptual? That's the passageway. That's the perfect reflection of the thought forms that are emanating at the schism point, right now. This is the star that Jesus talks about that is hung as a permanent beacon for you to identify. The star of Bethlehem, we call it in esoteric Christianity, and it hangs right here. "Well, it really doesn't hang right there." Yeah. Where did you think it hung, somewhere out there? Who do you think is reenacting the Christmas Story? Do you guys read Chapter 20?

You're reenacting the Christmas story, do you see that? You're going to go through what? The passion of your crucifixion, or *apparent* crucifixion, and resurrection, aren't you? Where is your Bethlehem, then? Christ is born, wrapped in swaddling clothes, in your recesses of memory, the cave of memory, and he escapes the Pharaoh, he spends time in Egypt, and he evolves up, and he ends up in the Passion Week in Jerusalem which is at Golgotha, which is the skull, and he undergoes, through the futility of his associations with God, say in the Garden of Gethsemane, which is... Come on! I'd like to have you guys embrace the truth here in Christianity.

You guys have all sat in your Gethsemanes, and you've been in the Garden, and you've had all your disciples desert you. How determined are you to overcome this last temptation to associate yourself with your perceptual self, rather than understanding that Thy Will will be done, that God's Will is literally going to be done? How many times have you said, "Why hast Thou forsaken me?" Are these the enactment of the illusionary man, Jesus Christ? Did he think of himself as illusionary? Don't be absurd! He thought of himself as exactly as real as you do, and if you think of yourself as real, he is you being exactly the same; there is no difference between you.

This is my whole teaching. You want to call that the Second Coming? There's no coming necessary unless it's the second one. Why? Because this has already all occurred. So I'm going to give you "second in time" for just a moment. But how can it occur outside of you? You keep looking outside of you for the Christ to come, as you did originally. Well, he'll never come. Why? Your imagery is a projection of the denial of his Christhood. Period! Why? It's the denial of your brother's Christhood, who is your Savior. Do you understand me? Can you hear this?

If the Christ is going to come, he would have to be in the imagery of my mind. Is there a question on this? If I projected, from my own limited associations, an idol, a thought form that I want to demonstrate as the Christ to me, I am inherently denying it. I am limiting it in my association. This is why the practice is non-judgment. Do you see? It has to be non-judgment, because if I judge it, I have condemned it to my own false associations, and am dying with it. Is the Christ then all around you every moment? Well, where did you think he would be? Who do you think he is? Who do you think the Savior of the world is?

See, you like it conceptually. You like the idea of the power of your own mind in this reference. What you really can't stand is that there is only your mind. You'd never do that. What are you going to do? You're just going to compare yourself with yourself. This is what you want to do: Release the comparison; undergo the experience of the transformation. If any of you have an idea that the *Course In Miracles* is anything but a course in enlightenment, don't come to me. I don't need your identifications and your mechanisms that you're using in order to define your determination not to get this. The last thing you want to do is get this. If you can't see that, don't come to me. You're obviously very very fearful of it. Why? It's true, and you're afraid of the truth. You feel guilty about it in your limited associations. You've separated yourself from God. You're literally attacking your Father. I'll give you this from the *Course* if you want it: You think there's a battle going on. But the battle is only going on in your own mind. You're asleep. God knows not of it, that's why, because the source is not real.

Now, can you find this out outside yourself? How can you, if the cause is false? This is just pure *Course In Miracles.* You study your effects in an attempt to determine how you're going to associate yourself with this. But the cause of it is not true. This is the whole beginning of the *Course,* and it's in the first three lines. Okay? The responsibility of subjective reality is very fearful to you, finally. It would have to be. That's where your fear threshold is. You can't stand your own thought form association, and you literally project them outside you and place them onto another image.

Look at all the sentences of the *Course* that say your brother is doing to you exactly what you think you did to him. Do you see it? Every thought that you're having is really emanating from your own associations with this. Now, if you can get a hold of this, what you'll begin to do is, instead of doing projections, you'll just begin to allow your mind to expand to the reality that is, where? All around you. It's all around you. Right now.

It's as though you're sitting in an egg, and you've reflected all of this within your own pattern. It's like you're going to crack this egg now and come out of here. When you stand out, and you look up at the stars, and you see these trillions of stars, you see three thousand million light years. What the hell does that mean? "The world will end in a billion years, and we won't be around to know it" and all the other nonsense that goes with that. Yet, what power are you using in your mind to know of that? All the power that there is in the universe. But you've got it contained within this… You're east of Eden aren't you? You're dreaming. You're asleep. Is reality all around you? "Well, how can I find it?" You can't.

The provision of the Atonement, which is what I am, and what you are too, is provided as a device (not real) to show you that you really never left; that you never came into the schism. Am I going to change the demands that you make on yourself in your temporal associations? I hope so. Will this be painful to you? Everything is painful to you. I'm trying to get you to get your pain over with, guys. You keep putting it off.

When I do an individual repair, it's not in association with that conflict, but with the whole conflict of you. Do you hear this? Rosie hears this real plainly because she's seen me do it a lot of times. But if you're going to enter into this association of thought form, I don't want you to be impeded by a karma knot. That is, there's no sense in you being tied up in a self-inflicted thought form — "karma" you call it — that's going to hold you from hearing what I tell you. And this is the whole teaching of "fake it till you make it." It's the whole idea that while you don't have the answer, if you'll make the commitment to it, everything will work, because each moment you'll disassociate from this crap.

This body — I pay absolutely no attention to it at all, none. Remember (this is the whole teaching), any time you pay attention to it, you've given it the direction, and it's telling you how it is. I know you're going to say, "Well, from now on the old man told me not to pay any attention to my body." And that's not what I told you. What I told you is, each moment that you accumulate a divine instant (that is a holy instant) in which you do not identify your limited associations, you save time. See, time is only happening each moment totally. The Atonement is nothing but the holy instant accumulated. Why? It's later on in time when you have raised your frequency of perceptual observation of yourself. You're literally getting closer to the truth.

Now, Jesus would say that can be a thousand million years off. Why? Because if you get caught up in the trap of, say, combatting sin, all you're going to do is fight with your own illusions, which is what occurs down in here, doesn't it? If you release that, you come into a more harmonious association within your own mind, because there is nothing but your own mind. I wish everybody in the world could hear this talk. Excuse me, I mean it's so vivid to me that this is the manner in which you do it, and it's so vivid to me that that's what this is [tapping his *Course* book].

Is there something wrong with the *Course In Miracles* being absolutely true? Answer me. Isn't it okay that it's true? Do you want it to be true? Well, why don't you let it be true? Why do you study its source? Why do you demand to know its emanations? Why do you ask: "Well, yeah, but who or what is that consciousness in relationship to me?" The whole consciousness has no relationship to you, none. You're literally in your own perceptual mind with a direct association in time, to your awakening procedure. I'll give you this. It's impossible you're not going to do this. What are you going to do instead?

Listen. Anything you would do instead of what I'm telling you, encouraging you to do, will be nothing. Each moment in your perceptual associations you're doing nothing. Nothing! You're not doing anything. You're just communicating with yourself and that's not communication; and if you think you're communicating here you're wrong. I'm going to tell you: dead wrong. That's why you're here: you're dead wrong.

You're searching for the living among the dead. They're not here. You're asking yourself your own questions. What Chapter is this? Chapter 17. Boy, some of that's real nice, and it's all in there. What am I doing here? I'm going to tell you it's true. The problem you've had is that you've never had anybody that told you it's really true. Or better, that knows it's really true. Uh, oh. You're going to say, "Well, how do you know?" — which is exactly what you asked the author of the *Course In Miracles*. That's the same as crucifying him. It's exactly the same as killing him. But you can't really kill the Christ because it's true you are really the only consciousness there is in all the universe. You are the only living Son of God. You are as you were created, perfect. It's not out there then, is it?

Questioner: Could you give me an example of what exactly is true communication? You've said it a couple of times and I just...

M.T: Here it is. See, I've answered your question before you asked it.

Oh, hey, that was pretty true. What's that? Ha ha ha! That's true, right? That's the truest thing I've ever done. Are you ready? That's the only thing I've ever done. Tough. Is this the only thing I've ever done? Yeah. Is this the only thing you've ever done? Yeah. What else are you going to do? The only thing you can do is hear me.

"Communication must be whole to be real." Want me to break that down for you perceptually? I'm good at that. That's why you guys got me, I've got a real good mind. "Communication must be whole to be real." Any attempts to identify our association are inherently false. It's the same thing as saying that each moment contains the whole thing and it would make absolutely no difference what I do. None, if it's whole, and it must be whole because it is all that I do and it's impossible that what I do, not be whole. That slips in the Eastern tradition to chopping wood and carrying water. I don't care. It's a delineation of the falsity. A whole mind does nothing. In a very real sense, I'm only doing one thing, and that's not real.

That's very interesting that you'd be here. Yeah. Are you back already? See some of you guys, a lot of you guys I know from World War II. Even though you weren't here. Some of you were here. Some of you I know from World War I, and I know all of you from about 1885 to 1905.

* * * * * * *

We all have the same memories of this. How long ago was that? About two minutes ago. See, you have a tendency to sequence time, and when you do that, you're going to get old. I'm a lot older than you; it doesn't seem like I am. I was born in 1886. I was killed in the First World War, and again in the Second World War; and I just got killed over here again, for the last time, I hope. I looked at the young marines on the truck going up to the front, and I recognized three of my guys, and myself. Can you hear me at all?

I was killed on Saipan, literally, and I lost this leg; and they gave me a new leg so I could come here and still be here. Is that what you can do with this? You can do that if you want to. You can be just as whole as you choose to be. What allowances have I given you? To die! I haven't taken death away from you. I gave it to you, see? Watch me, I'll die, Hah! Here I am. I'll die again. Hah! Here I am.

This is the whole practice of the Atonement. You want this or not? "No, I'll put that off, I won't die." How are you going to be born again if you don't die? You see? You are going to have to undergo the kundalini, the death experience, aren't you? How are you going to know you're whole in your own perceptual relationships if you don't bring them together? You identify that as the loss of self. I promise you that it's the finding of self. That's a sentence right out of the *Course*, isn't it? You think it's death. This is what you're afraid to do, isn't it? You'll do everything you can to protect yourself from the light that's shining right above you, and to maintain this identity until it falls apart. But remember that there is no death.

So you think there's reincarnation, that's nuts. The idea of reincarnation is the idea of sequential time. Time is not sequential, and in that sense literally all you are doing here is living; getting ready to die. But you never die. You've used death as a solution since the beginning of time, because what has a beginning must have an end. And if you know that you planned to be born, then you have planned your own demise. I promise you this is true. Your greatest threat from me is that I am taking that away from you. You don't think it is, but I promise you that the only reason you are here is that you idolize death. These are sentences from the *Course* if you want to read them. When you read those, what do you do, just skip over them real quick?

And then you come to the passages you like that say, "Yes, we are all going together to find…" Naaaa… that's just the mechanism. You literally love to die. The highest passions that you will ever have are always finally in conflict. Do you know that? Your frictions of love are inherently connected with hello-

111

goodbye, death, love, hate, cancer, and it's impossible for you in perception to dis-attach yourself from that. Why? That's what you are. You have an idea that you can have emotions. That you can have thoughts. What is it that would have the thought? You don't respond to me. You say, "Me." I say, "Who is that?" You're a big bag of meaningless memories, but you can take all of those memories which are in all of time and bring them wholly together and get a single moment of a reflection of the whole idea of the reparation, that is, the truth, if you want to.

What are the requirements? You have to want to. Okay? That's the end of Lesson 29. The whole *Course* is this. As long as there's value to you here, never mind how you define it — please can you hear this? — it doesn't make any difference how you define it if you cherish it. You could call it love, hate, murder, you call it being friendly, you call it all of the ideas of the laws of man. There's a sentence in the *Course* where Jesus says, it doesn't matter what they are, as long as you think you can tell the difference in them.

Listen! They're all the same. None of them has any reality in what you really are in the grace of God. If you'll let that begin to come into you, you'll start to feel real good. Why? You don't have to order your thoughts in relationship to yourself. You'll consider that to be weak, I'll consider it to be strong. You'll continue to defend yourself and tell me I'm weak for not having an opinion. You'll be wrong and I'll be right, but you can't know that until you come with me. You literally can't know it. Why? You're defending yourself from your own thoughts. "Blessed are the poor in spirit... Blessed are those who hunger and thirst after righteousness... Resist not evil." Wow!

Questioner: I feel like you're talking about very elevated spiritual concepts, and I feel from my reading of the *Course* that it's true, but I don't feel it really affects me. I wonder if you could talk about your own transformation and the stages that you went through.

MT: You'll just use that as a means to deny me. All mechanisms are false, but you use them as a defense for not getting this. Yes, I think there may be some value in how this occurred. Obviously, I didn't get it on a spiritual path though. I got it by giving up, and you won't like that answer.

I got it by giving up. I got it by seeing that no matter what I did I couldn't succeed. Period! Now, the outcome of that has to be demonstrated by your willingness to surrender your association with yourself; you can't get it any other way. I don't care what you want to call that, but you're always bringing into the situation your demand for recognition of yourself in that participation, and you're always wrong.

The reason that I'm a little step ahead of you is I had a higher ego than you do. That's a fact. Why? It had to be more demolished than you're willing to demolish yours. You're going to maintain that there is value in this association. There's no value in it at all, and until you come to know that, you can't get this. The only value there would be is in your coming to the conclusion of the futility of the relationship. If you can't get that, why the hell are you here? No pain no gain! Everything you plan falls apart. What do they call this, Bell's Theorem? The re-association of the consciousness at a higher frequency of coordinated thought form.

The universe is winding up, isn't it? So every time you formulate it, since it's in time, it's contained within the tension of your own mind, that must be relinquished. That will always be defined as pain. Why? The tension is inherently painful. The necessity to hold it back. You hold the pain off from you, don't you, in the formulation, say, of your life, and you plan it according to the tensions contained within your own memory patterns. They always fail finally and cave in. Really, the acceleration of time is only causing you pain that you refuse to accept at this time. You want future pain. Can anybody hear me at all on this? You're identifying yourself with future pain, and future gain, which to you is the same thing. You must bring the pain and the gain together at this time, or how the hell are you ever going to get it?

Okay, you can say to me, "No, I have reached a limited goal; I am now president of the largest corporation in the world." "No, I have succeeded, I've got a bottle of wine and I've got a refrigerator crate that's going to keep me warm tonight." Those are the same things. You've found a satisfaction in the limited association. Now, until you feel the frustration of the limitations of your goal... Jesus calls it your inability to fulfill your function, which is only creating. You must release the tension finally and die into it. It's not a statement of your own whole self. You only create. Your mis-identities in the limited association cause you to miscreate within the time framework of the demands you make on your own aesthetic distance, on the things that you deny are a part of you. Everything is a part of you. The admission of that is how you practice forgiveness.

The last thing you want to do is hear this. Why? You're contained within your own dream, within your own perceptual association. Now, what you're going to say to me if you don't want to hear it, quite literally — and this seems insane, but this is why it's an insane place... Literally what you're saying to me is, "I would rather get sick and die than hear you." That has to be true. Why? You already have been presented with the alternative. The question is not that you don't know the alternative. The question is, when are you going to accept it? I'm just giving you the whole *Course* here. It's impossible that you don't know about it. Any denial is an admission of knowledge.

Questioner: How do I accept this?

MT: You can't. There's no how to it, acceptance is relinquishment of judgment. You just did it again, you just turned it around and wanted to know how to do it. You accept it by getting some more pain. That will cause the acceptance. Not only that, but you'll inflict it on yourself until you get it. Are you going to study that? That's a fact. Why? Perceptual mind is what pain is. All you've done is give it to somebody over there — and refuse to accept responsibility for it, just incidentally. You're going to hold yourself in a definition of finding your way out of this. You can't find it unless everybody finds it. If I were you I'd practice a little give rather than identifying. The real trick to this is don't study it; give it. Listen to me.

Questioner: Give what?

MT: Everything. Don't ask what. If you defend yourself in any regard, you're going to get caught up in what? Reciprocity. What are you giving to? Nothing. If you give to nothing, you are giving to God, because God to you is nothing. I'm offering you the impossible, immediately. But remember it's the demonstration of the release of your tensions that is what the miracle is. Obviously, if your perception is the obstacle to the miracle, which is nothing but whole mind, when you release that tension of association, you're whole. Why? Wholeness is what everything is. You're the... This [pointing to a body] is the obstacle. This is pure *Course*, this is in the preamble to the *Course*. I can't teach you what love is, but I can show you what the obstacles are, and they're you! I mean love is going to be love, right?

I understand this appears to attack you, because you are defending yourself from it; and this is the ultimate defense. Why? I'm presenting you with the ultimate truth. You literally do not participate in your own Atonement. How could you? You're the falsity. You want to respond to that? If you're false, how can you ever find the truth? Respond!

You can't! You're false because you're false. There is no communication between falsity and truth. Truth is true and nothing else is true. Your needs to identify yourself are what the falsity is. You look for a middle ground. There is no communication between God and this. Except what? Your own bridge that's contained in your mind by the admission that you are created, and have the power in your own mind. And that's what I'm trying to give you, but you're afraid to take it, because you associate it with limited power structure, what you call perception, and you continue to defend yourself in your own miscreations with the things that are apparently outside of you.

"Power corrupts. Absolute power corrupts absolutely. "Everybody goes "Amen". That's crap, that's pure crap. Absolute power is God. I'll do it once more for you. "Power corrupts." That's why you don't want me to be all powerful. I'm inherently corrupt if I talk to you from whole mind. Can anybody hear me? That has to be so. I'm a total authority, and you cannot accept total authority. How many times do you have to accept it? Just once.

Once more: "Power corrupts (because when we get more we hold onto it) and absolute power corrupts absolutely." That's the most insane statement that could ever be made. It's the definition that God is corrupt, evil and death, and those that have the most when they die are the most successful. It's just senseless. You are the only living Son of God — you're true; you're in a dream, and I came to wake you up because you told me to. Why else am I doing this? Did I come uninvited? Impossible. You can misidentify me, but you have to have invited me because I'm in your mind.

Somewhere within your time framework you heard me and came to Heaven. Why? We already decided that. We're trying to decide whether you're going to do it this time or wait until some other time. You think there's another time, I know there's not. You ought to remember me. I owe you. You got my marker. You told me to come here and do this.

See, you guys think that we don't know each other. How the hell would we not know each other? "Well, I certainly don't remember knowing you." That's because you don't want to. I remember you. Now, will you remember me somewhere in time? Well, of course. Will you remember me perfectly? How could you not? You know everybody. I mean it's not that big a deal. There were only twelve of us, right?

All I've done is taken total responsibility for the screw up. Can you hear this? I was in charge of this that screwed it up, or you were, but I'm going to take it this time. See if you can hear this. We went out on a mission together and got screwed up — it's called a mistake in the *Course In Miracles.* We made a mistake. What did we lose? Communication. It was nothing but a momentary loss in communication. But at the time it was broken... I think it was a fly speck on the map or something. I don't know.

I'm trying to give you an analogy that would be more like a parable, perhaps, than your definition of it. When my mind speaks like this, it's speaking absolute truth to you. We got lost. I led you into death, and I accept responsibility for that, and I'll lead you out of this if you'll let me. That's why I got the job. It has nothing to do with good or bad or right or wrong. It has to do with my recognition of the mistake. It's not sinful, it's not sick, it's not going to die, and, finally, it never happened.

I have often told you, I got the short straw at the Master's Academy. I drew the short straw. Nobody wants to come down this deep in this crap. Do you think I am a number one savior? I was 242nd in my class. That's a sad idea isn't it? You're not sure you like that. You know, I always was disturbed there was always a doctor who graduated last in his class! So you're going to judge... Because I was 242nd, you have a tendency to say, "Well, can I have somebody who was a little higher in the graduation?" No, no, that's why you got me. [laughs]

When you get this deep, we call ourselves the dirty dozen. This is quite literally true. See, the difference is you're just a complete misfit here. I wish you could hear this. Because of the advancement of your karma association within your heart, this time in this frequency, you're aware that you don't fit. You have to be or you wouldn't be sitting with me. If you had been able to fit this together, you would have been the number one cello player in the Chicago Symphony, or you'd play the harp beautifully perhaps, and that has given you the satisfaction of your creative purpose. You guys are Jack-of-all-no-trades. You're good at everything, but you have no tenacity to pursue it, because you see the futility down the line of the accomplishment. That's why you got me. Isn't that funny?

I couldn't go to school. I couldn't understand why you would go to school and study something that was already known. Can you hear this? Yeah. Algebra, I'd say, why would you try to solve something for the unknowns? You must know what's in there already. Why don't you just put the answer down, and I'll...Yeah.

So you study the philosophers in relationship to themselves, and I tried to read the philosophers, and I said, I know that, I know that. You do, too. They come up with all of these dramatic perceptual things and you'd say, "I knew that when I was fourteen." There's a lot of you like this, that's why you're with me. You couldn't understand why the academia would go and study for eight years and come up with all comparative relationships, in philosophy perhaps, between Aristotle, or Kierkegaard, or Hegel, or the Existentialists, because what they were looking for was always obvious in your mind.

So you felt the frustration of not being happy with limited goals. Now that can assert itself in various ways. You can continue to do it, put up a façade and die with it; being a loving grandfather, knowing in your heart that you screwed it up again, but you won't know that until you pass through another physical death. At that time you'll remember it perfectly, because that's really what's happening to you now, but you don't know that. I can't teach it.

Time is collapsing each moment, and you're actually undergoing death experiences, right now. What I want you to do is undergo one and remember it perfectly well. The experience that I had that you want me to tell you about, was much more devastating than a death experience. See, I thought there was some value in death. The experience I had indicated that there was absolutely no value in me. That's why I don't give you any credit in your own ego. It's absolutely meaningless to me. Did I get that through the devastation of my own association? That's what I'm trying to get you to do. Can that be done gradually? I don't know. There's no definition for it. Is it necessary to salvation? Imperatively necessary.

See, the *Course* is a soft course in the hardest way possible because it's very unequivocal, but it appears to give you full license of choice, doesn't it? It doesn't recommend any form of discipline at all except the practice of the association. As soon as that practice becomes part of you, you will inherently do it because of the progress being made in your transformation. Outside of that it would be totally non-doctrinal and totally non-disciplinary. Do you see? As soon as you begin to see this, you want it. Why wouldn't you?

Now, as long as you think the alternative is going to satisfy you, you won't seek it. That's a fact. I can't do anything about that. Now you will demand from me satisfaction in your limited associations, and all I can say is, be happy. What else can I tell you? If you're determined to be the grandma, if you're determined to continue to authenticate yourself, who in all the universe is going to stop you from doing it? You demand that I give you recognition for yourself, but I can't, because you're no-thing. I can't give you recognition. I can only ask you to look at the power of your mind that's being asserted in your determination to hold onto your limited associations. Will you be the same after you talk to me? It's impossible. No one is the same after they talk to me. How could you be? That has nothing to do with whether you attack me or whether you re-devise yourself in another association. Do I use that? Sure.

People don't like the Teachers Manual where it talks about the use of occult witchcraft to the benefit, but I love black magic. I mean, finally the only thing you are attacking is yourself and it can appear to be very devastating. But pure black magic is pure light — intrinsically. Can you hear that? The moment you would demonstrate total evilness you'd have to be totally good. You ready? What's the difference between something totally evil and something totally good? You want to respond to that? What's the difference between something totally evil, totally separate, and something totally whole? Hmm? How could it be? If you were totally evil, you would be totally good. You can't be totally aware of evilness. It's a negative statement of separation and becomes inclusive. You can't be totally separated; you become whole. How could you not? Separation; duality, is duality. Your problem is you're judging separation. You have to choose up sides and what have you got? You don't have a whole on either side of you. This is the whole *Course In Miracles.*

If there is a whole, it's impossible that anything be separate from it. You know that perfectly well in your mind, therefore you must be included in the whole, but in order to know that you've got to take the separation and bring it into the whole association of your own mind. What do you have to do? Bring the evil up with the good and don't judge it. Your "reality" is based on the moral definition of what is good and evil and what is murder and what is okay to do and what is not okay to do. None of that is true and none of it is real. Do I have that a step ahead of you? If I murdered when I was seventeen, like these young guys are doing over there now, I was justified in killing people. Some deaths are okay and some are not. That's absurd to me. It's absolutely absurd. If anything dies, everything must die, and that death must be in my own associations.

For your perceptual mind to qualify the relationship of pain and death is absolutely absurd to me, and I couldn't stand it. When I came back from the war, I couldn't stand this place. Why? Because I'd seen thousands of bodies piled up dead, and they had no meaning in the association with life. If life ends in death, what the hell is the purpose in it? You give it purpose and tell me it's okay. That's okay, I can't stop you from doing that. I'm looking for people who don't want to base their life on death. Because basing your life on sickness and termination is senseless to anybody that would care to look at it.

Wow. At the time one of my best friends was killed, I suddenly was him. I knew perfectly well I was him standing there, that I was a part of this whole thing. Not by my definition of his personality, but by the certainty of continuing consciousness within this framework of apparent reality. And that is what I am directing you to now.

So I'm taking death away from you. Now what are you going to do? You say to me, "What am I going to do now?" This is the teaching of Jesus Christ. Here's what you've never been willing to do. I'm going to take death away from you. If I don't let you sequence time, everything that you're doing here has no meaning. Is there a question on this? How could it? If you have constructed yourself in this association which you have of yourself and are giving it value, you will fulfill the obligation of your own mind to die. If I take that away from you, the earth doesn't have any purpose!

That's a fact. This is the teaching of Jesus Christ. You're not from here, your kingdom is of Heaven; don't lay up stores; give everything away; don't resist. Do you hear it? This is what you won't do. See, you want the truth of it, but you don't want to have to... Jesus teaches, you are not a happy learner. You think somehow there is sacrifice involved in what you're doing which is probably the craziest thing I ever heard of. Somehow you don't want to give up the rotten stuff that you've got in order to know that you're whole. This is an actual conflict that's in your own mind, and if you don't think so, you are sadly mistaken. And unless you look at it you are never going to be able to overcome it.

The admission finally has to be that I'm not going to lose the things that I love if there is a God. I'm not going to let this consciousness (this is my daughter, incidentally)... I'm not going to let my daughter get sick and die by defining her as a body. The power is in my mind to do that. I tell you that that's a power that I have because this is my world. Now you say to me, "Well, it may be your world, but it's not my world." Crap. I am you in my world.

I don't know if you're ever going to hear this, but you're going to have to hear it sometime. The very simple reason that I am the savior of the world is because I saved it by coming to know its unreality. It has absolutely nothing to do with what you think I am; and what you think I am is the falsity of it.

I'll try something with you. When I leave here — it's hard for me to teach that — in just a moment, or now, or when I fulfill the contract I've got with the *Course*... See, I have a contract with Jesus and the guys in the *Course*, because you weren't getting it. You were fooling around with it a little bit. So that's why I do this, so that you can make the energy connection with the perceptual connection of the *Course*. Why? The *Course* is true. Now since I'm doing that, that must be the method in which you got it. Do you hear that? Good for you. This is why it says you've got to use the *Course In Miracles*, because you have no alternative to it. The *Course In Miracles* is the awakening, not by your definition of it, but because it says the truth. What difference does it make who says it?

So what they've given you is a guy you're sure to deny. Why? He is in direct association with you! He's not some idol that you can accept up to the point where he fails you in your own mind. He's in a constant confrontation with you. Why? That's what you need to look at. Since it's only your own judgment that keeps you from being whole. This is the practice of the *Course In Miracles* in non-judgment, incidentally. Does this require your admission that I am expressing to you later on within your own time field? It would sure as hell help you. If you can't tell the positivity of my statements, what are you doing here? The only definition that I will ever give you for honesty is constancy. I'm absolutely constant. And the awakening minds that are coming around me know that no matter how they judge me, I will be constant in this statement, and it's not tolerable to you. Well, if it's not tolerable to you, go away. That will not prevent me from being constant. It's your acknowledgment of our mutual constancy that is what salvation is, dummies!

You can't get it without going to it, without the admission that this is what you want. I don't care how you judge it. What's that got to do with it? That's all false. Is something happening to you in your mind when you're around these new energy fields? Oh yeah. That's not the point, the point is what are you doing with it in your own memory? Do you see? Each one of you has "peopled" (Jesus uses this) his own memory associations with a conglomerate of phantoms of unrealities and identifies them. He's really not communicating with anybody. Back to that once more.

So I'm bringing about a re-association in your own mind. It doesn't have to do with him. It literally has nothing to do with him. Can you hear this? This is only between you and me. It's subjective. It doesn't have to do with you turning to the guy next to you and saying, "Gee, it's certainly interesting what he is saying." That's absolutely meaningless. Who the hell are you talking to? Somebody who previously agreed with you and now perhaps is going to disagree with you? Or is going to find a re-association in order to sustain your identity of me in your mutual falsity? Do you do that? Sure. But until you're willing to accept the Atonement for yourself, how the hell are you going to get it? There is only yourself.

How many anti-Christ's are there? Answer. "One." Who is it? "Me." Well, if there is an anti-Christ, it would have to be you. It had to be you. Well, strangely enough, in any sort of reasonable so-called dialog, if there is an anti-Christ, there must be a Christ. Okay? This is exactly the same thing as totally evil and totally good. You can't be totally anti- anything because it's an objective association. The moment that you would become totally anti-, obviously you would include it all in. That's what I want you to do. Include all of your anti- in with the good. See what happens? You no longer have resistance in your thought forms about what you are. You don't suffer the conflict. It's forgiveness. Don't bring your grievance up to the present and hold it against your brother; that's you.

Can you practice doing this? Do you need to? You say to me, "Well, I need to practice forgiveness," and I say to you, "Why?" If that's your thought form out there, why is it so difficult for you to forgive your own thought form? You say, "Well, I don't know if that's true." That's all you could say to me. Obviously, you're attacking yourself, aren't you? Is that so? Are you really only attacking yourself? How can you know that? Respond. Don't defend yourself. Well, explain that to me. No. There's nothing to explain about non-defense. There's nothing more defensive than an explanation of non-defense. It's the same as the explanation of nothing. It's the same as the explanation of unconditional love. I'm not teaching unconditional love, I'm teaching fully conditional love. 'Without condition' has to be in your conception 'all condition.' I'm teaching forgiveness, which is inclusion, not subtraction. You're determined to subtract some of the things you've constructed from the reality of this; it won't work. You will suffer the conflicts if you do, won't you? And you'll get old and die.

Now, this afternoon, I'm going to stop you from aging, because I don't want you to get old. See, if you'd care to look at this with me, how the hell does an image get old? Answer me. If you're in an image here, how do I know whether you're old or not? What does old have to do with the image? Nothing, except what? You have brought your previous memories in the constitution of what you are into this field of our association. That doesn't make any sense to me. I don't understand it. I go to nursing homes, and the people that are sitting in nursing homes, if somebody hadn't told them that they were old, they wouldn't know that they're old. I used to go because I love 'em. I love old people... I'd go and... I would treat them like they were eighteen, and what happened? They became eighteen. I don't understand why, because somebody gets old, he's somehow different than he was when he was seventeen. It's absurd.

* * * * * * *

What would you do if you could get old and couldn't die? Do you just keep getting older and older? Answer me. You say, "Well, I know I can't die and obviously I'm aging." No, no, you're not. It's obvious to you, but not to anyone else, because there isn't anyone else! You take all of your previous memories, and bring them up into a sequential time association, don't you? You bring into our associations your previous experiences. Now your reality is going to be based on the terrible things that happened to you when you were fourteen and fifteen. That's sad. Why? All of your memories are only of grievance. It's impossible that that not be so because all of your memories are only conflictual. All family associations are conflictual, and you as psychologists ought to know better than to allow the consciousness his limited associations, and verify him in your demand that you share the mutual grief. That's crazy.

That is not to say that you not may need an identity as an alkie or as a molested child. You can have any identity you want to have, but it will not be true. If you need to look at the problem you've had in that association, for goodness sake, look at it, but don't hold onto it as your identity, or you'll be here a long time. You can build whole nations around the grievances of the holocaust that happened fifty years ago, or two thousand years ago. If your reality is based on defense of yourself, that's called the First Covenant, isn't it? That's a statement of reciprocity: "I will never forgive you, and I'm going to get even with you in some fashion." That's exactly what the perceptual mind is, but remember that it's only trying to get even with reality finally. It's trying to make a statement of itself separate from the wholeness. It constructs exchange in order to retain that identity. That is the First Covenant, "an eye for an eye." That's the setting up of the laws of man. Rhinoceroses do not set up legal codes. This is you, meeting yourself coming and going, isn't it? Suddenly you see yourself in an expanded frame of reference, and have to take responsibility for your environmental concerns. At that point it would be important that you recognize that your heredity and environment are exactly the same thing. This would be a quantum leap for you guys. There is no difference between heredity and environment if everything is already past. Is that so?

You are literally constructing an environment based on your hereditary associations. It is impossible that that's not so. You want to give some credit to environment, and some to heredity, but finally it doesn't make any difference. Everything is heredity. It has to be if it's memory. You say, "Yes, but I want to be afforded the opportunity to expand my mind and my consciousness association." Good. But where are you in association with your determination to solve the problems of the world, when they're in your own mind?

You guys have been carrying the placard 'ban the bomb' for a very long time. That's an admission of the reality of the bomb, and the denial that you're the cause of it. I don't care where you hear this, that's a statement of fact. When the bomb is banned here [pointing to his head], then there's no bomb. You can't heal something that's out there. The acceptance that you are the cause of this war is how the war is not so, not by directing it out there and trying to change the effects of it. Now you're going to say, "You're telling me not to change the effects of it." I'm not doing that. I understand that you feel the pain of your own effects. I'm directing you to the certainty that the problem cannot be solved, and you will attempt to solve it until you reach that conclusion. And you must reach that conclusion, because the problem is not real.

Does it make you feel good that the problem is not real? As you reach a certain point in your own association, that is going to make you feel very good. At that moment, you're going to be attacked by your previous associations that think that's very bad. Why? You're simply saying, "The world is not real. I'm going to withdraw from it and no longer participate in it." They'll say, "Well, don't be ridiculous. I mean, you have responsibilities..." You guys don't like this kind of a talk. This is lovely in the *Course* where it says they're going to say, "Don't look up! Don't look up! Stay down here. You have a responsibility with us to stay in this conflict, and die with us. You have a sociological responsibility," and they'll demand that you fulfill that. That's really the conflict that you're feeling. It has to be, because you're early in this association, and there is no definitive evidence of what's going on in your mind. We're too deep. [Privately to a participant] What has that got to do with it? It's too late for you to do that; it's already in your mind. It's impossible that this be too early for you to do, isn't it?

Does it seem like conflict to you? Yeah. Why? Guilt — you won't like this either — what is defined as guilt is only the ordering of your own thoughts. Can you hear this? It has nothing to do with whether it's good or bad. Can you hear me? If you order your thoughts, you'll be responsible for the consequences of your thoughts. Question? Jesus says it's hard for you to understand there is no need to order your thoughts, that is your conceptual associations, but if you do, you must assume responsibility for them. How would you not? You must be giving them value, or attempting to give them no value in your own associations. You can not not do it. What have you done? You've assumed responsibility for what you are in your own memory. You say to me, "Well, how else would I live? How else am I going to exist, if I don't do that?" You will continue to do that until you examine the source of the problem in the need for you to order your own thoughts. This is the whole *Course In Miracles.* As long as you order your own thoughts, you will be the creator of your apparent universe, and nothing can stop you from doing it. So let's not pretend that something is keeping you from relinquishing this. You're not relinquishing your own thought forms, literally, because you don't want to. This is pure *Course* now.

A slave to death is a willing slave. You want the sentence? Somewhere you cherish the associations that you are formulating, and there's no one that could take that away from you. Why would they want to? How could they? They're in your mind. Until you examine them, you will not let them go. Now I'm teaching you the *Course.* Until you look at the relationship of your own self in your own mind to the things you love and cherish, how can you possibly come to know that you love death? It has to be true. Why? It's in the power of your mind. Now we're teaching you the *Course.*

"Is there another power that will help me overcome this?" No, you're using all the power. But you will not make this true, guys. Why? It's not true. God suffers no conflict. There's no such thing as fear and evilness and sickness and death. It's not real. You say to me, "Well, we're all coming to know that." No, you're not. You're denying it. "Coming to know" is the denial. All spiritual paths are denials of God. Is there a question about that? "Well, aren't you giving us a spiritual path?" No, I'm telling you there is no path. "Yeah, but you gave us a choice." I gave you a choice because I didn't have any alternative.

Do you know how I can tell an advanced teacher of the *Course* from an unhealed healer? An unhealed healer will teach choice. Are there questions? I'll answer questions on this. You say, "Well, the *Course In Miracles* says there is a choice." No, the *Course In Miracles* says there is no choice. What does it say? Choice is an impossible situation that you have placed yourself in by believing you can choose between this and something else. How many times have you guys read this in the book? All I want you to do is look at it. That's what it says, and that's what it means. You go to all these *Course* groups and say, "We're all working together." No! You should sit down and say, "We're all working together not to get this." Is that true? Yeah, darn right it's true. You say, "Well, not altogether." And I say "In what regard?" "Well, I'm certainly practicing all of the principles of the *Course*." The *Course* has no principles!

It has one statement. It's not a perceptual association of the values that you've given it. That's just the denial of the Source. If the *Course In Miracles* is a scripture, is a message from God, it requires your acceptance of it in order to hear it. It cannot be gained by your examination of the source. That's what holds you in death. Is that too big a step for you? You say, "Well, I have a conceptual association with Jesus Christ that does not allow me to accept the *Course*." Really? Well, do you accept what the *Course* says? Insane! "Well, I accept totally what the *Course* says, but I want to teach it as though Jesus didn't write it." This is really double nuts now. Now we're into the double nuts. What we're going to do is acknowledge that the material is true, but deny the guy who says he wrote it in the material. That makes no sense. You think you're not doing that, but that's what you're doing. You're studying the cause in what you want the effect to be.

There's a lovely sentence in the *Course* where Jesus says it has to lead to insanity. Why? It's a disassociation of cause and effect. Everybody got that? When I give you a true message, you study me instead of what I'm saying to you. You have to, because you're in association with me about what you want to hear me say in your own mind.

How often do I tell you this? Just once. I only told you this once. You ought to be able to hear this. A lot of you guys can hear what I just said to you. I could have only told you this once, because it's the truth, and it would be impossible that you did not hear me. The part about you that's pretending it doesn't hear this is not. That's the moment of the schism; that's a not. Now you can hold that not-ism together, in time, can't you? But remember the source is not.

Is this too tough a message? It's the simplest message there ever could be. That's why it's not acceptable to you. It's the most difficult message there could ever be, because it's obviously the only message you have to hear. What other message would there be? God is. And you know it, and yet you deny that you do. Knowing something and denying it is obviously rank insanity, yet that must be what you're doing. This is Lesson 139. It must be that you know what you pretend you don't want to know, otherwise how do you know you don't know it? But if you say you don't know it, the thing that says it doesn't know it must not want to know it. Not wanting to know is not real. Is that in Lesson 139? Yeah. You guys take a lunch break, and you read Lesson 139 and Lesson 140. If any of you are still left here this afternoon…

So you're in what, competition with your own mind here? Yeah. "How do I get out of this, then?" It would help if you believed what I'm telling you is true. Do I have a reason to tell you this if it's not so? I see some people are saying that the *Course* is the work of an evil force. The study of the *Course* perceptually is an indication you think it might also be evil. So let's not be condemning the people that have formulated within their own minds. Nothing is more evil than your judgment of the *Course*, or ever could be; but remember evil is not real. If you didn't need the Atonement, I wouldn't be here.

I understand that you're denying God. I'm trying to get you to admit you are, so that you can see that it's not so. How else am I going to do it? You can not not be in Heaven with me. Not only that but you can not not be in another congruent association with me at this time right out of time, because it's in our mutual minds. As Jesus would say, we're standing together just across the border on this. We'd have to be. We're talking about it. Well, when is this happening? Now. When are we standing on the other side talking about this? Now. "Well, can I cross over?" Sure. "Can I stay crossed over each moment for the time that I'm going to remain in my perceptual association?" Positively. "What do I have to do to do that?" Don't be afraid, because you think crossing over is death. You call it 'crossing the bar' and you're literally afraid to look up and allow this awakening that is trying to occur in you now to proceed. Why? It's fearful to you.

You say, "What are all these strange minds doing around here demonstrating to this new reality? I don't think they ought to do that. People here will think they're very strange." What is more foolish to temporal man than a spiritual man? What could be more foolish than what I'm teaching you? I'm teaching you: Don't subsist. I'm teaching you: Don't lay up stores. I'm teaching you: Make no provisions. I'm declaring to you that this is not real. I'm telling you that you can't die and you can't get sick. That has to be foolish to you! Don't tell me it's not, because it is. One of us is wrong though. Now maybe at that point I could get you to look at the alternative. Until you examine your own relationship, you're just going to keep insisting that you are right in this, and until you look at the outcome of being right, you can't get this. Do you see? You have to look at the outcome of what you're doing, instead of burying it on your brother. Instead of letting him get cancer and die. If anybody gets cancer and dies, it's what? It's you. Why would you want one of your loved ones to get cancer and get sick? Answer me! And you tell me you don't, and I'll tell you, well don't do it then.

You want a key sentence of the *Course*? You didn't make yourself, you dummy. You keep trying to construct yourself using the power of God. You're determined to come back to the location of yourself in time rather than questioning the schism where that occurred. See, time and eternity are obviously the opposite. So you're held within that association of a beginning and an end, and you maintain to me that's life. How? How do you maintain that that's life? How would you know if you are alive, except by dying? You couldn't. You have constructed your life on dying. And now suddenly you're dead, but how does that prove there is life? See, it doesn't make any sense. It's absolutely senseless, and until you look at it you can't get out of it.

Life based on death is what death is. You want to write that down? Death is life based on death. What's the difference between life — if you're going to die — and death? Nothing. What's sickness but death? What you're saying to me is, "I'm going to get sick and suffer and perish, and then finally, as a relief for my pain," — what will you do? — "I'll die."

I got a good idea that I had when I was fifteen. "Well, if you're going to have to go through the pain in order to die and be in Heaven, then why don't we just kill ourselves?" Okay? How many times did you do that? How many times are you going to do that until you realize the futility of associating annihilation with eternity, which is obviously the dilemma that you're facing. You ought to start to hear me here. How many times are you going to cut your wrists and say, "I can't stand this"? You can't escape the problem through death because there isn't any.

So all you're really telling me is, "I'm alive." This is what I discovered just before my awakening — that I'm alive always, and everything is always dying around me. Statement of fact. The statistics are incredible. A million people can die, but it's never you. This is why you don't really give any value to life. You really don't care that twenty thousand babies starved to death in Ethiopia yesterday; you're concerned about one life in the Gulf. That's perfectly okay until you look at the absurdity of it. But regardless of how you look at it, you can't die. You say, "Well, I wish I could believe you." And I say, you don't have any alternative but to believe me, because you're using the power of your mind to deny me now; and it's impossible that you will continue to do that when you discover that you're causing your own pain. You literally will not do it. Why would you?

Is it necessary that you accept responsibility for the cause of this? How else are you going to get it? You are the cause of your own pain, right? Is all pain self-inflicted? Don't do it then. Stop doing it. "Well, that's easy to say." Well, that's easy to do, too. Don't do it. Don't blame your brother. Now you don't like what I start to tell you. Why? Inherent in you is the shared guilt of your own association. He has to be responsible for what's happening to you. Now it's gotten much too easy for you. You're going to say, "Well, we all know that." You don't know that. If you knew that, you'd be in Heaven. "Well, I certainly like the way you present it, teacher, and I'm going to consider it." Go ahead; what good is that going to do you?

You're going to have to accept it, guys. Did you accept it? Yeah? When? Now. Did you get it just now? I just felt that. What happened to you? You dirty guy. Did you see that, Rosie, did you feel that? She had a knot. We all came from the pancreas, the Pleiades; did I say pancreas? Is that the pancreas out there? Yeah! Did you all know that we all came from the pancreas? There are real esoteric talks about the relationship of the ductless glands with what is happening. That's well and good, but you'll have a tendency to reduce it and go to the Menninger Clinic to be studied about your new brain waves or something. Am I creating frenzies in your brain associations? Yeah, yeah. You're having what you term epileptic seizure associations. Can you hear that? If you've seen somebody in a grand mal, that's much like… The difference is that you are looking at it as beneficial rather than retracting it. Remember that all of the reality has always been around you, but the explosion of the necessity of the understanding in the perceptual brain literally causes a contraction which is a seizure. It's called a premature awakening, perhaps, which is the same as a premature kundalini awakening. Or through drugs you attempt to stimulate your endorphin associations; you can bring about some very bad trips in your association: schizophrenic, or paranoid, or manic depressive, which are the three things we're directing you to here. Can you get this outside of the religious vernacular? Yeah, but why should you, if the lesson is all inclusive, dummy? You ask dumb questions. "Can I get this without using the vernacular?" All the vernacular is unreal until you bring it into associations.

Some of you guys I know real well when I recognize you. Does that mean that our associations have always been pleasant? No, that means that they have always been finally unpleasant, somewhere. They're associated with love and death and all the things that we've done together here. But I wouldn't be here if I wasn't your teacher. You can deny it, but that won't mean anything to me. Why? I only teach one thing and you only deny one thing: me. It's impossible that I'm not true because everything is true. I'm teaching you to relinquish judgment in order to see that, rather than hold onto judgment and try to identify truth. That's crazy. You're trying to tell God what He is. He already knows. Who is He? You. There's so much energy here, we'll probably have to have a little quiet time.

I want you to take the reasonable accord of what I'm saying to you and bring it into this new association with you through the inclusion of your own concepts. Otherwise you can't get it. No matter how much illuminate energy I give into a conflictual association, until it's prepared to relinquish its associations it won't do any good. I suppose it'll benefit from it. Certainly, I have no intention of causing you pain. People who come into this association with this energy many times leave much happier. A lot of people go out and do astonishing things. That has nothing to do with what I teach. That has to do with their demand to remain here and accomplish something in sickness and death. Can I stop them from doing that? No.

In energy, this is a sorting out process where, if you are ready within time to bring your own associations into this, you become a savior of the world — this is the *Course* now — or will you simply remain 'no-thing?' Now you will not define yourself as no-thing, and you will feel the accomplishments of the power of your own mind, but you will also take on the responsibility for your time associations, do you see? Therefore, all of the things that you love and cherish will become rusty, get old, and die. I'm right back to where, if you don't look at that, you'll continue to do it.

Is there a change in time going on in this room? Very dramatic, okay? The only place there is in all the universe is here. When you came in the door this morning, you walked into a time warp. I wish I could teach you this. How can I do that? This is Chapter 13. Think of time as being nothing but continual congruent continuity of thought, see? All time is going on all the time. If you come into a situation locating yourself in space-time in your own mind, and let go of that association, it automatically will formulate in a broader, later range in your time associations. That's what's happening here now. You can call that a Holy Instant, but I'd rather just have you look at the fact that this is the time of your resurrection. In the *Course* Jesus must do it a hundred times. He says, "Today is the day you did it. Today is the day that you finally found it." Why does he say that? Because today is the day that you did it. Expect God now. How could He come if you didn't expect Him now? The whole problem is you put off the expectation and continue to participate in your previous thought forms. How can you get out if you do that? Answer me, somebody! You keep pretending you want to get this, but you won't do the things with your mind that you have to do to get it. You are the denier of it.

I understand that for the first time you are seeing a way out of this, those of you who are getting excited about it. I assure you, you should get excited, because this is the way out for you, if you're ready to hear it. Now, can you deny me and go back out into the world? Yeah, but I shortened some time for you, because this time, when you suddenly discover that you're dying and the heart begins to pound and you go, "Uh, oh...," you'll say, "Oh! Oh! I remember that now. I can remember now, I'm passing over. Ha! I'm out of the body and I'm feeling all of this lovely light energy that's always been around me." What's happened? For that moment I've disassociated from the body. Those of you who have death experiences have had this one. And it's real bright and you know every answer that could ever be, and it's getting better and it's getting better and — Auggghhh! Here you are again.

See, somewhere the two things don't meet, do they? Of course not. They can't. Now, all I'm really asking you to do is advance the time to your final association, so that you'll be here just a moment in the total reflection of your own reality.

Know ye not, ye must be born again? Are you afraid to do that? Yeah, because obviously you're afraid to die. Can you do it? Sure! I'm here to tell you that you can part the veil. In fact, in this quadrant the veil is opened. It got opened inadvertently; it got opened a little early. Do you understand that the plan of Atonement is totally flexible? Can you hear this? If you think it's screwed up here, you ought to see the order room right up in here. See, there's only just a Master Plan. There's only just a single whole plan, everything else is pure chance. Does anybody hear me when I talk like this? It has to be pure chance because nothing can be planned. I'm teaching you that everything is a hundred percent chance. That's how you can be sure it's okay. I want you to become totally chaotic in your associations. Do you think that God orders his thoughts? Well, you laugh at that, but God doesn't order anything. "God is perfect order." Crap. God is perfect chaos!

If each moment is only a whole moment, how the hell would you put them together? All you'd have is a split in the moments, guys. That's what I'm telling you. Now, you're going to have to do what? Order the moments! Do you hear me? You're almost hearing me. This is so fundamental. I'll open up the book and read it to you and you'll go, "Hmmmm." You've got your moments sequenced. At so many places in the *Course* Jesus says, you're always bringing to the situation your past. Yet the past is gone and has absolutely nothing to do with what you are now, unless you let it have everything to do with it. That's forgiveness isn't it? If you let your past have everything to do with it — that's the Atonement — your future then must have everything to do with it, because your past and the future are really the same thing. Now you've brought your past and your future together, and you simply begin to create. Why? You've got a perfect reflection of your own thought forms.

[Sound of timer going off] That's it! That was what I was waiting for. Is that you? Sometimes in the association, if you'd like to think of this like you fell into a well. Jesus says you're occupying a very, very tiny spot. Only you know about this, and it's like we're just going to take the manhole cover off of it. This is how simple this could be for you. It might help you to think of the sky as paper-mâché. I'm going to try it: the sky is paper-mâché, and there are little penlight cells being shined through, and you're in a cigar box. There aren't millions and trillions of stars a thousand million miles away from you. That's poop. Jesus says, if you reach your hand up, you can right reach through to the very furthest one, and you can just pluck it down and look at it. There, see? Got him! This is called 'swatting earths.' All it is is just your own association. It's very little, and it only lasted a second and it's gone.

Now, will that help you in your own dilemma? It will help you immeasurably in your own dilemma. Why? It's true, and I'm in your dream telling you it's true. And if you'll admit that you want this to be so, it will become so. It can not not, because you have just as much power of mind to assert it as you do to deny it. C'mon! But what have you admitted? That the power is in you. This is the best talk ever given on the planet. It's a good talk. Why? Maybe some of you are beginning to hear it reasonably. Not in a comparison of your associate thoughts about it, but by the whole premise that what I'm telling you about eternity, singularity, and reality is finally very reasonable. And that what you're doing in your own death associations is not reasonable. It's not fair; it's not just. And God is fair and just and whole and beautiful, and this is not, therefore, this is not real.

Let's see how we look here. You got all of this churning going on in your perceptions. What are we doing? Well, we're stirring up all of your past frames of reference, and you're looking to grab a hold of something that will allow you, what? Not to go through the transcendence. Why? Because this is the last thing you want to do. You can say, "Boy, I can hardly wait to do it." Not true. You can do it now, and that's what you're going to demonstrate. It's very important that you remember it has nothing to do with the guy sitting next to you. Nothing! You're going to maintain it does and you'll be wrong. And that includes what apparently is his illumination. You'll look at him and say, "Gee teacher, I sure wish I could do that. I'd be illuminated like you. You're a real Master Teacher." Pffffffft!

You can hardly wait to attack me. You are attacking me, just by judging that I am and you're not. It's the fact that I am that allows you to be, for goodness sake! Got it? Boy, A *Course In Miracles* is beautiful. Your brother is your savior, literally. Do we allow that I am a step ahead of you in time? Only as you have directed me. I already know who I am, guys. I'm the same as everyone. It's you that's trying to be different. See, reality is going to be reality no matter what you do in your own dream. How come I got this assignment to wake you up? How the hell do I know? My awakened minds hear that. How the hell do I know? I'm just here doing it, right? It must be that this is what I do. One thing I know for sure, this is all I do. You do a lot of other things, but I'm telling you, you only have to do this. And you must do this in order to be this.

Let's have a little quiet time, here. I'm just looking at this thing going on over in the Gulf. You say, "Well, how come you participate in that?" I say, I participate in everything. It's hard for me to teach that. Remember that, in your mind, if you repair a sparrow's wing, you've repaired the universe. It's hard to teach this. See, a whole mind does everything wholly. You say, "Well, aren't you admitting to the conflict of the war?" Yeah, I'm admitting to this conflict, but remember the conflict is singular to me. I can't teach that. Sometimes it's necessary for there to be conflict for there to be solution, because, as Jesus would teach it, peace is not truce. If the conflict is contained within the subject, it has to be in the object, and that's the necessity. The Christ face is not a congeniality of anti-Christhood. It's not antichrists getting together and defining the Christ; that's just a truce. Obviously, you brought those perceptions to eventually attack yourself in relationship with yourself. It can not not be so. In other words, anti is anti. Only you can be opposed to the truth.

Questioner: Sir, could you relate this idea of conflict to the Persian Gulf War?

MT: That's what I just did. The only reason you caused it is that you caused all of this. If you segregate it, you're going to have problems in the magic attempting to overcome it. You've allowed for that sickness rather than the twenty thousand people that died last night. I just told you that. You're saying to me the Persian Gulf is more important than the people starving in Ethiopia. You're wrong. Remember that you have constructed the whole thing in the unreality of your determination to find yourself in your own death associations.

You have a tendency to make death explicit. I know you do that, and I know that you mourn for something specifically dead in your own relationship, don't you? Why don't you mourn for everything? Why don't you mourn for every baby that ever died? Why do you take a specific case of an example of what's constituted as evil in your mind, and attempt to bring it to remedy by your limited associations? Now does that make me a pacifist? It has nothing to do with pacifism. All pacifism in perceptual relationships is sociological. It can not not be. Can you hear me?

The idea of peace is always, in the mind, connected to the idea of war. My idea of peace is not connected to war at all. That's the step out of the conflict that's necessary for the Atonement of your own mind. Are you the cause of the war? Yes, but only because you're the cause of everything. You're attempting to discern the relationship between good and evil in this situation. I know it's a tough step. Why? Because you don't want there to be the pain, and when you feel the pain, you have a tendency to give it more immediate direction. When you don't want to feel the pain, you have subtracted it in your own memory and paste it out among the people starving in Ethiopia. It's amazing how the mind really finally is not concerned about death except it comes directly into their own associations.

On page 5 of the San Francisco Examiner will be eight hundred people trampled to death at a shrine in India, and on the front page will be one little girl stuck in a well. You see, you're directly concerned about that. Remember if you're the cause of it, if it remains real, you can never heal it. Now does this make you not participate in what's going on in the world? Hell, no. Do anything you want with it. What I want to do is bring you into a new association with your inherent conflict. And that's the certainty that if any of this is real you've got a bad problem and that includes this. So I have no solution to that, except to tell you that God is only love, and that if you define sickness and death in your association, you are not love and therefore not real. And I don't want to take away from you the pain that you're feeling for what's going on in the Gulf. In fact, I want you to feel the intensity of it. Then perhaps you can feel the actual intensity of what's happening to your brother, and you won't be able to stand it, because that's how I got this. I can't stand the idea that those young guys are getting killed over there. Now you ask me, "What can I do about it?" I'll do anything you ask me to do about it, but I still can't solve it.

Jesus says, all around you these terrible things are happening. You overcome this, this happens, you overcome that. Why? You're holding together the tensions of those thoughts in your own mind. But remember finally that the solution is that the conflict is only in you. If you want to know the exact difference that Jesus would teach it's this: I am trying to get you to serve God rather than man. I know you don't like it somewhere. It's the same notation as 'good works avail you nothing.' It's very difficult for you to see that. Somehow inherently you want to say, "Yes I can do good works." Then I would say to you that good works avail you everything, but you won't accept that. You want good works to avail you in the limited association of your own mind. My admonition to you is to serve only God because that's what you are. Your service to man is service to evil. That has to be true because you have constructed the sickness outside of you. Everybody agree? I know you don't like this but you might as well look at it.

Of course, I'm not teaching you to subtract anything from your mind; I want you to include everything in. If you feel the pain of it, then the necessity is for you to look at that. I'm teaching the *Course* now. "Why is it this way? What have I done? No, I'm going to let this be released. My service is to the single goal of awakening, not to the service of the participation in my limited associations with death. While I can guise them in charity, they really are not. They are really a defense of my own mechanism of death." Fact.

Now, will you go through the turmoil of attempting to assuage your brother's pain? That's what identifies you as a teacher of God. That's in the *Course*. Why? You felt your brother's pain, and you want to do something about it. The wonderful admission that you are the cause of it will make you feel real good, finally. Why? You let it go. If you can bring the cause and the effect together, you have the solution. As long as the pain is out there, how are you ever going to solve it? It's a good question. Can we all set up a prayer tower where we'll all pray? Sure, but you've acknowledged the war. "Well, won't it work that the war be stopped?" Sure. Everything works. And then there'll be another one, and another one, and another one. Why? The source is here, not out there.

Is it okay if we have a little quiet time now? Or would you all like to take off and go home? We have to have a quiet time then because your minds are all like this, aren't they?

Don't prepare for your quiet times. Always find yourself with God. You make elaborate preparations for particular times that you want to do this. Some of my more advanced people enter into it all the time. They can hardly wait. They get alone, and they just enter into this communication. And when this is happening to you, I would encourage you to get out of the chaos and let it happen. You're going, "Oh! I feel this. I want to be with God. I'm waking up." And someone will say, "Oh, c'mon. Let's go bowling." and you'll say, "No, I don't want to do that anymore. I've got a book, and there's a guy that talked, and he said this isn't real and I can be in Heaven." "Okay. They come along all the time. They're always telling you all of these things."

Huh? Where are the losers? Here. Where are the winners? Those that believe this. Where are they? They're not here. Some of you can really hear this. The only place this is, is where you denied what I'm telling you. And you'll look for authentication and you've got a lot of people who are going to tell me, "He compares favorably with a guy that…. I went through that experience back in '67"… Pffffft! They're telling you about your experience. That's absurd! I want to give you your visions and your revelations. That's the necessity.

You're going to go out and try to describe what happened to you today. And everybody will say, "That's very interesting. Would you compare that with banging the gong in Tibet" or some other… "You'd better look out for him, he's forming a cult or something." That's the other famous one. The great cultist, Jesus Christ, the greatest cult that there ever was. Secret, desperately afraid it's going to be attacked and destroyed. You know what the cult is now? We've got it out in the open. It's right here. This is a miracle [tapping the *Course In Miracles* book]. You didn't burn it, you didn't destroy it, you didn't torture it. It's sitting right there. Then boom! As soon as they got that in, along comes you. Boom! Yes, that's true. Bang! Let's go! You're gone. Why? You can hear it. You didn't kill it before it had a chance to get in there. Are you crucifying the Christ each moment? Sure. This is a place of crucifixion, which is sacrifice, which is the need for you to relinquish something in order to have God, and that's crazy.

We'll have just a short quiet time. We only have two quiet time tunes. "I Can't Give You Anything But Love, Baby," is one; and we have Nat King Cole singing "Stardust." That's a great one. Shhh, shhh. How long did I stand up there? I'll do an adjustment. Not bad for a hundred and twenty, huh? Breathe… breathe on me oh breath of life that I may know eternal life. The conversion of earth, air, fire and water. We're going to bring about a Hermetic reassociation in your structure. Do you mean that the resurrection is physical? Yeah!

Don't be afraid to release; you're safe here. Many of you have protected this veil for a very long time. I understand what you've been through and you've tried to say this before, but there's no need to be afraid here. There isn't anybody going to do anything to you.

(Takes a sip from cup) Whoooo! That's left from yesterday. Did you feel that? It's cold Instant Folgers. Look at that. Is cold Instant Folgers divine? Yeah! Watch what happens. I take a drink of this. They'll call this the cold Folgers ceremony. [laughing] Listen! Oh my!

I'll be darned. Heh, heh. It's nice to see you again. That's nice; thank you. Do you see we're related, real close, you even look like me. Finally, we all look so much alike. [sound of sobbing] Look at this; see that caused that because that was so lovely because I recognized you. That's very normal to express gratitude in tears, you guys. Tears and laughter are finally the same thing. This is your way out, and boy, you feel the gratitude of finally fulfilling a function of this. And you don't know what to do and you go, "Oh, yeah!" Can you explain this to perception? Naaah, but you won't care. C'mon, c'mon!

This is Lance; do you know who this consciousness is? Oh, see that, this is Lance, feel that? See, each of you has that aura capacity and energy and when you come into that I'll be able to tell. I can feel you. Good, you look good. You'll be all right.

What a relief, eh? What a relief. Boy! What if this really is true? Why don't you just for a minute let it be true and watch what happens? See? Going home. Good, good, good. And, open. Good! I'm going to notch this up just a notch. Gently now. You can do this. See? You can do it. I know my own, guys. Lovely. Why not? Wow.

Oh, my. Good for you. See that? They feel it when you smile at me. It really helps. Oh! Careful! Ha! What did you do!? Oh! Where you been keeping that? You guys got private stashes of love. Jesus says, you keep them in a warehouse, all the memories you've got. When you get up to this point, you use them; by giving, the door of the warehouse opens. It's a stash of holy instances. That's a nice way to describe it. It's a stash.

Breathe. Oh my, oh. Oh wow! I'll just open it up for you. Why not? Can you handle that? Ha! Little more light on this. Shooosh! Whew!

See, it's always been right there, but you couldn't see it because you were afraid to open that up. Open that up! You don't have to be afraid. There isn't anything to be afraid of up there. You were just afraid of the passage. You're not afraid of what's up there; it's the passage you've been afraid of. See that's what we're parting; we're bringing that together and that springs out. You're going to be free now of this. Free. "What do I do, demonstrate it?" I don't care what you do with it, but it's here. Certainly you can't judge it by watching somebody else. Shooosh...good. Okay, that's open, see? Will that stay open now? Oh yeah. You may put a little piece of gauze over it, but that's open in your mind. Once that's open, you can't stay here long. See, look. Look at this. Uh oh. See?

Do you want this to happen or would you rather study it? It's okay if we were wrong about this whole thing. The hell with this. This is being recorded; I have to be careful what I say. I say the hell with this crap. This is hell. "Well, I wish I could believe you." Don't. Who's going to stop you? Did I go through what you're going through? Oh sure. That's why you got me.

Is it okay if I do this? You don't have to go out and talk about this. You just be here and do this. You don't have to write this up. I just want you to do it. There's a lot hanging out here, and I have to be a little careful. You guys do anything you want to do.

It's called the ascension. I'd get ready. You let these be very sacred moments in your memory. This is as sacred and perfect as anywhere in the universe, the spot where you make this declaration of wholeness. There is nothing more sacred in all the universe than this. Nothing. Where would it be? Where the ancient truth and pain and sickness have come together. At that moment is what the revelation is. Don't degrade it, just give it fullness, then it will be full. Don't question it. Just go, "Yeah!" It can only have the power that you give it and if you give it the power, you'll be out.

This is Lisbeth. Isn't that lovely? Look at that! That's beautiful, dear one. Ha! You use each other's high ranges. You don't identify them; you use the energy of them. See? That's better, that's better. See? Mmm hmmm. See, you've been wearing a mask of perception, and you're willing to take it off just for a minute, and that's fearful to you. But if you take it off, what will you see? The face of Christ. Of course. Why? It's just your projection. You always see what you want to see. You don't have to be afraid. There's nothing to be afraid of, for goodness sake.

Heh heh heh. Some of you guys I used to sing in the choir with. Gently. (Singing) La, dee,daa… good. That's not going to hurt you. "I wouldn't dare do that."

Some of you guys have got these deep things you keep bringing up here. "Oh, I'd better not let him see that." That's part of the process. "I'd better not do that. That's unforgivable." You've only got one thing you think that is unforgivable and that's the whole idea of you, and that's totally forgivable. Some of you guys are going through some very lovely experiences. How can I teach them that? I want to show them that.

See, everybody in the universe knows about this. You think it's a big place. No, everyone that needs to know about this knows about it and that's everyone that needs to know. Either that or it isn't. It's impossible for you to call on anyone within this whole thought astral association without obtaining this if you want it. There is no conflict in it. You guys have been living in your astral thoughts where you are in conflict so long, you don't understand they're just waiting for your instructions. You go through this scribe nonsense of listening to some other voice that has no more idea about the truth than you have. It's waiting for you to tell it what it is. You study your horoscopes to give you the answer. You're the horoscope. It's waiting for you to tell it what it is. How grateful they'll be, how loving they'll be when you forgive them your own thoughts. Jesus describes this very beautifully. They can hardly wait for your forgiveness. You know who wants it the most? God! If you can hear that, you're awake. There's a lovely sentence in the *Course* that says God asks for your forgiveness.

I'm putting some thought into this energy because I want you to stay with the thought. Why? So you won't come back down into this, because you begin to do that. Remember, this is in your mind and you won't do this. You'll come up to this and you'll say, "Gee, I want to be around this more. Now I hear what this says." Then your groups will change, then how you're reading this will change. Then what you're doing with your own goals will change. It has to, God has given you that. Otherwise you'd be stuck here forever. See, you have to be able to hear this. And it's that determination that's happened to you now; the incentive of the miracle. What's occurring to you now is entirely outside of your perceptual association. It appears to be perceptual, but it's a whole new arrangement of your light thought forms. It really doesn't compare to anything that happened to you but it seems very familiar. It's something you've always wanted to hear; it's something that you remember. It's an ancient melody. It's ever so distant in your mind, yet you can hear it because it has always played.

You look beautiful. We'll take a little break now. Share your loaves and fishes.

It would be very nice if you guys would stay in these high identities. That is, it would be lovely if you guys communicated, but not in the mundane fashion that you usually do, since that is what the falsity is; and the truth is that you are in an entirely different place in time than you were (what you constitute) three-and-a-half hours ago. You listen to me! Listen to me! Listen to me! This is a different time and place. Listen! If you let that be so in your mind, you will formulate this in a whole new relationship of time and space, I guarantee it. It has to be so. You'll still be in time, but it will be a new association, a new later association in light formations.

The problem I've had with this depth is you're all coming from different times, and you don't have a central location in your own great rays. Some of your centers are later than others, some are earlier, see? Some of them you met six thousand years ago. A lot of you guys have Egyptian memories that are extraordinary. But many of you now are being afforded memories of your future meetings. That's what I am giving to you. You can then take those meetings from ten thousand years from now, if you want to call it that, and make application to them in all the times that you've been associated throughout all of time. Why? All time is really going on at the same time. This is later than it was. If you can hear this, it will be very valuable to you. Why?

I want you to hold this form. Every time you don't hold this form, you're just going nowhere. This is your salvation form. I want you to be you. It doesn't do you any good to look outside yourself for an answer to this. If you'll be you in this new energy, I'll handle the rest. That's the admission of your Atonement. That will formulate in here rather than trying to find yourself in a mutual location. You can't — you're too different in time. You know each other perfectly well, but for each part of you that recognizes the other, there is another part that still is in conflict. That's why you can't communicate. I will be that communicating source for you if you let me, because that's what this energy is. It's a communicative device, and I'm teaching you to what? Be a communicative device, to bring all of those memories in, so that we can hold them in the mandala — Jesus calls this the Circle of Atonement — where each time we have a thought, it extends from us and becomes our associate perceptual reality in the objected definition of it. See, when that occurs, we have no conflict. That's love. Of course it's love. Love is what? Communication. It's the certainty that we all come from the same source and we're all there together. That's the fun part of this. So you can have fun, eating lunch. See if I can quit here now.

Are you sure this is what we're supposed to be meditating to? [jazz music in background]. Is my Workbook up there? How are we doing? Are we okay? Come on guys. This is Bob Scobey from San Francisco. He went to Chicago. Listen. Start out with Lu Watters in San Francisco, playing San Francisco jazz, traditional jazz out of New Orleans. This is the Dawn Club in 1949. You dirty guy; it's where we... it was me! 'Course I was only nine at the time. The Lu Watters sound was a particular ensemble of particular associate harmonics without a lot of allowance for spectacular musicianship. The requirement was to make the sound, and guys like Turk Murphy, who had Earthquake Magoon (who was in the city for many years) was an alumnus of Lu Watters. Lu Watters quit playing trumpet and bought himself an egg farm in Petaluma or something. My San Francisco memories are very old. Of course all of our memories are finally very old. My Sacramento memories are more recent.

So we're all memories. Some of you will discover that you've lost your grievance. And when it happens to you it's impossible to express it to a grieving consciousness. You'll go to a family reunion tomorrow and your sister and your brother and your ex, who has got the kids, or you or whatever it is will immediately begin to share grievous associations. They'll connect them to love, but the reminder will always be of the associate injustices that were done to them. This will always be true.

To deny that this is true is to deny this teaching, because it's necessary for you to look at what your relationships really are. This has nothing to do with what is good or bad. It has to do with the certainty that they necessitate mutual attack-and-defense modality. They can not not, because any opinion is a form of defense, and any rebuttal is a form of attack. And what you attempt to share in these relationships are mutual identities of attack and defense. This is the teaching of Jesus Christ.

Now, perceptual mind presumes that that's the way of life. And when you went to the reunion, they are all sitting down reminding you, perhaps, of how your father beat your mother, or whatever else occurred that caused all the trauma of your apparent present condition which is inherently traumatic. Strangely enough, a new mind, while it can remember the association of the apparent grievance, cannot identify it in the heat of perceptual value. Can you hear this? It's very easy to forgive if you can't remember the passion of the association. This is what will happen to your mind if you'll allow it to. You no longer need to retain the value of the pain in that association in order to keep your own identity.

* * * * * * *

Psychologists are out there justifying the possibility of grievance. And then asking the consciousness — after you've given him justification for it — to attempt to remove his own justification. It's absurd! You're asking him to repair what you've already justified in his own mind. Now what are you going to do? As an unhealed teacher, you're going to share that justification of the grievance.

Why don't you just say to him, "It's impossible to be unjustly treated"? You know why? He doesn't want to hear that. Are you going to hear me or not? He doesn't want to hear 'It's impossible to be unjustly treated.' Why? It's impossible to be unjustly treated! If he heard that, he couldn't stay in the world, could he?

It's impossible to be unjustly treated! You say, "Well, I can treat myself unjustly." That's absurd! You're not going to treat yourself unjustly. It's the same idea as you're causing your own pain.

Say you're working with addicts... He is inflicting pain on himself— that's inherent in this teaching. You know that before you go to the meeting. However there's a guy who cuts you off on the road — I always tell the story, because it's a good one, it's very basic — he cuts you off, gives you the finger, and you've got all the resentment in you now for what he did to you. You don't realize how true this really is. He's very happily whistling, and the more he's happy and whistling, the more you get pissed about it. But the fact of the matter is, at that moment you are inflicting pain on yourself. And all of the subsequent moments that you hold onto that resentment, you continue to literally inflict pain on yourself for an incident that's already past. If you don't forgive it, you'll inflict pain on yourself forever.

How do you guys ever get over being rejected at the junior prom? You never get over it. Do you like that? Ooooh, you hate it. He didn't kiss you goodnight, and you went inside and you had a big piece of asparagus growing right... Golly! And you go back and you relive it and you relive it, and you said, "If only I'd gone to the ladies room, I would have brushed it away, and things would have been different." There's your problem. You really think that had that not occurred, things would have been different.

Now this is where I've got to get to you. You believe because of that specific incident, all of the things that occurred have caused you to be where you are. It's not so. There's absolutely nothing specific about your past associate frame of reference. Quite literally one thing is no more valuable than another. That's literally true. If you're going to hold onto the fact that things could have been different, you can never come into the now. How the hell could you? You're trying to change the past, and if the past is gone, you can't change it. You see?

I know you guys do this; it's where you live. Your reality is based on your mother dying of breast cancer four-and-a-half years ago; and you're hoping that you don't. These are just facts. But you have it constructed in your mind so what happens? You get it. Why? It's the power of your mind.

So you're nothing but a bundle of associate resentments, or needs to identify yourself. The new mind that's emerging in you now will not be concerned about the past — this is the whole teaching of the *Course.* To relinquish the past, don't bring the past into the present, except the certainty (hear this. It'll really save you some time) that everything that possibly ever could have happened to him has brought him to this moment. This is the key to salvation. He doesn't attempt to sort out in time the various aspects that have brought him here. Why? He's going to be here anyway.

This is *Course In Miracles.* Some of you are really hearing this. If he's going to be here anyway, what the hell difference does it make how he got here? When they have come, they have come. When you hear this, you will have heard it. It's your determination to associate with your previous forms of reference that literally keep you from hearing it. Because by bringing the past association into this, you project into the future your previous associations and literally cover the holy instant. Does everybody hear this? How the hell are you going to work a miracle if you and I are so busy in our own memories of each other? The memories are not true.

Can you hear this? This association that's going on here has absolutely no reality at all. None. None. Period. Zero. None. Yet you're addressing it, so somewhere contained in this association must be salvation. But obviously it can't be in our mutual identities with each other. Where's it going to be? In our determination to seek an answer outside of our mutual identities. You can't do it any other way, and that's what forgiveness is. I want you to understand this. When I'm speaking this way, I'm speaking mechanism, I'm speaking literally of the manner in which you reach Atonement. You, individually.

Isn't it okay that no one could ever mistreat you? No, it's not okay. Because mistreatment is justification for your existence.

Questioner: What about the man who committed incest with his daughter?

MT: What about it? Who's the incester? You are. You want me to toughen this up for you, dummy? You're the cause of it.

You see? He's determined somehow to reject his incestuous attitudes.

Can I teach it to you this way? If anybody commits incest, it's you! That's why you're guilty. You're guilty of all the thoughts that you attempt to disassociate yourself from, and give it to somebody else. Cut it out!

Questioner: What about the girl?

MT: Heh heh! What are you going to do? It's exactly the same association. You're raping your own daughter. How do you want it? Nothing is occurring except it's in your own association with yourself. Fortunately, it's not real. If that guy really raped his daughter, you've got a bad problem. The problem's not his; it's yours.

Wow. What just happened there? He laid the blame on another guy. This is the pure *Course In Miracles.* I appreciate your doing that, incidentally. Why? It's pure *Course.* You want the sentence? You're blaming your brother for the things that you think you did. Fact.

Now, here's the problem. You want to do it this way? Can you be found not guilty of incest with your daughter? Yes, I find you not guilty. If it occurred, you're guilty forever. Because you are sinful in time. Because time is what sin is. You listen to me! It's your determination to hold on to the things you identify as being valuable to you and reject any other things. But they don't go out of your mind. You hear me? Does anybody really hear what I'm telling you? If you're the cause of this, that has to be true.

Now, what did he do? He denied that he was the cause of it. The reason he can't accept that he is the cause of it is that his reality is based on not being the cause of it. You ought to be able to hear me. I'm speaking to you very plainly. That way he keeps his identity with what you would call moral, I suppose. He places himself under the laws of man, and equates the good and the bad in relationship to things that he would never do, but somebody else has done. That's crazy. What he's saying is, "There are separate minds outside of me that would do that, but I would never do that."

Tough teaching, eh? Too bad. Give me another solution. Anybody? Give me another solution to this. If minds are separate, that is sinful. You would then be capable of committing a sinful act. If it's only in your mind, it's reparable because it couldn't be real except by your association with yourself. I'm teaching the *Course.*

Will you hang a guy who says this to you? Sure. You can't get away with saying, "If you lust in your heart it's the same as the act." This is Jesus' teaching. In fact, it's what he teaches.

"Oh, I would never do that." Really? Really? "No, I would never do that." Okay. Don't. What would you do? "Well, I suppose if I had to defend myself, at some point I would be willing to kill somebody else." When is murder okay?

I don't want to get into the taboos of incest; I can give you a talk on that. The necessity for the genetic association to broaden in patterns of consciousness without turning back in on itself. That's a cultural distinction that goes on in the creative purpose of perceptual mind, and it sets up laws that will best bring about the survival of the separation — remember that — not the survival to God. Fit sociological associations do not mate within inner families — I'll give you the answer to the taboo — and obviously they seek outside, which then becomes the taboo. But neither one makes it real or not real because it's not so. This is just an association of your determination to hold onto your limited thought forms in the identification of yourself as a specie association — man. Homo sapiens.

What is man? What is it that doesn't know itself, if the condition, which is reasonable, of wholeness, of beingness, is knowing who you are? Do you see? If you are under no laws but God's, which is the law of whole Will, why are you concerned about your perceptual associations, except to protect yourself from that Will? Yet you can not not be whole and perfect.

If you believe that God said "Thou shalt not kill," you're going to be here a long time. Can you hear me when I do that? What would God know of killing? No, these are man's laws for man. These are reciprocal laws of social relationships. Are they valuable? They're completely necessary to bring about the association of the consciousness with himself. He'll then continue to search within his split mind. He doesn't need a law except that his mind is split.

You know, a rhinoceros doesn't need a law to reach up and eat off a tree. A rhinoceros is God. Why? A rhinoceros knows what it is. It doesn't suffer from a condition you call 'rhinocerosism.' You think it does, though. Can you hear me when I do this? You've given it a separate identity. A rhinoceros doesn't want to be a buffalo. It's perfect in its own mind. I don't know how to teach it. Can anybody — do you hear this? Beingness is beingness. I mean, if there's a difference between a hippopotamus and God, it's only because YOU say so. God isn't saying so; and certainly the hippo isn't. He's being a hippo.

I am asking you to be who you really are, but you don't want to be. You would rather make up all sorts of names for stuff, to keep yourself separate from your own identity. But you can not not be the only living Son of God, because you are God creating. Okay?

Is that not okay? "No, I would rather condemn other people outside myself and do what I'm doing." Well, who's to stop you, for goodness sake? You do that. It will protect you. You can set up a defense, here, can't you? Lay up stores, and protect yourself from all the terrible things that are going on around you. I don't know how you stand it. I don't know how you stand this place. I don't know how you stand a place where there is incest. That's what I couldn't stand. You ask me to justify it. It's not justifiable. But it's not justifiable in ANY regard. All you did was pick something you would never justify, and look at that purpose of the conflict. Obviously there are a lot of things you would look upon as justified that many people would not, isn't this so? Now you're set up in jurisprudence, where somehow you're going to have to attempt to equate what is justifiable under what circumstances and you wonder why there's no justice.

You should not judge because why? You cannot. And you say to me, "Well, I can certainly judge limitedly, under the circumstances which are presented to me." What's that got to do with the truth? Doesn't that frustrate you?

You know what my son says — he's a lawyer — "Well, that's okay. That's the best we can do." He says, "We'll always do the best we can do under the circumstances, and that's what justice is." I said, you don't know the circumstances. He says, "We have precedent." I say, all your precedent is judgment and it's not so. You keep changing your mind about the precedent all the time. You keep rewriting history according to the dictates of what you want to be true at this time.

The greatest thing that ever happened to the world was the assassination of Kennedy. And you go, "That couldn't possibly be true." Why not? No? That couldn't be? Well, yeah, that's true. That's a true statement. It's a good thing that happened, eh? And you say, "No, it's a bad thing that happened. If that hadn't happened…" Now, see what you're doing?

Will the history of this war be rewritten? Hah, hah, it'll be rewritten as soon as it's not expedient with the terms that you're in, in association with what's happening now. That's what you're doing all the time. Why do you have to do that? You're judging your present condition on the past frame of reference. And if it doesn't suit you, you'll make it up differently and change it. You're your own history. Isn't that funny? But it's not stable. Why? Because it's gone. Can you hear this? If you base your reality on what's gone, you're not here either.

At no single moment is the body real. Isn't that so? It's always past. Let me see you not be past. Everything you think of is always just gone. You can't hold onto it. It's just gone. Yet you're here. So what happens? You just keep getting gone, gone, gone, gone…death. You take your goneness and project it into the future, and you're literally no-thing. In the *Course* Jesus teaches this as "you cancel yourself out". Both parts of you don't know anything.

There's a sentence in there, it's a lovely obscure part of the *Course*, that says you're canceled out. Both the thinker — the object and the subject — are not real. "Well, what can I do about it?" How the hell do I know? Are you satisfied with the condition that you're operating under? You say, "Well, I think it's going to be all right." HOW? How is it going to be okay? "Well, there's better things coming." There's some lovely *Course* where Jesus looks at that. He says, "Why, is there a price for better things?" You say, Yeah. Oh, yeah. You have to pay the price in order to have better things, don't you? How else will you know they're better?

How are you going to know you're happy if you're not unhappy sometimes? Isn't that funny? How are you going to identify it? Where's the problem? You're dealing from lack. You have a fundamental insecurity of limitation. That's why you can never be whole. Anything that needs anything is not real, if cause and effect are not apart. If it bases its reality on need, it cannot be so. It'll just provide for its scarcity. It can never find completion, because need is the denial of wholeness. I don't know where you're hearing this, but that's fact. You need nothing. You operate on the presumption that necessity is the mother of invention. And indeed it is, but nothing is necessary. Inventiveness is always an attempt to form a limited relationship and deny your own Creator. Nice lesson.

Do you want to keep the idea of that happening? This war, this incest he spoke of, and your daughter getting killed at the senior prom by a drunk? Awful! Awful! You say, "Well, I'm just going to have to cope with it." Why? Answer me, somebody. You don't really realize what I'm offering you. Why do you have to cope with the idea that your daughter got killed at the senior prom? Do you wish that somebody else's daughter would have got killed at the senior prom, so that yours would be alive because she didn't get in the car and I told her not to?

You wonder why you're guilty? How could you not be guilty? What do I want you to do? I want you to be totally guilty. The only way you can come to Atonement is by the admission of all of this being in association with you. You can't do it any other way. Isn't that okay? If reality is reality, the observation of it must be false.

You remember this: I'm not trying to take anything away from you. I'm trying to give you things, but you're determined not to take them. By your perception you subtract yourself from paradise. That's a fact. It's not open to discussion. How could you have a question? The question is that God is real, and your association with Him is not. He doesn't need your identification to be what He is. Do you see? Your demands for justification in your own perceptual reality are totally meaningless; they mean nothing. There is no such thing as time. Okay? If you think there is, why not take the moment that there is to see that there is not? How many associations in your definition are ready to hear this? How the hell do I know? The requirement is that you do, so you stop attacking the reality. Have you been attacking the reality? Certainly! You don't like to read this in the *Course*. What do you do when you read in the *Course* that you're attacking God because you're afraid of Him? Isn't that funny? Yet your mind is whole, isn't it?

What do you do when you're inside yourself? I used to do this all the time. What do you do? Just talk to yourself about this? How do you find a solution to it? I'm curious. This consciousness is finding a solution. He's going to hold onto it some way. But there's really no justification for it finally, is there? What would it be? Why would there be death and sickness? Help me. Why? Is it necessary in order to what? I can't get what it is you're trying to do. Do you want to prove that death is real to me? How do you obliviate yourself? You're in an impossible situation. And you say, "Well, I'd rather have this than the alternative."

This is lovely *Course* now. Why would the alternative be bad? You say, "Well, at least I have this. You can't take this away from me." This is actually what you do, isn't it? You hold on to this little piece rather than just saying, "I'm everything." Because everything is a threat to you. That's the way it is. How do you get out of it? That's an impossible dilemma. You'd rather have this than nothing, because you think that God is nothing. So you die to prove you're right. But you can't die.

What's the solution? You have to use up all your avenues of attempt to escape God. You won't do it any other way. You can sit there forever and keep demanding recognition for what you are. It's not real. I'm not quarreling with you; I'm just telling you it's not real. It has nothing to do with good or bad. It has nothing to do with incest and murder and rape. It has nothing to do with that. You already are killing the things you love. What difference does it make how you kill them if you kill them? Is this the way Jesus says you identify murder with love? Yeah. Does this mean that what isn't love is murder? Yeah. Because murder is death. Death is self-murder. If you kill your brother, you're killing yourself. You kill a part about you that you don't like, and try to save the part of yourself that you do, and you die anyway. The reason that I make this an imperative is it's exactly what you don't want to look at. Is this lovely consciousness provided for you to take a look at this? Sure. Why? Because this is the same thing you're thinking in your own mind. Is that different from what your mind thinks? Of course not. You're a human being, and you've set up a value system within you. When I tell you you're under no laws but God's, you positively reject it.

This is turning into a tough talk, but I don't care. Finally, you're going to have to look at the idea that you're causing your own dilemma. If you won't do that; if you're going to keep blaming something outside yourself for your problem, there's no sense in coming to me. You're a liar, and you've been a liar from the beginning, but you're not real. You do this but to yourself. Now, if you can look at it as just a little occurrence, which it is, just a little happening in a limited framework, you won't have any problem with this. I'm going to try this with you: No one knows about this but you. No one knows about this but you. This is just your own turning within yourself. You're in a dream. This never happened. That ought to eliminate the questions about the incest. If it doesn't, don't come to me. I'm giving you now the fact of the matter. If you're determined that this is so, there's no sense in coming to me. There's no sense in doing the *Course In Miracles*. That'd be senseless. All I'm giving you is what Jesus said, out of body. He tells you that you're not a body, that you've constructed this in your own mind, and what? That you're the dreamer of the dream.

Why isn't that okay? I always knew I was dreaming here. Somewhere within me I always knew that this was a dream. Is this a dream, now, going on? What are we going to do in our dream? Shall we talk about grievances? And all the terrible things that have happened in our dream? You tell me the things that happened to you, and I'll tell you the things that happened to me. But we're really not communicating, not really. Evil cannot be shared, Jesus would say. Separation really can't be shared, because it's based on not knowing. We can only approximate it and utilize symbols to represent it, like I'm doing now; do you see what I'm doing?

Would it be better if I didn't speak at all? I don't know. I have to use this devious method, because you have constructed this devious method not to know the truth. That's a nice sentence in the *Course*. Remember where it says that? You speak in these weird tongues in order to keep yourself from seeing the truth. Then you share that limitation, as long as you don't have to do a confrontation with your own reality. Then you share the guilt of the terrible things that you and I did together. But it's not real.

Am I telling you what you don't want to hear? Of course! This is the only thing you've never wanted to hear: That you're perfect. Why? If you're perfect, what would be the sense in this?

So, you told me to come here in this time, and tell you that you're perfect. And to tell you that you're waiting for yourself later on. Is that true? It would have to be true. Otherwise what is it you're looking for? See, it would be impossible for you to be searching for Heaven without having found it. Wouldn't that be true? I'm here to remind you that you found it. And you'll say to me, "Well how did I get back here where I don't remember finding it?"

It's amazing that when I offer you eternity, many of you look at it as some sort of sacrifice. "Look at all the lovely things I'm going to have to give up."

Questioner: I would like to suggest that there's another plausible cause why I'm unable to see it; that is, it's virtually incomprehensible.

MT: No, no, it's totally incomprehensible.

Questioner: It's very, very difficult to understand for most mortals.

MT: Mortals aren't real, though. More than that, it's impossible for mortals to understand eternity. That's why they're mortal. How many times am I going to have to do it for you? I just keep doing the same thing over for you. Mortality is what time is. Time is constructed not to be eternal. How could it understand it? You're right on. You can make it very difficult, but the idea that it's difficult to come to wholeness is crazy in my mind, not in yours; because you want to construct difficulties in being whole. But why would it be difficult to be everything? Respond.

Questioner: Difficult to be everything?

MT: Yeah! That's what you are. Why is that difficult?

Questioner: My experience is that I'm one thing at a time.

MT: That's why it's difficult for you to be everything. But if you're one thing at a time you're going to hold yourself in time and suffer the consequences of what you call a conceptual time association. Do you have the power to do that? It's not whether it's good or bad! You're the one who's going to have to look at your determination to hold onto it.

Is it valuable for him to do that? Sure! He's a shill. I put him in there to ask these questions. Ha ha ha! Do you know that that's true? You know that already. It's a big con game. I have to stimulate some sort of response in the conflict that you're feeling, otherwise you won't deal with it. That's what I do. But remember that I'll always stay with the constancy, and you will always stay with your determination to die. That's what makes our dialogue finally possible, and I'll call it dialog in this sense. Because if it's necessary for you to have the atonement, or the At-One-ment of your mind, this is what you will be. Remember though that you are the denial of your own perfection. That's what I told you this morning. You actually think you have a choice in this matter, because your reality is based on choice, which is what sequential time is, isn't it? Choosing between things. Do you have a choice, really? If you ask the question "Do I have a choice?" you must have one. But remember this: If you brought your cause and effect together, you could only have one choice, and that's to see that this is not so and that God is. That's A *Course In Miracles.* And each moment that you're tempted to give credence to your associations, you look at the outcome of that purpose, you step back from it, and you stop doing it. Each time you step back from that limited association, you save yourself time because you're not tracking off into another direction. Your way becomes like a razor's edge.

Jesus calls this temptation: "Oh, c'mon and do this with us." This is in the movie, the *Last Temptation of Christ* — lovely — where the cross turns sideways and the little lovely thing comes up and says, "Hey, it's all over. You've paid your dues. Now you can come and be human. Now you can come and have a family." Jesus says, "Oh, did I really do it?" She says, "Yeah, God would want you to come and be human here, and share these things with us." [Whistles] That's what? That's your last temptation. The last bastion of your defense is human love. That's a sentence from the *Course*. Why? We can't take love away from you; we can only ask you to look at what you're doing with your own creations. I'm going to give you your love, and I'm going to ask you why do the things that you love suffer pain and death? And you're going to tell me, "There's nothing I can do about it," and I'm going to say, "Why?" That's not love, then. What you're going to share is not being able to do anything about it, aren't you?

Gosh, you guys look familiar to me. Well, did we come into this mess together? Yeah! You were the navigator. In fact, you're responsible for the whole screw-up. I didn't give you that message, I gave you…See? Isn't that funny? It's a little bit like there was a spot on the white linen tablecloth, and you quick tried to blot it out. And it just kept getting bigger, and bigger, and bigger, and just kept spreading more and more. You didn't hear the "olly olly oxen free" and you came back in… Jesus says you forgot to laugh. Remember that in the *Course?* Suddenly it got real serious. We were fooling around with the moon maidens…no, that's another one. We landed on this planet… See, this can be anything that you want it to be.

All I want to assure you of is that you're living in a time illusion. You must finally see that this is an amnesty bill. You've been doing jungle warfare, but you've only been combating yourself. There is no battle going on. This is the key to salvation. The conflict is only in your own associations. Everybody hear that? Then don't be conflictual. Truth and love is all around you, while you sleep. How am I getting through to you? I'm pounding on your shell. It's like you're down deep and we're hitting a pipe, and you can hear the boom, boom… "What's that?" you go.

I wish I could explain to you what happened when we lost communication with you. The reason why this is so difficult...I can't explain it. See, at the time of the schism there was a displacement that has taken longer to repair because what's happening is ... there was a particular refraction that occurred in this association, and a lot of you for the last forty thousand years have been coming up to a particular spot and you bump against it and it's not there; it's off just a phase off to the left. Now, if you hold onto an identity of an association with me, the image will be dim, won't it? For just a second you might see that, then that gets fearful to you because it gets too bright, and you're unable to correspond it with your right brain. You still have some drama playing out that makes you fearful of that revealing. This is the necessity for the holy instant. Why? Because you're very much afraid of finally removing that veil.

Was it removed this morning? Yeah. Let me see where you are, here. The necessity for this is for you not to think in this association, but to release up to this. What happens when you do that happened to you at lunch. Your re-association with the other consciousness is dramatically different...and it can be very dramatically different. You formulated this rather than this. This will never work. You try to make holy relationships out of your special relationships. You can't. You've designed them to keep them apart. The only way you can do it is common goal. But see how easy it is with common goal. How easy you can have a perfect love relationship here if you'll admit to an absolute common determination to do this. What does that require? That you include everything that you do in with that goal.

Is that what these awakened consciousnesses have done? They have no conflict with each other at all; at least it doesn't last more than a second. And that will always be in regard to what is the best thing to do to bring this about. There is no conflict in what we know is so. The idea that you could actually share in this whole goal is an incredible feeling of ecstasy and happiness beyond anything that you've ever thought.

You have never ever been willing to make a complete commitment to anything, because perceptual mind literally cannot do it. It will always hold in reserve the idea that it can choose to do it or not. You have no choice in this matter. Everybody hear me? You have no choice but to awaken. You have no choice but to awaken now. You have made a decision within this time association to hear this. There's no sense in denying it.

When you go back and read the things I'm saying to you now, they'll stare right out at you from the *Course*. You'll go, "Oh, yeah! That's what he said. Oh, yeah!" You can see it differently. Rather than covering those real emphatic statements, you'll begin to say, "Hey! This is what this says. And this is what I'm doing."

Is this the way out for you? Yeah. Are you going to choose to come out now? Or are you going to choose to get sick and die again? You want to follow me, I'll take you out. You say, "What qualifies you to be able to do that?" And I say to you, "I have no qualifications at all." You say, "Then how do I know you're the savior?" And I say, "Because I have no qualifications." Some of you really heard that. I'm totally unqualified to do this. That's why you picked me. Somewhere you had to know there were no qualifications for this.

Was my awakening spontaneous? Hey — all awakenings are spontaneous. Can you hear it? When it happens to you, it's always a complete surprise. A lot of you are experiencing these holy instants, and they're always a complete surprise to you. When you go back and try to define them to somebody, they go, "Oh, yeah." But they don't see that that's not what it is. For crying out loud, I'm teaching you to the experience. Well, have it! If you can put it into a frame of reference, it has to be in the limited perceptual relationship of what you identify as atonement.

I'm astonished by what you guys classify as master teachers. It isn't that they're not true; it's that you deny them. All teachers are true. I can't teach that, can I? An unhealed mind will give you qualifications for what constitutes your awakening. If I do that, you be sure and tell me. If I tell you that there are qualifications for you to do this, you tell me. Except your own little willingness to do it. Obviously you have to see you have the problem, but that's the qualification.

The more you see you have the problem, the more the solution will be there. And when the problem becomes total to you and not solvable, that's what salvation is. It is not something else — not where you solve the problem and then recognize salvation. You listen to me. You ought to start hearing this. The solution is in the relinquishment, not in the determination of the relinquishment. This problem cannot be solved. The recognition of that is what solves the problem. No other way.

Jesus teaches this again and again and again. All he really says is, "The problem's not real." Somehow you want to solve it, and I can't take it away from you. Why? Because you've always solved it. And you've always solved it in the manner in which you thought was best for you to solve it. Wouldn't you do that, reasonably? Isn't it necessary that I eat? Isn't it necessary that I pay the rent?

Yet if you do Lesson 76 it will say, "No, none of those things are necessary and that is what is keeping you here." And you'll say, "That's why nobody does the *Course*." And I'll say, "That's right." You say, "Well, nobody here does that." That's right. They all live within the framework of their associate bodies. I don't know what they think of another trillion stars, and three thousand million other consciousnesses here. They're constituted so little that there's really no breadth in the expansion of their own mind. I belabor it.

Now, when you're ready to hear this, you will hear it because you already did. Be sure you have this. It's impossible that anything that is happening to you has not already happened. There is nothing that you are going to do that is not a part of this whole plan. You don't do anything accidentally in that sense. You can't, because all you've ever really wanted is happiness. And since that's all you can really be, you must be that. And you will search for it, and that's why you're here. You're searching for love and peace and happiness, and I'm telling you that you can't find it where you're looking; but yet it's all around you.

How much value is there in what I'm telling you? Each one of you — can you hear this? — represents a hundred million associations. When Jesus tries to express it in the *Course*, he has a particular problem with it. You don't realize how much your individual mind is actually affecting everything in the universe. I'm very much aware of it. I'm going to use you whether you're going to get it or not. Every time I address you in your own drama association, I'm doing a major repair in the whole universe. Jesus says to you, you don't realize, when you do your own atonement, how much you're really affecting. Everything within that total time framework, regardless of where it is, benefits from your re-association at that time. Can you hear this?

Not only that, but it's possible for any association that you've ever had to benefit totally from it, if you can get enough insertion — this is what the *Course In Miracles* is — at a depth of where the chaos occurs. Jesus says you're affecting constellations thousands of things out. You have no idea of the power of your own mind, quite literally. I do, though — and I'm going to use it. And you say, "Well, I want to be a savior along with you." Come on! But you're going to have to use what? The power of your own mind. And certainly you're not going to do it if you think there's something outside of you that can harm you and cause you pain. Right? How could you?

It's not a big deal being the savior of the world; but it's the biggest deal you'll ever do, because it's the only thing you have to do. The idea, if you care to look at it — and this is in Chapters 29, 30, and 31: The simplicity of salvation is incredible. All it says is what you think you're doing never happened. But still you must do it in your own mind, right? Because you're the cause of it. See?

Is it possible to love without judgment? No, not perceptually. But it is possible to bring all of your judgments into a whole association of yourself with what you are and create from that stance. Do you think I can't tell the difference between what you constitute good and evil here? Of course I can. That's why I can teach you, because I can show you that the difference doesn't matter. Because I still have in me when it did, and I demanded that I be given credit for the difference so that I could identify myself. And it won't work.

So the miracle of the solution occurred at the turning of your will and your life over to God. This is the *Course In Miracles*; this is the Twelve-Step Program. All I really teach is turn your will and your life over to God. What did you think that this is? How could you fail if you did that?

The problem you have is you keep taking it back. Turn it over. Now, the demonstration of the miracle that occurs at the time that you turn it over authenticates your determination that you weren't the cause of it. This is what all addictive programs teach — that by yourself you couldn't have done it. This is my whole teaching. You couldn't do it by yourself.

Do you like the word surrender? Obviously what I'm asking you to do is unconditionally surrender. Did you think I was doing something else? Do you think the *Course In Miracles* is anything but a course in unconditional surrender? That's what it is. And it means unconditional, because unconditional surrender is inherently unconditional love, because it removes the obstacles of the conflict that you refused to surrender to. Is that demonstrated as a miracle? Hey! And it will be so miraculous you can't believe it. Because it occurred despite you, not because of you. And that's what the miracle is. Showing you that despite everything that you did, it worked. Not because of you, but because you determined that you couldn't solve the problem.

I want this on the tape, because this is how I got this. I'm not teaching it necessarily the way I got it. I used up all the alternatives, and I couldn't die again, so I was caught. I'm pressing you to use your alternatives, without giving you the allowance to escape. If you can hear this, it'll really help you. It's just like you're in a vise. I'm pressing you to keep looking at your situation, and use up the possibilities of succeeding in the limited goal, and at the same time I'm taking away from you your escape hatch, which was death.

And now you're caught in the terrible gap: you can't solve this problem, and you can't die. Now you're in Gethsemane. This is the dark night of the soul. Everything you do does not solve the problem, yet there is no other solution that's available to you. Can you guys hear me when I do this? This is actually what's happening to you in your mind.

Your solution has always been to avoid the problem. If I take your avoidance away, you're forced to look at the problem. This is exactly what the *Course In Miracles* is. Now what are you going to do with it? You're going to have to undergo a change of your mind in regard to — this is the Hermetic philosophy — it's the bringing together in distillation of thought forms into a brighter association, because we plug up all of the manners in which you can escape. We used to call this 'the twelve gates of Jerusalem.' And finally you've got no other way of expressing yourself out, and you literally open your crown and come out the top of your head. That's the initiation process. You've resolved the conflict within your own mind. This is *Course In Miracles.*

Will you do this? Sure. Are you doing it now? Sure. Does it make you happy? I don't know. But if you're unhappy with it, you'll go out and find happiness in your limited pursuits. They will then turn to rust and rot and you'll have to look at them again. And you'll keep doing that. Why? Because it's in the power of your mind to do that, isn't it? And that's what you're going to do, until you finally say to me, "I have no need of this." And I'll say, "Good! You have no need of this."

"I don't need to get sick any more to get the sympathy that I think I'm entitled to. I need some attention. After all, I should be entitled to it. I've been unjustly treated long enough. I've given, given, given, and got nothing back. I'm going to stop doing that now; I tried giving and it didn't work." It worked perfectly.

Can you give without expectation of return? Can you understand there's no such thing as exchange? These are all sentences from the *Course.* Can you get hold of the idea that you only give to yourself? You projected it out there, right? It's a thought in your own mind. Who are you giving to except yourself? Why do you limit your own self? Why don't you just simply give yourself everything?

You say to me, "Well, if I gave it all away I wouldn't have anything left." And I say, "That's crap. You'd have everything immediately." Because the process of giving away is how you know you've got it. Until you give it away, you can't possibly know that you have it. How do you know you have anything until you give it away? You hold it as a thought form in your own mind, and store it up in here, and pretend you're going to use it later on. That's absurd! The bank goes bust and you've got nothing. You just lost it. Whew! I don't know how you stand it. You keep laying up the security that's necessary, but until you use it you can't know you've got it. That's the parable of hiding the shekel — three brothers, one hides it, the other gives a little away, and the other guy just gives it all away. And God comes back and says, "That's the way you do it."

You gotta give it away to know you have it. You're hiding your light under a bushel. "I wouldn't dare give it all away." Then don't expect to create, because creating is giving, and God only gives. He doesn't know anything else because there isn't anything else. Is everything I'm telling you true? Yeah. Does everybody know this about this? Sure. Does everyone in the whole universe know about Heaven and God, and all the things I'm telling you? Yeah! Of course!

Why? That's the condition of reality. Well, how come nobody here knows it? Because you created them in your own mind to share your own disillusionment, to share your own denial of it. Okay? Everybody got that? I'm going to stop doing it now. I want to be sure you understand what the *Course In Miracles* says. That's what it says. That this is your world; that you've created it in your own dream; and if you want to let those things out there influence you in regard to what they are, if you want to be at the mercy of the things that are going on around you, you're perfectly capable of doing it. You might even like it. That way you can get somebody else to tell you how you are. And if that doesn't seem crazy to you, I don't know. How could they possibly tell you what they are —what *you* are? Can they judge you? Can you judge them? Nah! So that's your relief.

Is this the new you that's emerging in this new idea? Sure. Will this take a little time to settle in with you?

The reason I'm giving you a hard message is you have a tendency to float into your energies around here. You guys have so much contact with whatever you do out here, with masters and energy and all that, and you can't get it the way you've been doing it, because they are forcing you into an identity. You see, I'm trying to give you all of you to transcend that.

I don't care how you identify me, it won't be true, until you see me as whole, and at that time you'll be whole.

Questioner: If I didn't want it, why do I do it?

MT: You do want it. You cherish death, because all the things you love are connected to it.

That's not too tough for you if you want to look at it. Otherwise, why is it everything you love dies? You say, "I don't want them to die." Then they won't, but neither can you, because you're the constructor of them. So the necessity is to make the declaration, "I can't die." Then neither can the things that you create. Why? Everything creates unto itself. If you formulated yourself in your genetic association to teach something to be separate, that is precisely what you did with your children, and so did I. So we taught them the autonomy of self- expression, taught them how to cope with sickness and death. Why? Because we come from that genetic association. You'll always reflect to your creations what you are. This has to be true.

What I am telling you is, what you are is unstable. So you end up in difficulties with your own offspring because you've introduced judgment unto them. Physician, heal thyself. The only teaching of the *Course* is for you to come to know who you are, right? Do you know who you are? But certainly if you know who you are, you are eternal; because the condition of knowing who you are is what eternity is.

Jesus says it's difficult for you to see that sickness is a choice. Yet I must admonish you that everything is your choice. And it's directly connected to the statement that you never do things for the reason you think you do. You've always got the association of your previous identities in your attempts to be sick contained within your own mind. Nobody can take that away from you. Not only that, but you can always find verification for it, can't you? You created the verification for it in order to keep your own identity, didn't you? Will they bring you back the answers that you want to hear? What the hell other answers would they bring you back? You constructed them to tell you what you want to hear, didn't you? Remember what Jesus says in the *Course*: You send out all of these thoughts to bring you back what you want to hear, to confirm yourself in your own associations, don't you? How do you get out of this? Change your mind about what you want to hear.

Is this a practice? In time it would have to be a practice, wouldn't it? But remember that you can't practice anything to a future fulfillment; that the practice is the same as the accomplishment. That way you won't feel disappointed when you fail, because this is a place of failure. That will make you constant in your pursuit of this, and will show you that infinite patience will bring immediate results. If you're going to do this, the idea that you're failing will not really concern you because you've always failed.

I'm very much aware that my message can't be heard by you. If it could be heard by you where you are, it's not true. When you healed teachers go out and try to teach this, do you think that our dear brothers aren't feeling the frustration of trying to express their revelation? What do they really give you? Vision. I'm just giving you a re-vision of yourself in association with all of your own things.

I can't teach you my personal revelation, that's absurd. How would you possibly know about it? But I can show you that you can come to your own revelation through the re-visioning of your own mind, through the utilization of the non-judgment of my revelation. This is the way you should do it, if you're going to teach A *Course In Miracles*. These are sentences directly out of the *Course*. Revelation is personal. But remember that reality is ultra-personal. It is only you. Isn't that funny?

You want me to check and see how much longer you've got to do this? They asked Jesus, "How much longer are we going to have to do this?" and Jesus says, "God knows." That's in the Bible, of course. There's no answer to how long, is there? You keep saying to the old man, "How much longer?" "I don't know; I thought you knew. Did you get some late word that I don't know about?"

I've been out a long time. I'm left over from the previous insertion. I told you that already: we lost your savior here. I don't know where they can hear that. We lost your configuration of what was going to be your savior; he fell off the truth wagon. That happens. Rosie hears me perfectly.

See, you never get it until you got it. The guy that was groomed in time to get this, slipped, and he fell into projections. He didn't complete his own treatment. You ask me, "Who is that?" I'm not going to tell you. If you ask me who it was, the true confession would be: it was you. But that's changing it a little bit. Because there was a consciousness that I am directly associated with that couldn't make a breakthrough in his own kundalini — couldn't come to his own full Christhood. When you can't do that, you always end up teaching a form of time association. You end up giving value to the association. Why? Because you haven't completed your own process.

So I'm what you call "an understudy". I literally was inserted into... and, you know something? I know it; I know that I'm not from here. In fact, I had a lot of leave time coming and I got a memo if I'd take over this and wrap this up, but they didn't tell me what was involved. "It'll take you just a little time. It's in quadrant 77. Just stop by and do that." I don't know how much of this you're hearing. When I get to this level I'll always speak in parables.

So this association, which was not on a spiritual search in the sense that you are doing, had just come in a lot of karma memories with enough frustration to have used up most of the

175

necessity to retain this limited idea of identity, i.e., my name, who I was when I was here — remember I'm looking at it now as pure energy, not as personality. Personality doesn't have to do with it. But this was ready to some extent.

If you listen to the history of my name, of Chuck, you would say, "Oh, yeah, I see how you did that, and how you did that," but at the time I was doing it I had no association with it being a spiritual search. None. That had nothing to do with it. Except I felt the frustration of being here. So that the insertion into me was positively spontaneous.

Obviously it involved the relinquishment of my own associations, and the demonstration of a miracle within the addiction program, where I felt the intensity of the pain of serving my brother, but a lot of people feel that. Then I felt the frustration of not being able to complete it, but a lot of people feel that. That's where you are. Now I'm here to tell you that that absolute feeling of frustration… You did it in two parts. First, I am here because you asked for help. I want you to hear this if you can.

Somewhere within this immediate time frame, you asked for help. And you REALLY asked for it. And you meant it. That's a prayer, isn't it? Well, the moment you really asked for help, a whole new association of thoughts formed, because you no longer held it in the stricture of the need to satisfy your perception. That's called the prayer of abandonment. "Father, into Thy Hands I command my spirit. Help me!" Do you understand this?

Remember that we're not at all concerned about what you're asking for help for, but only the fervency of your prayer. Can you get this? This will be nice for you; I haven't given this talk in a long time. I think I gave it in Denver… It's like it rings a bell. It's as though… "Help!" It doesn't make any difference what you're asking for help for — you could be the worst sinner in the world — an incestual rapist — all you finally did was ask for help.

Meanwhile you've got the Pharisees standing outside saying, "Well, how come I have done all the good things and this guy asks for help and gets it, and I don't?" Because we're not concerned about your definition of what help is or what you need help for; we're only concerned about the totality of your necessity to get it. Got it? Because you gotta ask for it in order to get it. You addictive people know how this works. As soon as you need help totally, you get it. Until you do, you won't; and you get as much help as you think you need and no more. You can call that a bottom if you want to.

But I'm telling you that the only prayer you would ever need is "Help!" and "Thank you!" isn't it? Because if you asked for help you must have gotten it, and the admission that you did get it makes you grateful. I don't care whether there's evidence that you got the help; that has nothing to do with it.

Somewhere you asked for help or I couldn't be here. You must have felt the frustration of not being able to solve this problem the way all the people around you apparently did. Whether they couldn't or could in some way, you always felt different. "God help me!" and whappo! Why? It would be impossible for you to ask for it and not get it if you really meant it. You know the problem? You asked for limited assistance. It isn't that you don't have the power of your mind to work the magic. I watch you guys at this level work magic all the time. You really think that's great. "Now, watch me get the parking place."

Notice how everything formulates in the power of my mind to bring that about. Do you do that? Sure. Sure. That's what you wanted and that's what you got. You know what the problem with that is? You denied somebody else the parking space. Uh-oh.

Questioner: There is no one else.

MT: Oh, yes there is. If you thought you had to have a parking space, there is. I'm not going to let you off the hook

177

that way! Otherwise you wouldn't have had to worry about parking.

No, no, no, you used the power of your mind in magic to bring about that occasion. If that occasion was brought about to your benefit in the limited association, somebody else suffered for it, and if you don't think so, you're not hearing me at all. You got that? That's called karma. I'm not going to take it away from you. What goes around comes around. Any assertation that you make in the power of your mind, in your attempts to gain, cause somebody else to lack. "Eat your dinner, they're starving in China." And I would say, "They're going to starve in China whether I eat my dinner or not." Terrible!

You always feel guilty then about the assertion of your own mind, but you continue to assert it, in order to what? Demonstrate the power of you. This is the power of the evil; separation. This is the temptation Jesus was put through; after the baptism, he's put through the temptation to assert the power in the limitation during the forty days in the wilderness. "Show them how much power you have; jump off the cliff and God will save you." "Thou shalt not tempt the Lord thy God." Why? You'll fall down and get killed on the rocks.

The idea that you cannot get killed, and using your power not to get killed, is not what the answer is. You can move mountains. I want to give you that power. All I'm telling you is, however you use it, you will be responsible for it. Isn't that so? Does somebody disagree with this? If you're going to understand the power of Science of the Mind, you must understand that you will be responsible for that power. Usually, you'll go through a period of not wanting to hurt your brother. You'll say, "Let's all be nice." You become a counselor, and for some years everybody comes to you to settle their problems because you seem so balanced. You seem to be able to deal with it because you console... Somewhere you still hold onto your prejudice, and finally you determined that, even though you were the counselor, you didn't have any answers, although you might have used the power to do that.

Remember Chauncey Gardener in [the movie] *Being There*? Chauncey was not capable of conceptual relationship thought, so that everything he said only reflected back what the consciousness wanted to hear. He's a perfect counselor. He did not understand the problem at all. Now, the Holy Spirit understands the problem perfectly, but He knows it's not real and in that sense He doesn't understand it. But Chauncey would just say, "I understand." "I think what our insightful friend is saying…" and then you'll reinterpret it in your own mind to the capacity of you to identify that nonjudgmental association.

This is what I'm doing with you. I have no opinions about you at all. My mind is not capable of an opinion. It would be senseless. Why would I have an opinion? About what? Now, I can give you that reflection, if you'll see that any opinions we might have about each other will have no value. It's not necessary that you know anything about anything.

Am I too good to be true? Sure. What I'm offering you is absolutely impossible. Be glad! What if you could really accomplish it here? Do you hear me? That would've meant that it would have had to have been real in order for you to overcome it. How would you ever be sure it was really overcome? You couldn't. You can't stand for a forgiving God, did you know that? You're very suspicious of a God that forgives you totally. Nothing is more sinful than a totally forgiving God. Why? If He recognizes the crime and forgives it, He's not all good, not in any sense.

So, God does not judge. Can you get that? Is that okay for you? Who wants God to judge? Everything does not judge, right? How could it? So stop asking God to judge this. Does established religion — Christianity — do that? Of course not! They construct a God who conceptually judges them in association with the things that they do, don't they? And you say, "Well, I don't want to associate with a religion. Christianity does that. They say God sent his only begotten son to be killed. And I know that's not true." So, what do you do? Do you form some other establishment that justifies you, secularly, the Kiwanis Club, or the Philatelists, or something?

Philatelists are stamp-lickers. I don't know where that came from — "You're a philatelist." That's the old political campaign: "I don't want to say anything about my opponent, but I understand he's a philatelist. Isn't that awful? And his daughter's a thespian." [More laughter] Ahhhh. See? We hear what we want to hear, don't we? "I think he matriculates too!" You hear what you want to hear in this regard, because you hear it in order to satisfy yourself. And you like the idea that your brother is fallible — and it's necessary to justify your fallibility. Jesus teaches this as guilt: He must be guilty along with you. And once you do that you can never get out of it.

That's why I stopped by here to tell you that it's not real, and that if you want to come home, it's okay. And if you don't want to, you must mean that it's okay with you not to, because all I could possibly do is offer it to you. But your original attack on God is senseless.

Is this really happening to your mind, that you're going to change your mind? Sure.

What occurs all the time here — see if you guys can hear this — remember that you guys are going through your own personal perceptual atonements — individually, aren't you? That's what's happening here now — within your own association. Sometimes this can appear conflictual, because you hold onto it in a limited frame, and you assert energy rather than releasing energy. That's what you're doing now; I just saw you do it. Don't do that. This is a release, not an identity. The level at which some of you have got this is not high enough to be stable. The stable level is up here and that veil is open for you. If you don't move up to that veil now, you're going to start feeling the frustrations of the world real strong. Because you've learned some fundamental lessons, and you're going to go out and — whappo! — it's really going to hit you. And you'll say, "Why am I doing this? This is futile." Or you'll go out and try to teach it in limitation, and be attacked because you're teaching. What you call teaching is not what I'm instructing you to do at all. I'm instructing you to BE YOU. With this energy it'll work perfectly. Why? You're teaching all the time. Everything only is an expression of what it is. It requires no reciprocation at all; and, in fact, if there is reciprocation, it's false.

Jesus says teaching on earth is literally exactly the opposite of what teaching is. You are going to be you regardless of what you do, so you're actually teaching each other in a total karma association all the time within the Great Ray association. It doesn't make any difference what you say. Sometimes you'll say, "Well, is it necessary that I talk at all?" I don't know. I do, so you must need me. Otherwise you'll keep formulating it in an association.

Did you hear what I'm telling you? Of course. What would there be not to hear this? In a very real sense, I'm only instructing myself. But remember, I'm only instructing the one single part of me that for a moment I can remember didn't know this. That's why I'm the savior.

Questioner: You haven't spoken about guidance, and I know in San Francisco there's a lot about, "check with guidance, check with guidance." Can you...

MT: Sure. The way you ask it, all guidance is false. You've limited the association and are asking for guidance in a specific identity. All you need ask for, ever, is total guidance, then the result won't concern you at all.

You're asking for a result of a problem. C'mon you guys! You've denied the miracle by asking for guidance in the limited association. I know. It's important. I understood what you're saying, and this is inevitably where the *Course* falls. Why? Because you need an assertion for dividing up the problems. The direction of the *Course* will be that you only have one problem, regardless of how much guidance you ask.

You can hear this. You inevitably ask for guidance only when you identify a specific problem. "Holy Spirit told me don't put onions in the potato salad." So a lot of the counselors are saying, "We don't deal with the *Course* because we send them out with the Holy Spirit and they all get different answers" and then they come back and they look for a consensus of what the Holy Spirit is saying. It's just so crazy!

You can only hear what you want to hear! Ha ha! My favorite joke: the guy coming out of Reno, driving out and he's got two hundred bucks left. The voice says:

"Turn back!"

Oh! Holy Spirit! And he turns back.

"Stop at Harold's Club"

Oooo, he parks his car, he gets out, he's all excited.

"Go to the roulette table." "Put your money on 24."

Mmm... [wheel stops at] Number 36

"Oh, crap!"

I hate that when that happens! That's awful! Who can you count on?

There's a tendency with awakening consciousnesses to gamble. It's a very amazing thing. They understand that all odds are finally the same. Many of them in this relinquishment will go through periods of gambling. Oh, I betcha! So did I!

Questioner: There's a card room here in San Jose, and actually I was thinking about stopping before I go back.

MT: You already won! You have everything.

But the tendency to take a chance statistically will come into a whole mind, because it realizes that when it wins, it had just as good a chance to win as anyone, regardless of what the odds were. And what it says is, "It's proper for me to make the application of that power in my re-association to bring that about." Some of you have become very clairvoyant.

... literally. And you're going to say to me, "Well, no, because I don't know when it's going to occur." I'll say, "Yes, you do, because any death is all occurrence, all the time."

When Jesus teaches salvation, he teaches time is a sleight of hand. And that the time that you were saved was always the time that you were saved, even though it appears to be quite arbitrary. That's exactly the same thing as death, because the time that you go through the death experience has to be the time that you went through the experience. That is to say, putting off death is what death is. It doesn't make any difference whether it's cancer or a beer truck that runs over you. At that moment you're dead, and then still alive to observe yourself dead.

So indeed you can be prophetic. Can you do telekinesis? Yeah. Can you levitate? Oh, c'mon! This is nothing but an assertion of your own perceptual mind. What are you going to do with it? Join the circus? Can you use it to advantage, if you know who's the winner of the horse race, for example? Certainly, but somebody else is going to lose, or is going to suffer because you won. You say, "No, I didn't affect... There wasn't too much karma in it."

And that happens to you. Just before the derby, suddenly you know perfectly well who's going to win the derby. You know. Should you go and bet on that? I don't know. Will that

183

horse win? Probably. It's statistically possible for the horse not to win, because you could affect the odds sufficiently to cause a re-association in time. I don't want to give this talk.

But generally speaking, at the level you're at, you're very able to see what's going to occur. And it may very well flash in your mind. In that sense, it's what they call checking the akashic record. What you do is you just KNOW that's what happened. You didn't arrive at any conclusions here. Did it happen? Yeah. Will you use it to your own benefit? Yeah. Will it cause somebody else concern? Yeah.

What are you going to do with it now that you've proven it? Keep doing it? In order to what? Accumulate power in your own associations? This is the devil. This is the idea that you can gain power in your own limitations. But what happens? You always lose. Jesus says in the *Course*, you sell your soul to the devil, which is literally the assertion of your own power, you then have that power, but to what advantage? You've proven that you can have the power, and then what happens to you? You get sick and die. He claims your soul, if you want to look at it that way.

So, I can't take your power away from you, but I can ask you to use it in order to escape the illusion of death. And that's exactly what I'm doing. And if you'll believe me, you will see immediately that you're in Heaven with me. Until you do that, you can't see it. Somewhere you're going to have to accept what I'm saying is true. Until you do, you can't get it. You might as well hear this now. This won't cause you a lot of delay. Finally I'm teaching acceptance. There is no other way you can get it. I have to be right and you have to be wrong.

You have to say with me, "I can't die. There is no death." Obviously, the moment you believed me, you could never die. Why? You believed me! And the power was in your own mind that had constructed your death. Is this so? How would it not be so, if death is your decision? Do you need somebody to tell you this? Yeah! You need a savior. It's not in your own construct, because you're constructed to die. Is that faith? Yup. Finally. It's also true.

So the question is only this: Do you really not want to die? Now, if you can come to hear me, you're indicating to me, "I'm not satisfied with dying anymore." I don't care what you say to me — that's just an indication you're going to stay a body, and die. Who could take that away from you? No one!

But, "He that believeth unto me will never die." That's a statement of a whole mind. Why? The whole mind knows that the limited association is not real. Can you accept that? From the *Course?* From anyone? No. Not totally, because the moment you do, you become the savior of the world. You could not not be the savior, because that consciousness is a projection of your own mind. And the moment that you would forgive him totally, he becomes your savior.

Is this hard for you? Do you do the *Course?* This shouldn't be too hard for you then. It's a course in forgiveness. Why do you keep asking questions about it? If that is a projection of your own mind, it must be perfect, if your mind is perfect. If your mind is not perfect, the fault is yours, not his. Doesn't that make sense?

He is only going to tell you what you want to hear from him. Right? He'd have to be. That's what he's doing. Now, when I tell you that you're perfect, you don't want to hear it. That's all. Is that why you asked the question? Yes. Is that why you got the answer? Yes. That means if you're not hearing it, it must be because you don't want to. This is lesson 139, that I know all of you read at lunch. Somewhere, what's going to occur to you is that there really is a God. That will have nothing to do with what God is. It'll have nothing to do with the identity of it, will it? It'll simply be a statement that God is a fact.

I'll give you a statement of fact: God is a fact, and He has nothing to do with the world, and this is not real, and there is no sickness and death. Everybody got that? What else should I tell you? The question is not that what I said was true. The question is whether you want to hear it.

Yet it is impossible, if you ask the question, "Is there a God?" that you do not know that there is one. Would that be so? Why else do you need to ask the question? Yes, there is a God. Yes, there is eternal life, and all life is eternal. Yes, there is not pain and sickness and loneliness, strife and anger, and all the things that you seem to see here are not true. That's what this says [taps the *Course* book on the table] on the first page. That's what I'm here to tell you, to give you this association.

It's easier for you to deny Jesus than it will be for you to deny me, because he is not going to attack you. He just keeps offering it to you. I'm a little more confrontative with it. If you're going to teach this now, this is what he wants. He wants this. He wants you to make the declaration of your own saviorship. Do you have to see that you are the cause of this in order to do that? Sure. What's wrong with that? Then you won't keep persisting in denying your own reality.

Well, is the *Course* written by a consciousness that's not in a body? Yeah. Could something in the body write the *Course In Miracles?* Sure. But it wouldn't need the body, would it? Is this just a dream? Yeah. Can you reduce this in your perceptions as you read it? It's tough, but you've been doing it. Not only that, but you'll search, in the *Course* now, to find ambivalence in the simple statement of the *Course.* Why? I've given you allowances for choice. Do you see? This will end this now. I've given you an allowance for an impossibility. Now, you can go to the book and prove that somehow in your perception you can make a choice about this. But the fundamental teaching is that you have no choice.

Don't "uhh" it. This is what I want you to start to teach. That way you can get it. As long as you think you have a choice, you literally won't get it, because you are having a choice. Now you can say to me, "Aha! I've got you here. You're allowing me to make a choice." Yeah, you got me. If I'm going to be a savior, I have to give you that choice. But it's not real. There's no such thing as a savior of the world. At least not for more than a moment. Is there such a thing as the Holy Spirit? Why do you need a Holy Spirit? The principle of Atonement was introduced at the time of the schism; otherwise there would be no necessity for it at all. It's not real! This is all an illusion. All perception is illusionary.

I'll give you the top — this is the whole Eastern teaching, incidentally. This is the certainty of the illusion, la mère (the mother): Are you determined that you're going to formulate this in your own limitations and express yourself? Sure. And what I'm telling you is not feasible in your own relationships. You really don't want to know that you're whole and perfect, otherwise you wouldn't ask questions.

Questioner: It has to do with guidance. Judy was asking you about that a bit ago. In Chapter 30 there is the section on Rules for Decision, which does seem to suggest that asking for guidance is something that we should be...

MT: You always get what you ask for. So the question is what are you asking for? I just covered it. You'll always get what you're asking for.

Questioner: That wasn't my question.

MT: You ask for guidance, you're going to get what you want. What's your question?

Questioner: I don't understand very well this section on rules for decision. I was hoping perhaps you could say something about it.

MT: Ask me.

Questioner: Well, it does pertain to asking for guidance, and it tells you to think about the kind of day you want to have, the kind of feelings that you want to have, and the things you want to happen. How specific is it okay to frame this?

MT: Totally, because you can't stop yourself from doing it. This is the part of the Text that's going to go into the Workbook. Actually, it sounds more like Workbook than Text, doesn't it? That's because it's at the end, and now they're going to introduce the manner in which you can do this. Remember that the premise, however, is that you really don't have any choice. As long as you want to remain in the mechanism, you can do so, yes. And as long as you think that sin is real, you're going to have to address the illusion, aren't you? Why? Because you've got it out there as conflict, and you're going to have to look at it. That's the whole teaching. Obviously, that's what you've got to do, yes, you ask for it.

At some point, you would want to address the certainty that you're the cause of it, however; that you're the cause of your own conflict, and that the association that is asking for guidance is not real. Or, that the association that asks for guidance gets it immediately to the idea of what he has asked for.

What happens is this. As soon as you're given a mechanism, you use the mechanism. That's exactly what you're doing now. I can't take your mechanism away from you. All I can do is ask you to look at it. Why? The mechanism is not true.

Questioner: I'm sorry. What mechanism are you referring to?

MT: The mechanism of having to ask for guidance. That's the mechanism I'm referring to. The mechanism of having to ask for guidance is not real, because the consciousness that is asking for guidance is not real. Of course you're going to use the mechanism, but at what point do you put away your toys? I told you, you have no choice in this matter. Asking for guidance is an indication that you have a choice. I gotta give you that. In that sense, it's a progression.

I'll tell you why you ask for guidance. I don't get into this. Here's why you ask for guidance in the Workbook. The manner in which you have constructed the problem is false. And at the time you address that association you have already solved the problem in association with yourself, and it's inherently conflictual. If every time you come into a situation, you say, "What I have brought to this is false. I do not know what this is, I'll let it go and ask for help." That's guidance. That's perfect. Do that.

Now finally what happens is this: The miracle begins to occur. Instead of finding yourself in the deep crap, you've let the deep crap go on the outset of the authentication. Can you hear this? You were inherently in conflict with the association that was outside of you, regardless of how you define it. You're going to ask for guidance in how to look at the problem. Why? You know — if you're going to do the *Course* — that the way you're looking at the problem is not so, and you're getting back the frame that you have established in your own mind to bring about the relationship, and you're hearing the answer that you wanted to hear.

When you ask for guidance, you say, "There's another way to look at this; I'm wrong." Why? You are wrong, because all of your perceptions in association to what you think you are, are not true. These are the first twenty lessons of the Workbook. You don't tell it what it is, what do you do? You ask it. Ask for guidance on what it is. Good! Sure! But as soon as you identify it, it's too late to ask for guidance, in the sense that you now want to determine how you're going to be guided by what you have constructed objectively, and that's where you'll have the problem. You'll let sin be real, and then try to repair it.

Obviously, you can't know you have a problem until you experience the conflict within your own mind. That's a true statement. The closer you get to the truth, the more inherent will become your conflict with the world. You literally can't stand it. Everything seems like everybody is just battling everybody else, and of course they are. So you try to get out of it. Maybe you go in a nunnery, you go to a priest, you go up into Tibet and search for truths in here. I know you do that.

What am I telling you? It's only in here. If you seek this, you'll find it. Is there guidance available to you? Yes. Need you use the mechanism of perception in order to get it? Obviously, or you wouldn't need the Atonement.

If you put faith in the mechanism, you will inherently fail — this is in the *Course* in several places — because the mechanism is not true. What you're saying is, I will use the power of my own mind to come to the truth in perception, and you can't. The mechanism is the release of the necessity for judgment. This is only to teach you to know that you don't know. I'll do it in a double negative for you if you want. That's the teachings of the *Course.*

Questioner: I'm confused about what is the meaning of the mechanism? Here on page 582, it talks about the three separate questions to ask...

MT: What do you want me to tell you, buddy? You're doing that right now. All this really does is to give you an allowance — I'll do it once more, and then I'm going to stop it — it gives you an allowance for a new way to look at the problem, rather than seeking the solution of going to the office for the last twenty years. If you really decide you don't want to go to the office — you want me to show you how this works? — all you would really have to say is, "Screw the office. I'm never going to go to it again. I'll ask for guidance on something else to do," and you'll get it, because you're determined not to do that. Will the result please you? I don't know, but at least it's an assertion of your determination to relinquish your previous association. This is the Workbook of the *Course*. I'm trying to give you what you want and more, and you don't want to take it.

All decisions are made by you. All guidance is only to yourself. If you don't ask the question, you can't get the answer. Every question that you're asking will come back to you in exactly the answer that you want to hear. You cannot get guidance that you don't ask for. If you ask for total guidance, you have to relinquish all of your perceptual ideas about the necessity for guidance. That's what the miracle is.

Is the miracle all around you, working all the time? Sure. You're the one that asks for guidance within the limited framework of what you ask. By opening it up in the Workbook, it's going to tell you, "Ask it what it is." "Who are you?" I don't say to you, "Hi, I'm Chuck. Let's ask for guidance in how we're going to handle the day." You can do that if you want to, but it's absolutely meaningless. You've already decided that you're going to be in association with that.

When you go to teach this, they will always fall into mechanistic defense. This is what happens. Justification for the idea of spiritual progress. There's no such thing. Justification for a spiritual path. There's no such thing. Jesus says in the *Course*, anyone on a spiritual path has his hands over his eyes. This is what you're trying to do. You can't do it. That's what he says. I mean, if there's a spiritual path and you're looking for God, why do you need guidance in finding God? It's senseless. You don't need guidance to find God, and anything that needs guidance is not real. Be glad! What if you really were separated and needed true guidance to get to God? God would have to acknowledge that you were really separated from Him.

Who are you asking guidance from? Your own whole Self. Because you must know the ultimate Answer. You call that the Holy Spirit. Do I tell you not to ask? I don't care, but you're only going to get the result that you want. I went in a circle. All power is given unto you in Heaven and earth. That's not a big deal. That's what you are.

Can you go out and teach this? I don't know. I think I'd teach it as an experience, and try to stay out of the repartee. It's meaningless. I allow questions and addressing, because there are some very fundamental necessities in the admission of what this really says. That's why I came here. I want you to look at what this says, and stop trying to define it in your limited associations. It just simply says this isn't real. How many times does it say this isn't real? About thirty, forty. Will you come to know that this isn't real? Sure. How else would you be able to ask if this is real? You must have come to the conclusion.

This has been a very eventful occurrence. We're going to have a little quiet time now. Boy, a lot of you guys are really familiar to me, you know that? See how quickly we get familiar?

This initial purpose is what we call a sorting out. What I'm telling you is true. We used to call it sorting the wheat from the chaff, because this message is real high. If you want to hear this message, it'll be very easy for you to hear. If you don't want to hear it, it simply means that you're in a choice of a situation where you are still deriving satisfaction from your limited associations, which are death. Wouldn't that have to be true? And as long as you continue to do that, you won't hear this message. All I'm really doing is to encourage you — this is called speeding up time now — to look at your problem, and ask me how you're solving it. You're going to have to tell me, "I'm solving it by death, or by my associations." And I'm going to tell you that won't solve the problem.

When you have tried enough to solve the problem and have not been successful, you will begin to hear this. Why? This is the only solution. There is no solution but this. If sickness and death and the earth are real, there is no God. This is a sentence right out of the *Course.* If there is a God and wholeness, then the earth, sickness, pain and death are not real. There's no sense in equivocating this, if you're going to attempt to teach it. These two things do not know each other. If you attempt to formulate reality based on your conceptual associations with death, you will fail, because concepts are not real. That's how simple this is.

So, now, the psychology is to relinquish your own possessions. If you are possessed, if you are the devil, you are holding onto idols, or thought forms, in your own mind, that constitute your reality. And you cherish them and you give them value. I am teaching you to be dispossessed. How do you do that? Give it away. This is the part you hate to hear the most.

If you want to do this, finally, and it can't be defined, you're going to have to give away your own idolatry, your own association with yourself. You can't get it any other way. Yes.

Questioner: Since you're always choosing, that means that you make the choice to leave your body. What happens to your body?

MT: My body's not here. There isn't any such thing as a body. People have the idea that in the future you can lay your body down. That's crazy. If you can't lay it down now, when would you lay it down?

Questioner: How does it look to your family?...

MT: You mean, how does it look to your family? Are you going to trick the old man here? I'll tell my story sometime, if you come back to it.

I was in a very social situation when I started into my awakening. Did it create problems? A-ha-ha-ha-ha. O-ho-ho-ho-ho-ho. But, you have problems anyway. If you're going to have problems, have them going to God, that's all I can tell you. How long is it going to last? Just long enough for you to see that you can't escape anything by disassociation.

A lot of you get a little piece of this, and you think, "The hell with it. The *Course* teaches me to give up my family, throw everything away, and go to Heaven." The *Course* doesn't teach that at all. The *Course* teaches you only to give up your whole self, and definitions of what that is are what the falsity is.

You can make mistakes, and you can finally say, "I find myself in an impossible situation." Why? You've changed your own mind, and you are no longer who you were last week. Now the question is, are you going to allow that previous association to hold you in the bondage through the obligation and guilt that you feel by your former karma? That's a problem for you. Do you hear me? Because all relationships here are special.

Fortunately, there's such a thing as a miracle. Fortunately, it's going to work despite you, and fortunately, not in the manner in which you thought it would work. Never! [laughing] The manner in which you constructed it to work contained the falsity of your need to disassociate and re-illusion. Nothing ever happens for the reasons that you think it does. When you released your possessive specialness, which wasn't real in the first place, there was a whole reformulation, including that consciousness, to the full benefit of the harmony contained in reality. This is the miracle, guys!

Motivated action is death. Of course! All action is death. You need do nothing but change your mind. That may appear to be conflictual, but it's always been conflictual. You've always just buried it. You say, "Well, how much of this am I going to have to go through? The situation I'm in now... I've got children... I'm a grandfather... and I love them all... and you're going to take that away from me."

No! But I think you ought to look at what's happening in that association. What you have constructed in your family unit, in order to attack God. Why? They are the constructs of your mind.

Jesus is a little... he says you've got to hate your brother. I don't tell you that. But I want to give you the total love of you, and then ask why are you doing it? Will the miracle work if you do this? It must work, because your perceptual mind is what the obstruction is. Can that be demonstrated here? Sure. The reason it works perfectly is because it's perfect. Each moment, everything you're doing is bringing you to paradise. You're the one that insists on sequencing it in your mind. Do you want to grow up and get cancer and get old and die? Well, then don't.

You say, "Well I'm caught up in things that I formerly thought that I had to do, that I'm associated with." That'll be all right. You make the commitment. You say, "No" — remember this is the power of your own mind — "No, I want to do this." May that cause what you classify as a disillusionment? I don't know, but anything that can be re-illusioned wasn't true in the first place. You were determined to make it true within your own framework. There are some lovely things in the *Course* that say, "Let the dead bury the dead." Remember that the responsibility you feel for this is an attack on God.

I'm tired of tough talk here. Obviously this idea of friendship and all that, is a direct attack on reality. Why? Because it results in death. So it appears to you that I'm taking away the things that you love. But you love them only to suffer the loneliness and pain in association with the love. Could you just once love them totally? Yes, but you'd have to do it with no judgment, and then you could never lose them, because you've lost the judgment of yourself, and you're no longer participating in the exchange.

Whenever you begin to talk this way, it's always because you forgot there is a God and a miracle and truth, and that this is your dream. And that includes me. All we're really going to do here now is dream a whole dream together. Can you do that? What would stop you? Did you do it? You're doing it now. Is it inevitable that you do it? Everything is inevitable. Be glad! That way you don't have to decide whether it has value or not.

Are you ready? One more sentence, and I swear I'm going to stop. I'm giving it to you right out of the *Course*: Everything should have total value — is worth valuing totally — or it has no value at all. Now you've got no problem. You just value everything perfectly, but to do that you've got to not judge it. And if you don't judge it and value everything, they'll say, "You're crazy." You turn into a Job; the Lord strikes you down, and you say, "Thank You, Lord." That's progress, though, eh? You still think there's a sacrifice connected with your determination to find it. Jesus would teach you there's no such thing as sacrifice; it doesn't cost you anything to be with God, because that's where you are.

Does this appear to be a complicated and difficult message? Of course; to those who want to complicate it. What am I really saying? I'm saying the same thing over and over again. I never say anything but what I'm saying. Every time I speak, I'm saying exactly the same thing as I always say. I'm just trying to penetrate your perceptual associations with what I'm saying.

All you're determined to do is to hold onto what you thought was true last week is true today, and you're full of crap. Everything you brought in here was absolutely meaningless. That's what salvation is. [laughing] The whole teaching is to come here naked. To come here without the judgment. That's why I say, come here just as you are, and let it be. Don't try to judge this in association with your previous things.

"That's hard to do." Why? "Well, I'll lose my identity..." Yeah! "But it starts to work, and I get scared, because suddenly I begin to feel these strange things happening to me. I'll lose my mind." No, you'll find your mind. You've already lost it, in your own mind.

What you classify as paranoia, schizophrenia, manic depression and all that, are all efforts of reality to penetrate your shell of denial. Without exception. I'll give a talk on that sometime. Isn't that nice to know? You feel paranoia because there's a lot of things around you all the time.

When you expand your consciousness, you really get the feeling that something is around you, and you're absolutely right. And that scares you, so you take a drug to bring yourself down out of the fear that you have every right to feel, because there are things around you that can hurt you. Obviously, the whole *Course* is nothing but a lesson in schizophrenia. It's the idea of a split mind, one of which is whole and the other isn't, and they are in conflict.

Manic depression is what I teach. I teach you to be totally depressed, so you can enter the mania side of your reality. When I used to teach this, when somebody would express depression to me, I'd say, "Go into your total depression. Don't try to recover from it." You want to write that down? That's important. Don't attempt to recover from it. Go through it. If you're going to experience the pain of your bottom, let your bottom come whole again with you. That's the quickest way to get out of it. If you cover it, you'll remain with a defiled altar that you're fearful to look at. You'll then construct your reality on being unwilling to look at the fateful moment that brought you into this in the first place. Do you hear this?

What's the difference in bottoms? "It seems like I've paid all my dues and that I ought to be able to…" You're not the judge of it.

I sometimes tie this in with the Twelve-Step Program, because that's the way I got this. And boy, does it tie in with it. I'm going to make a comment about the Twelve-Step Program in case somebody is listening to this.

There is a point where it's necessary for the consciousness who is an addict to re-associate himself in a new factor of his determination that he is powerless over something, and that by asking for help he receives it. This is the *Course In Miracles.* It may very well be necessary at that point for him to have a re-identification, say, as a recovered addict, because that's a statement of the wholeness of him in that association. It's a discovery of himself. If there's any dichotomy between the *Course In Miracles* and the Twelve-Step Program it's that I am teaching you that all identities are false. So that if you are working a program that says, "I am a recovered addict," or "I'm a recovering alcoholic," it's very important that you keep that identity, so you won't fall into the temptation of the original powerlessness that you could not exercise over the drug. And in that sense, having paid my dues again in this regard, all I can really offer you is this: All Twelve-Step Programs that are real programs are spiritual, because it is a totally spiritual program, and it has nothing to do with self-identity, but with the relinquishment of the identity. And then it'll come together real good for you.

To a mind who needs the identity of being a recovered alcoholic, what I'm teaching may not be apropos. Bless his heart! If he needs that identity, let him have it. In the direct assertion that he is aware that his recovery was beyond him, he is teaching the *Course In Miracles.* To the direct application that he had something to do with his sobriety, he is denying his own program.

And I know that you need treatment centers where you can give application of the problems that an alcoholic so-called feels, but you remember this: There's only one problem, if you're working with an addict, and that's his addiction. You guys begin to counsel him as though a lot of other problems caused his addiction. That's a lie. If you're going to focus on the problem, the problem is you. And the solution has to be in your certainty that you cannot overcome the problem by yourself. This now becomes the *Course In Miracles*, and this is obviously the first three steps of the Program. Everybody got that?

All good programs say, "I had nothing to do with my recovery." All of them. Any time a program, within the scope of the counseling, indicates that you had something to do with your recovery — you listen to me, addicts, if there're any here — you're going to get in trouble. Why? You begin to get into the driver's seat. All good programs know that they got it through the grace of God. For crying out loud! That's the whole teaching! I'm here through the grace of God, and the certainty that I couldn't do this myself. That's what I'm saying to you now, about the *Course*. You came to me through the certainty that you are what you call an ego addict, a humaholic. You're addicted to everything in your own mind in that association, and that's a fact. And actually you're powerless over yourself — that's a true statement. I wanted this on the tape because there's a previous talk that I gave that's circulating around the whole world. It's a good talk on the relationship between the *Course In Miracles* and the Twelve-Step Program.

Is the Twelve-Step Program valuable to you in the *Course*? It can be totally valuable. All it really says is, I'm powerless, there's a Power that'll help me to sanity, and I'll turn it over to Him. That is the *Course In Miracles*! The *Course In Miracles* does not have purgation, and it doesn't have inventory, but to any *Course In Miracles* groups I would ever direct, I'd say,

"Look at your guilt associations, and repair your home front!" For crying out loud!

You can't overcome the guilt if you don't make the amend. It doesn't make any difference whether the amend is accepted, but you have to make it. Your fear that it won't be accepted holds you in the bondage of the non-necessity to make it, and you're wrong! You're going to carry that as guilt down in here, and you'll never get rid of it.

This is how I woke up, incidentally. This is what I used to teach; I still do. Make the amend.

You got a grievance against somebody? It doesn't make any difference how he responds. What difference does it make how he responds, if you've accepted responsibility for it? This is the *Course In Miracles.* You're determined to get a reciprocal response from him that would share the judgment. You're wrong. You're totally guilty and he's totally innocent. Now you can get it. Can you teach that? The power is in the admission, not in the demonstration of reciprocity. Hell, I taught this mm-mm years ago.

You're afraid to make the amend. You haven't spoken to somebody for twenty years. Some of you guys... it's really sick... You've got that all buried down there. I always give this talk at the end: Why don't you just go to the telephone and pick it up? — I know you guys have one of these in your mind. This is in the *Course* too — just pick it up, and dial it, and say "Hi!" and then just shut up. This is letting the decision be made for you. This could be very valuable to you. Don't immediately say to the consciousness, "Well, I just called to tell you that I'm sorry for all the things..." That's not going to do any good. All you did was re-create the problem.

You guys like this kind of talk? It's a lovely talk.

What you're really saying is, "I don't know what the

solution to this is, but I'm going to look at the problem and not try to find the answer." The answer is there in the love you have for the guy, for crying out loud! It's only your own pride that doesn't allow you to simply say, "Hey." Do you need to say "I'm sorry"? Then say you're sorry! But you say "I'm sorry" and then you say, "Well, will you accept that I'm sorry and some of the responsibility for this?" That's sharing the guilt. [laughing]

Really, that's not the problem. You're fearful of the response. He's liable to say, "Well, you s.o.b., you call me after all these years." A lot of times when I use to teach amends, and I did this for many years, I'd say go make the amend. And the consciousness would make the call, and discover that the guy didn't even remember it. Those are always amazing. The guy would say, "I don't know what the hell you're talking about," and for twenty-five years you've been carrying this. Uhhhh!!! All pain is self-inflicted. But if you have a problem out there, for crying out loud, look at it. It makes absolutely no difference what the response is.

You can't do anything about a consciousness that wants to be a slave to its own grievances, and if you think you can, you're wrong. Advanced teachers will discover this. A slave to death is going to be a willing slave. If his reality is going to be placed on holding a grievance against you, there's absolutely nothing you can do about it. Stop trying! Your job is to see him as whole through the assertion that you're making to this.

Questioner: How does that square with letting go of the past?

MT: It's the same idea. If you have a grievance, it means that you haven't let go of the past, have you? You specifically held onto it. Why? It appears to be a grievance for you. You say, "I don't want to look at that. That's not what I want to look at." I'm not telling you that it's necessary for you to look at, but if it is necessary for you to look at, it's necessary.

People used to say to me, "Is it all right if I just make the amend in my own mind? It'll hurt everybody if I bring that up again" This is the ninth step. I didn't mean to get into this talk, but if you need to make it, make it. But don't look for the result. Why? The problem is in you, not out there.

Once more — it doesn't make any difference how they respond to it. It's your admission that it was a problem in your own memory. That will become very natural for you as you progress in this.

When you go to these gatherings, all your brothers and sisters are going to tell you how awful things were, and hold onto the grievance — this was the beginning of the talk; this is the end — it won't bother you in the least. That's not to say you won't remember the past, because you'll remember it perfectly. It just won't be a grievance to you. What will you say? "Gee, if that hadn't happened, I wouldn't be here now." "I'm glad that my father did whatever he did; that taught me all the lessons that I had to learn..."

* * * * * * *

If you grieve in association with them, you have entered into consort with the necessity that you retain death together. This is a very high program. But remember there's a God, and that reality is all around you. Then it'll be a lot easier for you. You won't have to study your own associations with it. I already took death away from you anyway — what are you worried about? Why don't you just believe me? Can you do that? You'd be in Heaven. You are.

I always end up saying that. Why? That's the truth. Can you teach that? Sure. Do you have to fake it 'til you make it? I won't care. If it's the truth, why don't you fake it 'til you make it? Oh, I wouldn't dare go out and say, "I'm the only living Son of God." Why not? You are!

Questioner: The book says we only made one big mistake, and you phrased it as we got lost. I don't understand how God could get lost.

MT: He couldn't, but you could, because you apparently are. I'm not going to take that away from you. I understand where the paradox occurs, and that's really what you're looking at, isn't it? The idea of recovery is what the idea of being separate is. If you didn't need Atonement, I wouldn't be here. That's pretty simple, then. But remember that this is totally you. There's nothing outside of this.

Are you asking whether God knows about this? No, He doesn't know about it. You and I got in it together. Don't you want to hear that? We're the cause of this together. We have to be, because we're in each other's minds, aren't we? All I want you to see is that we're finally totally in each other's minds. Jesus says, you can't remember the one single incident that we did together that got us into this.

You're trying to study it and find an identity with me. You can't. It won't work that way. You know me, though. I know you from last week. You were with me on my last death episode. A lot of you guys were. I know ya. We know each other real well. So what we're determined to do now is to dream a true dream out of here. Why? I know you out of time. I can't tell you what you are out of time, except that you are as God created you and you're perfect. The requirement is that you love.

So, this is a course in Atonement, in the changing of your mind, that's happening to you now. The requirement is the experience of the transformation itself, not the observation of how it's going to come about, not the mechanisms that are going to bring it about. None of those you need be concerned about.

There is a God, and when you bring together this association of yourself, cause and effect, you will be real and in Heaven.

Now, the parts that you've been avoiding in the *Course*, that cause you to keep all sorts of books about what it says, and attempting to study it, true and false, mean absolutely nothing. Don't do that anymore. Look at the sentences that you have been previously afraid to look at. I looked at some of the little cards that you guys make up, and they're real soft. They have a tendency to say, we're all working together on this. Because we gave you that mechanism, and you take it.

Not so. You are the dreamer of the dream. This is your world. Finally. When you depart the world which you thought was real, where is the world? There isn't any, is there? This is your construct. When you're not here, there is no world.

Never mind all of these things you made. You can't be in Heaven and something else in hell. This is hell, and you can go to Heaven by this re-association. How simple then is salvation.

Final comment. A lot of you are undergoing real dramatic changes in your, what you call, aura or energies. You ought to be able to feel it. I would really like to validate it for you. If you won't limit what's happening to you now, and take full advantage of it, you'll be out of here in a flash. All you really had to do was take that little willingness and say, "Uh-oh! This is what I've been waiting to hear." Why? I'm telling you what it says. "This is what I wanted to hear. This is what I'm going to do now with what I am. I'm not going to die anymore." Because that's the choice that I'm giving you.

Questioner: You say fake it 'til you make it. Is that what you do?

MT: That's just a denial of my Christhood. Any other questions? All you did was deny your own reality. You made a jerky statement about it. I told you at the beginning of this that you don't believe anything, that everything is fake to you, and you just verified it.

Questioner: By wanting to get out of here, aren't we making it real?

MT: Of course, but what's your alternative? You think it's real. Otherwise you wouldn't need the Atonement, would you? You're always looking for another way, aren't you? That's why you're here. Search you must here, because that's what you came here for. You came here to find happiness and truth, didn't you? I'm telling you it's not here.

So the necessity to know it's not here is not to give it value; then the reality will be all around you. It would have to be, if you're the obstacle. You've constructed what you think salvation is, right? It's not that. You don't even know who you are. Why are you trying to do this? Stop it!

That's the most fearful thing. Jesus says you don't know who you are, where you came from, how you got here; it's silly! I looked at that when I was about fourteen. I said, What is this? How did I get here? "We don't know." Where do I go when I die? "We don't know." Where do I find out? What are all those things? "We don't know. Don't bother with that. Just stay here and live this life and die." Crazy! But that's what they ask you to do, and you're saying, "There's something wrong with this."

Do not underestimate the insanity of this. It's totally and absolutely insane. The idea that you're going to take your mind and direct it to a judgment of what God is, is absurd. Can you judge me in this regard? Uh-uh. That's why you can't find the Christ. He's all around you, but you keep trying to determine what He is through your own judgment. And your judgment is absolutely faulty. You have no frame of reference for what reality is. None. You can't remember being whole. If you did, you wouldn't have to do this.

You only do it once. And you must have done it, because you have it in your mind that you're doing it. This will turn into a game of kicking it back and forth. Now you go out and find some more pain, and you say, "Maybe this is right. Maybe everything he said to me is true. Maybe this really is not a real place." But remember that it will occur from you; there's nothing in Heaven or earth that will force you to do it unless you decide you want it. You can give me all the constructs of your mind that you want. What are you going to prove? Certainly you're attacking me, and you're going to prove that I'm not real. But that's because you attack everything. Judgment is what attack is.

I must be making some progress; I allowed questions. I've never allowed questions before. Is that a corruption on me, or is that okay? You guys ask good questions. The reason I let you ask questions is some of you with real open minds see that the question doesn't make any sense, yet it makes perfect sense to the consciousness that's asking it. That way, you're able to compare where you are in that association.

You guys think I'm teaching non-judgment. I'm teaching discernible judgment. But judge only to the criteria of eternity rather than to the association. I'm not trying to take judgment away from you; that's impossible. You're going around practicing not judging your brother. That's absurd; you've already judged him. You can hear all this. It's in the *Course*, and it's lovely.

We must have a little quiet time now, guys. There's a lot happening in the world now. You take this new you out from here now. If you've allowed yourself to be new, rather than hold on to the association, you will begin to go through a lot of experiences with this energy. Take all of those experiences and make them a part of the whole Atonement thing that's happening to you. Do you see that? What have you got to lose? Why don't you just take a chance that what I'm telling you is true? Are you going to take a chance on

God? Sure. But you've certainly used up a lot of your other options, haven't you?

Thanks for giving me the job, letting me fulfill what I do. This class will be graduating …right here…well, it depends on a couple of things that have to happen. What are they? I don't know. Maybe you would just as soon do it now. You can do it now if you want. "Oh, no I couldn't." Yeah, you could.

I have to tell you, this is the time that you chose. I was tricking you. Now I've got you too close to this, and you don't know what to do. Always before you've turned back when you got to this point. There's a lovely sentence in the *Course* that says, you've come up to this point, and always said, "No, no." This time you're going to go through your transformation. That has to be all right with you, though. Otherwise you'll be very afraid, because you've always been afraid to do this before, haven't you? This morning you weren't afraid of what you felt; you were only afraid of the relinquishment of yourself in order to do it. The loss of your need to identify it, for example. The admission that you in fact are whole mind.

We'll have a little quiet time, guys. You look beautiful. Just a little quiet...

Good. Infinite patience brings immediate results.

Am I too hard on them, teacher? I love them. What are you going to do? They'll get it. That's better. You ask me to teach you. I say I'll do the best I can. But I can't let you get sick and die anymore. You told me not to let you do this anymore. That's what I'm trying to do.

You be happy with this. (humming) O-ho, you've got Celtic energy that's just beautiful, Druid energy… lovely, teacher… nice. You populated monasteries in medieval Europe for four hundred years, that energy right there, nice. I know you guys. It's lovely.

[Brief sound of sobbing] You should be happy about the darn thing. I'm not going to let you die. Ridiculous. I already took care of that little thing you have. You don't have that anymore. Now what are you going to do? Get something else? Okay, go and sin no more.

I wouldn't bury that. Just let that come up; that'll work good for you, teacher.

Well, at least you're afraid it might be true; and you're afraid it might not be true. That's good progress. But you're going to have to have an experience. You're not going to get it on this side, you gotta get it on this side. Come on up here. It's a process. There you go... C'mon up, c'mon. Get up to this; get up to it.

You're fine. There's nothing to be afraid of. Don't be afraid. There's nothing to be afraid of. Don't be afraid. You're right at your break point. You don't want to be afraid of that. You don't want to go through that again. There you go! That's better. Do that! There! See that? You want to open that up. You want to open that up? There! Look at that! See, you never had that. That's okay. That'll make you eternal, won't it? Hang around.

What you get is what you got, teacher. Don't miss it. C'mon, c'mon. You guys are all over the place. Don't try to traditionalize this. Your traditions are the falsity of it. Come into this and you'll be just fine.

We have a guest coming in here.... Now, you can part that right there... Sure... Wow. Some of you guys are astonishing. You have no idea what you've done. There! Nice! That's nice, teacher! Go like this. There you come.

See, it's real thick for you because you're working off your male. I'm going to get you some more female. You males are afraid to use your female. You females are afraid to use your male. It's funny. See, this is creation. I'm going to create. The awakening is the awakening of your female, the activation of your potential. There. It has nothing to do with gender. I'm talking about male/female in the sense of potential and fulfillment; artistic association, you call it.

Is there energy in this form? Aha! There's energy in the motion. Gurdjieff used to teach a particular dance where there would be conflict, confrontation, resolution.

Where do you hold onto yourself and keep formulating? How the hell do I know? But the more spontaneous it is, the more real it is. When I went through my awakening I had some extraordinary happenings. Why not? You don't get it by limited self-identity, that I'll guarantee you. Afraid to be who you are. It's senseless, but you're afraid somebody else was going to judge you. Gosh, it's crazy. Yet it's only you who have limited yourself, you dummies! Stop it!

I was doing ballet and still wearing wing-tip shoes. I was going through my process. Did you think I got this going mmmmmm? No, I was out there. That's why you got me.

You look beautiful, guys. You have a lovely association going on here of love at a real high level. Your break came with Hana and Ritah. See? Here's where they are. That's what you guys have come up to, so this is really simple. What I've done is given you a little confrontation here. I want you to know how much I love you. I don't want you to slip off on me.

It's like going fishing. Some of you hop into the boat, "That's what I want." For others we use a particular form of lure, and fish, but we get you all eventually. Your problem is, after the resurrection, you've been fishing out of the wrong side of the boat. This is one of the great miracles after the resurrection: Jesus told them, "Throw your nets over the other side." It's on the fulfillment side of you, not this side of you.

There's a notation whether you need to formulate into a spiritual association. You already are that. Call yourself anything you want, but as Jesus would teach it, you are the church. I'll be final with this. I don't want to hear any more talk about churches. It's impossible the Christ, or reality, does not formulate on you, because you ARE the church. The church is the necessity for the establishment to come to its own reality. That's why you have to locate yourself wherever you are. In the *Course* Jesus uses the word "church" in this reference. I must build my church upon you because it's you that needs the church. My church is built on Peter, because it's Peter that denies me. If you are the denial why would you not have to have an association to come to that truth? I don't care whether it goes this way or not. That has nothing to do with it.

But if you think the *Course In Miracles* is anything but spiritual, you're just deluding yourself like you always do. The *Course In Miracles* is a spiritual thing, a religious…, a coming whole thing, it doesn't have to do with therapy. Therapy will be totally involved in it; how could it not be, if the miracle is only the Atonement? But not allowing it to be, or to be embarrassed by your own spirituality is nuts. There is a God, and you're finally going to have to say yes, this came from there, and that's what I want. If you're too embarrassed to do it, at least do it in your heart. At least make some sort of confession to yourself that you didn't make yourself.

You inevitably will find other consciousnesses. Are they in an organization? Only of commitment. These brothers here, my teachers, don't analyze themselves in their association at all. Well, not very often. If they come to me they must learn they must relinquish their perceptual associations with themselves and only teach this is what we do, which is what the *Course In Miracles* is. Will you succeed if you do this? You cannot fail. You've just never attempted it before. If you attempt it, you will succeed. If you don't hear anything else, hear this: You have to go there to get there. You have no frame of reference for having gotten there because you haven't gone there yet, in that sense, even though the journey is long over.

Am I telling you what you want to hear? Ohohoho boy! You can hardly wait to hear this, I know! At least over here you can hardly wait to hear it. Over here it might be a little early for you. You love the old adage, "When the student is ready the teacher appears." That's a true statement. Why? Because he has constructed the teacher in his own mind. The *Course In Miracles*, which is the direct route to reality, speeds up time by presenting the teacher to you before you think you're ready to hear him. This will really help you if you can hear this.

You think you're not ready to hear this. But as Jesus would teach you and I'm telling you, you must be ready or I wouldn't be telling it to you. "Oh, I'm not ready for those experiences." Or "I'm going to practice the Twelve-Fold path and come to it this way." No, no. This says if I said this to you, you must be ready to hear it. There's nothing qualified about it. It is not a condition of hierarchies. It makes no allowances for degrees and intervals. You think it does, but it doesn't. It takes all of that out of it.

This is the direct way. All you really needed was a teacher that said, "Yes, this is the direct way. This is the spontaneous occurrence by the admission that there is no way. All ways are false." Doesn't that make you feel good? Now you don't have to be concerned about finding a way to God. Is that the same as not doing anything? Yeah, sure. Will it work? Yeah. "Well, it didn't work before." I know. Or, it worked perfectly. You've never had this direction before, if you choose to accept it. Nobody comes to this that already "has it." You wouldn't need it if you'd done that, I understand that. I just can't let you get away with murder when you're with me.

I don't come out like this. This is ready. We've got a lot hanging out here, and you immediately began to attack it, and I'm aware of that, because you've always attacked this because it's not possible. But many of you now can hear me, I know you can. Will you all hear me eventually? Sure? And did? Sure.

211

Jesus teaches it this way: We're asking you to come into this perceptual time frame, the one that you're in now, and come to light. Time is a sleight of hand. You've been presented with the opportunity, in this time warp, not somebody else, not a hundred years ago or next week, to actually wake up from this dream. In that sense, it's a configuration of unity. Why? Because you do it in a relationship. We can't get you out of relationship. We're not going to isolate you somewhere, where you practice going to God. We're going to make you confront yourself in relationship with yourself. That generates the friction of the release that provides for the Atonement. That's what you're experiencing here.

It ought to make you feel real good. If it doesn't, Jesus would say, "Why don't you look at it?" It must be that you're feeling sacrifice about it. Be a happy learner. Why aren't you ecstatic to find out that none of this is real? I was. Ohoho.

Some of you I'll see tomorrow. Some of you I'm sure I'll be seeing later on. All of you I am with.

This lovely new energy, you let this formulate now in this area. All of these other consciousnesses come in and say, "What's going on?" You say, "I don't know, but I know that I'm different than I was, so it must be *A Course In Miracles.* I've discovered that the *Course In Miracles* is not studying what the *Course In Miracles* is. No, the *Course In Miracles* is the miracle." If it's a course in enlightenment, it's a course in enlightenment, not the study of the method of coming to enlightenment.

This is all in the *Course*, but once you begin to experience this, you say hey, I'll be darned! It is so. It does work. Why? It's been revealed. You've uncovered that. Now you say, "Hey, that's what I'm going to do. I want to do that." Will you face the conflict of other people saying, "Yeah, but what about it?" To the direct extent you really want to hear it, that won't bother you at all. As soon as it doesn't bother you, it'll change because you had set it up as a conflict to deny what you're doing. It's trying to trick you. Jesus teaches it: Don't look up, because if you do you'll lose all the things that have been holding you down here. That's some of the most beautiful *Course* isn't it?

I encourage you to look up and see the bright light of reality, which shines directly above you; a light that was placed there at the time you think this happened is shining on you right now. That's in here (taps *Course* book), and that's what I'm telling you. Are we a moment later in time than you are? Yeah, but time is not real. You can get this any time you make a decision to.

There's some real bright lights that shine, do you see that? See how much you've changed? You'll go home and look at each other and go, "What's that? What happened?" You became one-eyed. Remember the teaching? This is the Holy Spirit isn't it? Came together. Suddenly you go, "Oh! Now I can see through." This is the *Course In Miracles.*

Take this very instant, now,
and think of it as all there is of time.
Nothing can reach you here out of the past,
and it is here that you are completely absolved,
completely free and wholly without condemnation.
From this holy instant wherein holiness was born again
you will go forth in time without fear,
and with no sense of change with time.
Time is inconceivable without change,
yet holiness does not change.
Learn from this instant
more than merely that hell does not exist.
In this redeeming instant lies Heaven.
And Heaven will not change,
for the birth into the holy present
is salvation from change.
Change is an illusion,
taught by those who cannot see themselves as guiltless.
There is no change in Heaven
because there is no change in God.
In the holy instant,
in which you see yourself as bright with freedom,
you will remember God.
For remembering Him is to remember freedom.

Expanding
The Holy Instant

The energy that you're feeling is real bright high energy. It's coming from the consciousnesses that have been at God's Country Place. It's very noticeable. You will get into this now. See this?! It's difficult to demonstrate a Holy Instant — feel this — because it's experiential. It doesn't have to do with your ideas about it.

I'm going to let it hang out a little bit here. Let's see who we got. You guys aren't going to hurt me or burn me or anything, are you?! I want you to get the idea that it's okay for you to have a process. If it's not okay for you to have a process, you're never going to get this. You've got to let it be okay to demonstrate for God because the ritual of worship is a demonstration. I know that you feel, "I don't want to do that. I don't want to be a Shaker." (Are you familiar with the Shaker movement?) We call ourselves Wavers, or something. The direct contact, obviously, is the insertion of a range of electromagnetic energy; you can call it energy if you want to. But you are nothing but an energetic association. The admission of the fact that you are more than a body, that you are an accumulative Great Ray association, as Master Jesus would teach you in the *Course,* is very valuable to you.

What the hell is the sense of doing *A Course In Miracles* if you're not going to go through a transformation? I want an answer to that from you so-called *Course* students. It's absurd. The *Course In Miracles* is the course in enlightenment! It's not a course in practicing forgiving your mother-in-law. It doesn't have anything to do with human beings. It has to do with God! This is the God contact! If you don't want to contact God, don't come around me. I'm contacting God. I mean God. Not your idea of some sort of religious association of perceptual connections between what defines God. God is a fact! We are experiencing a fact. Maybe for the first time in your perceptual life you could actually have a Godly experience! You'd be embarrassed by it. You'd be ashamed by it. You'd say, "Well, I wouldn't want that to happen to me. I wouldn't want to really make a confession that there really is... I have to keep this veil on top of me. I've got to crouch around."

If you feel what's going on here, you can get an idea that these consciousnesses are undergoing, literally, transformations of their minds. If this doesn't occur to you, what are you doing? Are you going to stay here and just study your own associations with your own thought forms, you *Course* people? Your projected thought forms have nothing to do with reality at all. Nothing! They have nothing to do with reality. You don't know what they are.

You must be what you are. And this is what's happening here now. Does this disturb you? Are you fearful of somebody that would stand up and suddenly you feel this in your head? "I'd better run away. I'd better get out of here. What's happening to me? Why am I feeling this?" You are an emerging species. You are becoming Spiritual Man. You are the forerunners of a new reality. Someday I'll teach this with no religious significance at all to give you a fundamental idea that you are undergoing an evolutionary process of your mind.

What do you think your mind is for? Why do you hold it down in this range of associations of the form? Where does your idea of God come from? What's wrong with us contacting God? I can't even get you to talk about God here! "We don't talk about God here. Well, we talk about Him on Sunday. I don't mind admitting it, but you've got your God and I've got my God and meanwhile we'll struggle with this." That's not what I declare to you. I'm declaring to you that there's a God! You say, "Well, I don't doubt that." Then I ask you why you are sick and in pain and dying if there's a God? Didn't God make you perfectly in the certainty of His own reality? How come you're not that, then? "Well, I'm undergoing a process." Okay. Let's undergo a process then. How else are you going to do it? What are you going to do? You're a body. I see you sitting there looking at this. You're doing this in your own mind.

If the *Course In Miracles* is not a course in atonement or enlightenment, what is it? Where did it come from, all these written words in here? Who wrote this? Who directed this? Where is he? Watch your mind shut down on this. Where's the guy that wrote this? Is there a separate place from this? This wasn't written here, was it? Helen Shucman didn't write it. Would you dare admit that this was written by a consciousness transcended out of time? Throw out the religion. It doesn't have anything to do with being crucified on the cross. It doesn't have anything to do with the conceptual comparisons of the man Jesus with the Gnostic traditions of the third and fourth century. That's just absurd. I'm talking about the declaration that there was a man who underwent an experience of resurrection, what you term two thousand years ago, and is now directing you, out-of-body, to the declaration that *you* are in that process yourself. How you could look at the *Course* and not say, "Wow! Could that really be so? Could this really be happening to me? Where did it come from? How did it happen to come here now? It was never here before." *You* were never here before. You were never in this dream before. This is the culmination of your associate dreams in space/time. This is your going out time. This is your growing up time. This is your maturation. This is the time that you chose to wake up. The *Workbook* lessons for this morning will demonstrate that to you; that this was the time that you chose.

"Well, do I have to have an experience?" How else are you going to keep from dying? You've set yourself up to die. You're a human being on the planet. You were born here, you have children, you have a family, and you're going to die — unless you're capable of disowning your associations with sickness and death and declare through the revelation of your mind that you're not going to die. You have to do it. Otherwise, you're going to die because you have designed yourself to die.

You don't have to take notes on this. You have already designed yourself to die. Why? You have designed yourself to take notes so tomorrow you can study this. There isn't any tomorrow. What's tomorrow? I don't understand it. When is that going to be? That's today.

I'm supposed to deliver a message to you: This is the last day. So if you still feel like you've got to make some telephone calls, you better run and make them. I'm very serious. You guys who come unto your altar and need to make your amends, you better get out and do them. Clean your act up. Some of you guys got real crappy stuff. The *Course In Miracles* doesn't teach amends — well, it declares it through love. But some of you guys are carrying a lot of grievances and junk.

This is a carry-over from what I told you last night. You got one. You better take care of that. I know you guys perfectly well. I was a human being. Don't fool me with your resentments. Some of you have been carrying them for forty years, thirty years, twenty years, this morning. Some of you had a couple of bad ones this morning.

Do you understand what an amend is? Anyone? It has nothing to do with reciprocity. Stop it! Stop thinking that an amend has something to do with the response that the consciousness gives you. Do you want to hear this? It has nothing to do with the response you get. You call them on the phone and you say, "Wow! Hi! How are you?" and "I love you" and that's it. You're so determined that you need to be somehow justified for your own grievance. Stop justifying your grievance! I'm back into the Twelve-Step Program here a little bit because this is a part of that. You're held in the bondage of your determination to defend yourself in that relationship idea. Cut it out! How are you going to change it except in your own mind? It has absolutely nothing to do with the response the consciousness gives you. Is there a question on this, you non-amend-makers? You're carrying your pride. You've got all sorts of pride about the situation. You're very fearful of what the response is going to be. You're very guilty about the things which you've done. The whole basis of this teaching is that's okay, that you're carrying the guilt of previous associations in your own mind. But the only way you can do it is to clean it up. Who cares what the response is? Then become non-defensive. Do you find yourself in conflictual defensive associations? That's what your relationships are. They *are* conflictual associations. Of course. They are arbitrations of death and sickness.

Some of you undergoing these experiences at high levels are finding a considerable amount of conflict in your special personal relationships, but nothing is more conflictual than the relationship itself. I assure you of that. Your relationship is based on some sort of equanimity, some sort of balance of separation, a determination to die. So you may well undergo some conflicting associations. If you walk up to a special one and say, "I've decided I'm going to commit my life to God. I've decided I'm going to take this seriously. I've decided I'm not going to die. I've decided I'm not going to get sick anymore. I've discovered that sickness is a decision, and I won't get sick anymore." He says, "Ha ha ha ha! Well, just wait a minute. You're going to be just like the rest of us. You'll be just as dead as we are." They will tell you this. From deep experience. They'll tell you that. "It will catch up to you."

My sister has all of the resentments that I gave up. So does my brother. Those are my Nazareth connections. My sister is a totally absolutely resentful consciousness. She's very determined that this is a place where you must die in order to be in Heaven. She's a Christian, a Christian as she defines herself. The necessity to die is a part of the religion of Homo Sapiens, of the religion of man. It has nothing to do with God at all. God does not demand your death.

I didn't mean to get into this talk. How did I get into this? Every time I open my mouth, I get into a talk. We're talking about Holy Instants. Do you understand that any opinion is an attack on God? Do you do the *Course*, guys? I mean, I'm just giving you the sentences. Any opinion you have about your own relationship is an attack on reality. God doesn't know about it, but you do, and you attack Him and He doesn't respond. You demand a response, and He won't give it to you, so you curse Him for not answering your prayers of death. He doesn't answer your prayers of death because He can't hear you. He doesn't understand being sick.

What does God know about sickness and pain and death? Nothing. *You* know about it. How about the devil? He knows about it. He's a force that's opposed to God. Does God know about him? "Yes." Then He's not all-powerful if He can't do anything about him. If He could do something about him and doesn't, He's not all good. I don't want anything to do with a God that allows the devil. You have him. All you've done is projected your own devilship, your own separate association with yourself, outside of you, and given it an objective reality, the same as you've given God an objective reality, and you're caught between the devil and God. Whose side are you going to decide to be on? What qualities do you think that this consciousness would have, this evilness, that would be different from that consciousness. Obviously, this perfect, loving God is allowing this perpetration of this evil thing. That's absurd. That's senseless. You have that if you want to. I would never know what side to choose. Which side do I choose?

God is going to have to define to me what He means by evil. This is what I went through in my awakening, for you guys that struggle with this. All I ever asked God was to tell me what I'm supposed to do. But He never answered me. How about, "Thou shalt not kill?" Is that one of the commandments of God? That's a commandment of man. God has nothing to do with, "Thou shalt not kill." He doesn't know about death. I don't know where you hear this. That's Jehovah. That's the god of Abraham. That's the First Covenant, isn't it? That's the exchange. That's the idea of: "Thou shalt not do that, or this will happen to you." That's the idea of an eye for an eye. That's the First Covenant. God is the God of love. He knows not of death. He would never command you not to kill. He doesn't know what that is. How could He?

The basis of this teaching is that evil is only separation. You are separate from God; therefore, you are evil. But evil cannot be real. Therefore you are not real. Now you can be happy. Well, be happy that you're not real. Some of you addicts that are here used to do the *Twenty-four Hour Book*. And there's a lovely *Twenty-four Hour Book* that says, "Wear the world like a loose garment." You're caught in a box of time and space, and the whole basis of this teaching is to allow you to relinquish your own associations with the thing that you are demanding redress for.

All human consciousnesses are only grievances. You hold on to your past associations and attempt to change them in the present, and that's impossible to do because they're based on something that happened a year ago. How are you going to change it if it's gone away. If you base your reality on what's gone away, what good is that going to do you? I watch you guys go through counseling sessions in order to justify the veracity of your grievance, and it just really gives me a pain. You got an idea that you're going to form groups to justify the things that happened to you twenty years ago. And you get together and say, "Well, we were all beaten with lollipops." I don't care what you tell me. You're going to justify yourself to hold on to the grievance instead of undergoing the experience of forgiveness. Some of these groups are support groups for support groups. They're coming up with a support group for a support group for a support group of children who had grandchildren who were alcoholics. Just nonsense! Anything to keep a mutual identity, rather than undergoing the experience of saying, "That's okay."

"Well, after all, if these things hadn't happened to me, I wouldn't be this way." You're caught. You will never get out of it. What a terrible situation to find yourself in. These things have all happened to you, and all of a sudden you're standing here, and that's already happened.

The transformed mind undergoes this and it discovers that forgiveness is forgetting. My mind that went through a transformation is very capable of remembering exactly the same grievances that my sister holds against the occurrences in my framework of time. You and I share a same time framework. I'll tell my sister, "What a wonderful time it was to be alive in the thirties." I know I don't look that old, but that's because I underwent my awakening. And I say, "Gee, remember the family and all the loving things we did. And we would go and get a cold root beer." And my sister says, "What are you trying to tell me? What do you mean it was good? Your dad was drunk, and he fell down the stairs, and we didn't have anything to eat." We lived exactly the same experience, exactly the same experience. Now, did I practice giving up the resentment that my sister exercises against my father? No. I love my father's weakness. How can I say this? I love him for being exactly what he was because if he hadn't been what he was, I wouldn't be what I am now. What did I do? I took the apparent adversity of the grievance and turned it into a benefit. This is the whole teaching. This is my whole teaching. I'm really giving it to you here, if you can hear it.

Everything that could possibly have occurred to you in all space and time, every karma memory, most particularly the memory of this world, has brought you to this time, to this place, right now. All of those memories can be brought together, and you can call this forgiveness if you want to, so that you have the capacity to remember the now, to say, "If that hadn't happened to me, wow, I wouldn't be able to be happy and joyous today. I wouldn't be able to be me." Because, you listen to me, no matter what you pretend or what you do, you are going to be you. I'm telling you, you can decide the kind of you that you want to be, and that is by giving up the grievance of the associations with the past. The past cannot be corrected. It can be forgiven and forgotten.

You'll go to your reunions, and the whole basis of your reunion will be based on grievances or associations of your family connections. You will sit down in a chair, and they can hardly wait to remind you of all the terrible things that happened. The reality of the human race is based on coming together with declarations of the fights that the sisters had. And finally, as you go through your maturation, you'll sit there and say, "Well, why can't we all be loving?" In fact, this is what you always did. Most of you were always the counselor in the family, anyway. Well, see, you're making a little more progress in that regard. And finally, you'll be sitting there, and they will absolutely insist that you hold on to the resentment, and if you don't hold on to the resentment, they will inevitably attack you for siding with the other consciousness. And if you don't do that, they'll attack you simply for remaining neutral.

See, the perceptual mind is a condition of attack and defense. I wouldn't want to be here. Listen. These consciousnesses that are undergoing high spiritual experiences have no problems giving up the earth. Your value systems that are set on the grievance do not understand a transforming mind. A transforming mind takes a look at a human being and says, "Wow! I'm glad I'm not that way." Do you hear me? I mean, they're really glad. I'm *really* glad I'm not a human being. I don't want to carry your death and grievances and the things you want. You demand that I do. You demand that you're going to give me an identity in relationship to what you think I ought to be with you, and you're wrong.

My mind is different than yours. Your mind can be like mine. Your mind can become like these minds have become, but it's not there yet. That's a decision that *you* have to make through the laying down or the relinquishment of the things that you cherish here. There's no such thing as sacrifice. You're not going to give anything up. You can't lose. The idea of loss is absurd. Why would you lose the things you love? Nobody ever answers me to that.

So you accumulate and use it up and get sick and die. Go ahead. Get sick. Die. Who's going to stop you from doing that? You're using the power of the universe. The power that you're exercising is exactly the same as the power of God because that's what it is. There is only one power of mind. You can take that power of mind and hold it in a perceptual relationship, but you can't make it real. Illusions combat illusions, not God. You don't believe that. You actually think that somehow you're addressing an issue of reality. You're not.

You *Course In Miracles* people ought to look at what the *Course* really teaches. If the effect is not real, the cause cannot be real. You keep trying to give yourself a real cause and then say, "Well, my effects aren't real." That's not what it is. This is not a real place. Your conception of your association with yourself has no reality. This is the whole basis of the *Course In Miracles*, that this is not real. Now you say, "Well, why does the *Course In Miracles* give me a choice in this matter?" It has no alternative because it's faced with the impossible situation of your belief in choice. No choice is possible in this.

If I can get you now to see with some degree of certainty that the enlightenment experience that you are undergoing is inevitable, you'll stop making pseudo, unreal choices about your determination to die. You have no real choice, as taught by any awakened mind, to be sick and die. You're trying to counsel that way. It won't work. If you give them that, they're going to take it. They're then going to tell you they're in a condition of free will where God gives them the right to get sick and die. That's crazy. Wholeness does not know of sickness and death. You better make that step, or you're just going to be out there, counseling to death. Why? You have projected the image of your association onto your patient and literally you're killing him by allowing him to express himself to you. That's a fact, incidentally. You enter into his plight. You can't help it. All unhealed teachers do. They start out with a provision of the justification for the possibility of the sickness. You're a liar. He's a projection of your own mind where in associations you can attempt to appear in unreality.

Is this too tough a lesson for you? Leave. You are going to tell me that guy is sick and then try to heal him? How the hell are you going to heal him if he's really sick? What is it that's sick? If you don't ask that question, you can't get this. You'll repair that with some sort of magical treatment, everything from booze to aspirin to some sort of laying on of hands. He'll simply reillusion into another definition of his false self. Do you understand me? You haven't cured him of anything. What you've done is alleviate his magical associations with his own sickness. "Well, you're not going to die of cancer. Now you're going to get hit by a truck tomorrow." Or something. Getting hit by a truck is exactly as sick as dying of cancer. Not only is it exactly the same, but you have made a provision in your karma associations to be killed by a truck. Everything happens because it happens. Everything happens at your will. There is no alternative to this. You don't like that? Too bad.

I'm teaching what you must term "conceptual reality". There is nothing objective about reality — subjective reality. This is the *Course In Miracles*. This is the declaration of all whole minds. There is nothing outside of you. There's no such thing as Newtonian physics. There's no such thing as separate objectivity, other realities. The whole basis of the *Course* is you are caught in thought forms that establish a distance between the thoughts that you had in your mind about a chair and a table and a Lesley speaker, a nice Lesley speaker. Now, do I have memories of this Lesley speaker? Sure. Is that Lesley speaker being manufactured in my mind? Yes. Yes, it is. If you really begin to do the *Workbook* of the *Course*, the first lesson will be what? You don't know what anything is. It seems as though you know that this is a chair, but remember, that has been established in your conceptual relationship with yourself.

I'm going to show you what the *Course* is trying to get you guys to do, you so-called healers. This is a chair, right? Not so. It is only a chair because within your own memory of your reflected perception, you have made it a chair. You don't know what this is. How do you know what this is? You don't know what you are. You don't know how you got here. You have no idea. Now, we can agree that this is a chair as long as we just want to associate in our own perceptions with what it is. Do you agree with me? Let's you and I get together, and we'll have a relationship based on this chair. And that will be perfect as long as we both just think it's a chair. The problem we're going to have is that because you are separate from me, your ideas about what this chair is are not the same as mine. And if you think they are, you're wrong. Now, we can establish a temporary association with the chair as long as you don't say to me things like, "Well, I much prefer to have a padded chair rather than a chair like that." And I say, "Well, I don't know. What's wrong with this chair." You say, "Who made it? It's not going to last very long." We're caught. "How much is it worth?"

You and I are caught, describing ourselves objectively. You say, "Well, that's okay. All of my relationships are objective." Of course. You possess associate thought forms about yourself. You hold on to them, and they rust and die. This is exactly the same as an idea in your mind. The idea in your mind will rust and die. This will rust and die.

What's the practice of getting out of this? Ask it what it is. Just ask it. Say, "What are you?" to that chair. Wow! Wow! Wow! Look! The chair! This is the seventh lesson in the *Workbook.* The chair is God. This is godly. Sounds like pantheism. The chair has chair gods. Everybody has their own god, but there is only one. As a matter of fact, the chair god has got a better god than you've got. The chair god knows what it is. Just like God is a hippopotamus because he doesn't question it. I mean, there's no difference between a hippopotamus and God. *You* just think there is. Why? You've got an objective reality that has given that a sense form.

This is *Course In Miracles,* and I'm going to get in a holy instant just for a minute. Actually, you are really only establishing yourself each moment. Otherwise, you could never get out of here. You have in you each moment the absolute capacity to change your mind because time itself is not sequential and has no real longevity. This is Chapter 13 of the *Course*. It has longevity only in your own perceptual thought form associations that you hold by your previous frame of reference. "This is a chair. I am a body. I can sit on the chair and be a body and have a heart attack. Ooohhhhh! Call the medics!" You think that I didn't just have a heart attack and die? You're wrong. I just had a heart attack and died. You guys get a little defensive. If I really begin to present you with what you're doing in your own mind, you won't like me. You're defending yourself from heart attacks. You watch your cholesterol. What are you caught in? You're caught in the thought forms of your own associations of body. You are not a body. You are as God created you.

Once you begin to study the cause-and-effect relationships with your body, you'll be caught forever. You will never get out of it. You can't get out of it. How could you? You've given separate identities to the functioning of your own wholeness. You doctors treat patients like they're hunks of pieces. It's astonishing. You've got specialists in everything. Just imagine that! A doctor specializes in a particular thought form of the association with the apparent symbiotic relationship of something he has no idea of. He's a plumber. It has absolutely nothing to do with what consciousness is. Wow! Is that something! Why would somebody want to do that? Healers? You've already acknowledged the sickness. Now you've become a specialist, a proctologist or something. The whole world is nothing but a species of proctologist. I know you don't like that, but when I see what you guys do, you're always just peering into your own self. And you defend it, too. You can defend this if you want to. Some of you really defend it. "I wonder if there's that in Heaven? Gee, will I be that in Heaven?" That's what you say to me.

So you are in a form of objective reality that precludes your coming together in your real associations with yourself. And this is the lesson that we have come to learn today. Now, this is literally true if this image that I have made with my mind is sitting out there as you is a body. I'll teach you the way the *Course* teaches this for a moment: At no real time is the body there at all. It's only a projection of your own imagery. Does everybody see that? You make up the images out of your own memory.

So the holy instant, then, will be the time when suddenly this takes on a different aspect of reality to you, where you lose your objective associate identity with it. That's an experience. That has nothing to do with you. You can't accomplish this except by looking at the absolute magnitude of what I'm declaring to you, and you're very frightful of doing it. I'm literally telling you there's no such thing as objective reality. Contained in you right now is an idea that this consciousness in its persona, in its personality, is real. You positively have projected that out from your mind, you've given it a separate identity from you, and then you question it in your own relationship. The consciousness literally cannot give you any response except what you have dictated in your own mind, and if you think it can, you're wrong.

Why do you continue to study your ego, your personality relationships? What good are they going to do you? I'm going to give you a big one: You literally are not communicating. Stop pretending that you're communicating with your own projections. You're communicating only with yourself, and that is not communication. I know you think it is. I'm telling you that you're wrong. I'm telling you there are no such things as separate thoughts. Take a bite of it. This is the teaching of the *Course In Miracles*. There are not separate thoughts going on in somebody else's mind separate from yours. You better be thankful there aren't because if there were, your problem is literally not solvable. If that consciousness really has separate associate thoughts from you, how are you ever going to get to know what he's talking about? You're just going to have to agree on a temporary association with him. You are not communicating with him. Stop pretending you are. That's a big step for you.

"What do you mean by that?" you say. "Well, let's get together and decide what we mean by that." How? You don't know who *you* are. If that's a projection of your mind, it's impossible that he is going to give you any message that you do not want to hear, so let's not kid ourselves about this. That includes the message of your death, his death, and every possible idea that you cherish in relationship to your conceptual self. That's what this says. This is *A Course In Miracles.*

How you could fall down into the idea that the *Course In Miracles* is an exchange in perceptual relationship is absurd to me. It has absolutely no meaning and no value. The declarations of *A Course In Miracles* from out of time are that time is not real, that this is not real, and that it never happened. And that the practice of coming to know that is a fallacy! The practice of coming to know that is illusionary but it's the only alternative. I am going to give you, through this mechanism of transformation, a new dream. It will still be a dream, but it will be the bringing together of all of your memories into a harmonious association. It's still an image. It still appears to be separate. It gets brighter. It makes you happy. It makes you joyous. You lose the conflicts that you've established with that consciousness to defend your own associations with yourself.

I don't know whether you're hearing this. You ought to wake up and hear it instead of trying to counsel that everything's going to be okay. The counseling is it's not going to be okay. All awakened minds or progressive minds who have turned their wills over to God counsel that the world will never be okay. The problem of the world cannot be solved, and if you'll stop trying to do it, you will discover that *you* always were the problem, and there never, ever could be a problem except as you have established it in your own mind. Until you stop trying to define yourself in relationship with your own mind projections, it is impossible that this can occur. Why? You have the power of your mind to hold onto it and die in your own karma drama. And you do.

Fortunately, fortunately for you, since you invented time, you can change your mind about your conceptual associations with it. Time has no longevity more than an instant unless you give it that. Not that that instant is true. But that instant of the time of the apparent schism is what? The closest that you can get to reality. When would that instant be? When? Now! It would have to be now. If you have shortened time — this is pure *Course In Miracles* now — if you have shortened your perceptual determination not to die, you haven't laid up a store that's making provisions for you to die. That's absurd. Why are you storing things up? You're going to die, anyway. Why don't you use them now and give them away in love? "Oh, I wouldn't dare do that. How would I keep myself?" From what? You guys go, "Oh oh, I wouldn't dare do that." Until you do that, you will never be alive. Some of you hear this. I know a lot of my people hear this very plainly. That's why they protect everything by giving it away. If you hold on to a perceptual idea of yourself, you protect it. You project it into the future. It rusts and you die along with it. And you tell me that's okay. Well, go ahead. The whole teachings of Master Jesus Christ of Nazareth are you should live in the now, don't plan for the future, consider the lilies of the field, don't defend yourself, and you would be in Heaven; and you are in Heaven because you did that.

The problem that you're having is remembering that you did it. It is impossible that I am presenting anything to you that has not been done in your mind. Where do you want to hear that? If I'm a construct of your mind, it must be that you have already remembered and ascended into Heaven following the schism. It's impossible that not be so. Isn't it? If perception is only past tense, how did I get into your mind in the first place? How come I'm telling you this now? What do you do with it? All I've ever done is tell you this. All I've ever done is tell you this. All I've ever done is tell you this. All I've ever done is tell you this. All I've ever done is tell you this. All I've ever done is tell you this. All I've ever done is tell you this.

Literally, all I have ever done is tell you this. You can do all sorts of things if you want to. They mean nothing to me. I am what you call a designated whole mind. This is what I've got going on around here. We're very much aware — this is pure *Course In Miracles* now — that we have undergone transformations of our mind that give us the single provision of showing you your own reality. We do nothing but that.

The exact difference in my mind and yours is not honesty. It's constancy. And that's what you can't stand about me. No matter what you tell me about yourself, I'll tell you you're perfect and happy and in Heaven. And you'll say, "No, I'm not." And I'll say, "Yes, you are." And you'll say, "No, I'm not." And I'll say, "Yes, you are." You'll say, "No, I'm not." And you'll go through another death process, have a heart attack to prove that you're right. And then you'll come back to me again, and you'll say, "Well, ha! This time I've got it solved. This time I'm going to be a human being on the planet earth, and I'm going to live to be hmm hmm hmm." And I'll say, "Well, it looks like you've got a pretty good thing going there." "Other people outside of me are dying, but I'm okay." Who is to stop you from doing that? No one. Death is a decision. Can you hear this? All you would have to say to me is, "I don't want to die." Try that. Say, "I'm not going to die anymore." All: I'm not going to die anymore!

That's what this teaching is. Now you have an awakened mind; you have gone through a process. So the show we're taking on the road is: "Swear not to die." What you just did assured you eternal life because life is eternal. You can quarrel about that with yourself, but it will be to no avail. Why? You made the one true statement that it's necessary for you to make. If time is death, eternity knows not of time. Time knows not of eternity. Time has to be death because it's born. Anything born has to die. The quicker you can do it, the more you can see there is no time. The whole teaching is to be born and die each moment. That's the Holy Instant.

Now, the unholy instant is your stringing together of your dead associations. The Holy Instant is the accumulation of a new you through the declaration of your reality, which will shorten time because it cleans up your previous perceptual associations that have accumulated in your own genetic memory, what you call your *I Ching*, what you call your akashic record. You search your akashic record for a solution to your problem. It's not there. It's literally not there. You are caught in time of thought-form association. You say, "Well, I went into an astral plane, and I was instructed by a Hindu priest." What the hell good is that going to do you? He can't tell you anything you don't want to hear.

The one thing that you're very afraid to hear is that God is real and that you're actually in Heaven. That's why you're afraid of God. Since you have to defend yourself, God appears to be outside of you. You have to project *your* wrath onto Him and make a wrathful god from which you protect yourself. It's crazy, but you do it. What am I here to tell you? Quit doing it. Stop doing it. Don't do that anymore. Stop doing that.

Well, that's better than you were yesterday. Coming along a little bit there. I've never seen anything like that. Some of you guys get really sunk down into this. "I wonder, what's this all about?" Why? Your condition is to defend yourself. Like that. Just like that. "What does he mean by that?" It's what you do. If you defend yourself, I must be attacking you by what I say. The only way you can know I'm not attacking you is by not defending yourself from this. This seems far too outlandish for you to be so. You would much rather write your own prescriptions, the answer to your own mind. And you're wrong. I am giving you a completely outlandish, insane solution.

Whole mind has to appear insane to perceptual mind because it has no guidance system. It simply declares love. And that's what you're deadly afraid of. Why? You would lose your associate consciousnesses. The things that you love would live forever. If there's one thing you don't want, it's the things you love to live forever. You really can't stand them fundamentally. They are attractions of your hate and disassociation from other thought forms. Everybody hear this? The reason you guys don't want to live forever is because it's finally very painful for you. You think that eternity is a long time. It has nothing to do with time at all. So you can hardly wait to die finally to get out of the pain and tension that you're in.

I'm not going to let you die anymore. Now what are you going to do? You can insist that you're going to, but I know you perfectly in my mind. I know you. I know you intimately within the last two hundred years. We know each other. All of us are what you would term quick reassociations. If you guys look around, you'll see consciousnesses that you have been in association with intensely in the last two hundred years, and you know it. You just keep writing different scripts for yourself and hold yourself in a particular coordination of what you want that consciousness to be. What are you going to do with me? How did I get stuck into this, then?

Now you've really got a problem. Why? I'm making you address your own problem, and you don't want to do that. You're the cause of this and therefore you're the solution. You would much rather share sickness and death with me as you have projected me so that I can give you a value in association with our mutual bodies. Don't tell me you don't, because that's what a human being is. Not only that, but it is expressed as love and *is* love.

Dear ones, I'm not trying to take your love away from you. I'm just trying to give you whole love rather than discriminatory death associations. That requires the confession that everything that you love gets sick and dies. Is that a true statement? Don't give me this, "It's going through a transition and everything is going to be okay." That's senseless. Jesus in the *Course* says, it's a strange idea that somehow a part of you would die and a part of you would be real and go on. That's absolutely senseless. If anything dies, everything dies. Wouldn't that be so?

There is no death. "How can I come to know that?" Bring your associate consciousness, what you define as a body, into a whole thought-form relationship. This is called in the *Course In Miracles* the "face of Christ." These consciousnesses who are undergoing this transformation are literally having bright images of their own thought-form associations. They may see your face, for example, as the Christ. The practice that we'll do this afternoon is to look through — this is the *Course* — to look through the consciousness that you're sitting with. You guys may want to do this in therapy. You're starting to do it now because you feel this opening up in you. What? We begin to look through each other rather than establish in our reality here. As long as you defend yourself in thought form, our reality has to be established in what we would call an aesthetic distance between us. This is pure *Course* now. We have thought forms that we bring together and project from us and mingle in some sort of pool of consciousness and defend our own associations with ourselves. We now have what? Maintained a distance between ourselves and associated ourselves by our own projections.

I am showing you that if you will release your opinion of me, you will discover that through your own creative mind you have extended me from your wholeness, and since you are whole, the consciousness that you're identifying with is whole. This is a process of the relinquishment of judgment.

Now, my mind, which is in spirit, what we call the opening here — Jesus calls this "looking through" — I'm only seeing you as a whole consciousness in my association. I'm not thinking the way you do. You're beginning to release it now. "Oh, I wonder why you're wearing your earrings, and you've got a..." This is what you do. "How did you get here? Why are you sitting there? Who are you? Who does your hair?" I'm not doing that. I have absolutely no concern about what your name is.

When you do your workshops in this, stop wearing identification cards, for goodness sakes. What you're doing is condemning your brother to death before you even meet him. "Hi! I'm John. How long have you been doing the *Course?*" "Well, I've been doing the *Course* for seven or eight years. I'm a doctor of ploopi-doop." "Oh, is that so?" "Oh, that's nice. What do you study?" "Well, I study the glaciers on the moons of Jupiter." "Really? Well, that's interesting. I studied the beetles in the Brazilian jungle." It's all just bleahh.

What are you doing? Keeping your own identities. You're holding on to your own self-assertions in order to keep your identity. But I'm a great threat to you because I only love you, and boy, if there's one thing you're not going to take, it's that. There are some lovely sentences in the *Course* where Jesus says, boy, if love gets too close to you, look out. You're going to back away from that. There has to be a justification for love. Your mind is a justification for your limited love associations. The idea that you are whole and beautiful in God's sight is impossible for you because your identity is based on not being that. You don't have anything to say about it. So let's give up your own self-identities in these Holy Instants and then we can come to know who we are.

I didn't mean to get into a talk. I never know what I'm going to do. Is this being recorded? Are you guys still with us, out there? This tape will be available at God's Country Place. The first three years after my awakening, and still, I wouldn't allow any sort of taping. Awakened minds have a natural aversion to associate judgment because this kind of talk is inherently crucifictual. I'm presenting you with the reality of you and there is a defense that you have built in not to hear the simple teachings of Jesus Christ or what I am saying to you. In the *Course* Jesus says you crucify the Christ each moment by your refusal to admit your own Christhood. You literally kill yourself, which is exactly what you've been doing. Don't do that any more. And you will be whole and free.

It's not too early for you to do this now. You stop looking for the Second Coming outside yourself. The Second Coming is you changing your mind, if you want to use it in the religious vernacular.

It's impossible that you are not both the Christ and the anti-Christ. The part about the Christ doesn't disturb you as much as the part about the anti-Christ. But if you're not the anti-Christ, who is? Can you understand that you cannot be opposed to anything in reality? That all opposition is false? That all negative-ness, that is, a disassociation from anything, is a declaration of less-than wholeness and is literally impossible? You cannot be separate from reality. Never negate. All negation is an opinion. My teaching is to agree with everybody. Don't defend yourself in any regard. Have no opinions about anything. Be weak. Be meek. Be poor in spirit. Step back. Be number two. Let the world go. Don't succeed. Give up stores. "Well, that's an impossible message, I don't want to hear that." Don't!

Is this the message that you must hear and practice? Yes. Now, watch your next response: "Well, nobody here does that." That's what you're going to do. You're doing it right now.

"I know, but all around me are these images and certainly none of these others consciousnesses are doing that." No, and never will. They literally never will. Why are you trying to change the effects? All of your counseling is an attempt to change the consciousnesses sitting out there. The practice is to change *you*. Do you see? You project it outside of you and you demand of that consciousness sitting there that he change his mind. That's the craziest thing I ever heard of. It's impossible. There's no way you can do it. I know that I'm teaching, "In your weakness is your strength." In your total weakness is your salvation! Why? You're in competition with God and you will not succeed. You think that you will, but you won't. You can't because you are perfect.

You can say a million times, "How did this happen?" I say to you, "What difference does it make how it happens?" Wouldn't you rather have it not be so? Why would you want to get cancer? I'm really curious. And you say to me, "Well, I don't want to get it." Then why do you get it then? And you're going to say to me, "I can't do anything about it." And I'll say, "That's crazy! That's absurd!" I'm telling you that it is crazy and absurd for you to get cancer. I don't very often do this, but I just straightened something out in you. Did you feel that? Now, that's a little plus that goes along with this. Yes, you can feel that, dear one. That's a new frame of reference I gave you in regard to your cancer. "Oh, I don't have cancer." Yes, you do. If anyone has cancer, you do. And you had it. You don't have it anymore. Do you know that you decided to die of cancer? That's crazy. Don't do that. That's a fact. And you know it and I know it. But now it's not going to happen. And you say, "Well, maybe I'll die of something else." No, no, it's too late. In the *Teacher's Manual*, they say, "What's the difference between healing and atonement?" They're the same thing! If you are whole in any regard, you're whole completely. You keep dividing up your own sicknesses. It's crazy.

Am I a healer? I'm the greatest healer that ever came into the earth. I'm the only one. You guys can't hear this. I don't care whether you hear it or not. If there is only one sickness, there's only one solution. That has to be me. What's your salvation? Believe me! You would have to believe me. Obviously that would be the requirement. Why? I'm a projection of your denial. Is it really that simple? Of course it's that simple! If I'm only a product of your mind, literally all you have to do is declare your brother to be the Christ. This is the *Course*. Do you guys do *A Course In Miracles* here? Yes?! Well, I'm giving you the *Course In Miracles*! Do you like that or not? You're my savior. It makes absolutely no difference whether you think you're my savior or not, I'm certain that you are. In that I'm redeemed. Thank you for saving me from this. I don't care whether you're the cause of it or the effect of it. Why? The cause and effect aren't apart. I could not care less whether you believe that Jesus Christ wrote *A Course In Miracles*. Remember that Jesus Christ is the *Course In Miracles*. He is not an idea about it. Jesus Christ can be a separate conceptual observation that you have about Jesus in your own mind. If you do that, then you have to separate the Jesus that speaks from what Jesus says. That's absurd!

If cause and effect are not apart, a whole mind is what it says. You attempt to judge what I tell you based on how you've constructed me. That's crazy. You've got your cause and effect apart. You are very determined to give the previous consciousness an association of two thousand years. You can well do that, but the only conclusion you can ever arrive at is that Man-Jesus, is man ascended; that you, Margaret the Christ, are Margaret in sin or sickness, unreal, going through a transformation and coming whole. That process is singular! There aren't multiple separations. How absurd. What would be the difference if you are separated from the whole? Why do you want to have a multitude of differences in relationship to what you are? Don't do that. That's the way you hang on to your illusion. You think there are degrees. You can't tell the difference between happiness and pain and sickness and death. So don't do it any more.

Have you been undergoing Holy Instants in the last hour? Yes! That's what's happening to you. Can you feel it? Yes! Did you pull it back down into your own false crap? I hope not because each moment I'm offering you salvation. You say, "This is too good to be true." No it's not. I'll get you now or get you later. And there is only now for me. There might be later for you, but that won't do you any good. Who did you think your savior was? I'm here! I'm telling you this now. All I'll ever do is tell you this. You say, "Well, later on somebody else is going to tell me." No, that will be me. Isn't that funny? You don't like to hear this. Can anybody really hear me? How many can really hear this? Obviously one separate self-identity would be the same as them all. You can divide up and judge your savior all you want to, but it is through your judgment of him that you deny his saviorship. It's impossible that I'm not your savior. It's literally impossible because I'm standing here telling you I am. Not only that, but I know it. Are you required to know that I'm your savior? It has absolutely nothing to do with you. But you're not going to like this, because I'm going to say to you that if you persist in your own perceptual mind, you have no reality to me. That's what your salvation depends on. Your determination to see that as you present yourself to me, you have no reality. Otherwise you will continue to judge me in our associations which are what our falsity is.

All an awakened mind does, and some of you guys are really beginning to do this now, is declare to the student his own unreality. "Let it go. All of your judgments of what I am are false." I'm making a declaration of whole mind to you. All judgment is false! Each time you come to me (and you have asked for me as an advanced teacher), I will deny your relationship with me and tell you that you are whole and perfect. You are determined that you will bring your self-identity to whole mind, and it's not possible for you to do that. Literally, it is not possible! But remember that I can only be a projection of your mind, and through your relinquishment of judgment of me, you will be saved and whole and remember Heaven. This is *A Course In Miracles*. This is what I'm teaching — subjective reality. Am I really in your dream telling you this? Yes! Did you really hear this in your dream? Yes! How else would you be hearing it now? It is impossible that you do anything in time that you haven't already done. Isn't this so? Tell me something that you haven't already done. Come on. You say, "I don't know what I haven't already done." Sure you do, as soon as you tell me, it's already done. Why? Perception is always past tense. Everything has already happened. In your own dream, you keeping re-living the same dream over and over. You play different parts of it. This is Chapter 26 in the *Course*. It's just your dream.

Well, where will the world be when you're not here? No where! There isn't any such thing as a world. Jesus in the *Course*: You really think that you came here at a particular time with a world only waiting for you to be saved. Not so. You brought the world with you when you came. You brought all of these shadow figures. That's what Jesus calls them. You brought all of these shadow figures with you to justify your relationships in your separation. That's what you've always done. You've been untrue from the beginning, haven't you? Is this too good to be true? Or too bad to be true? Sure. But it is. Now you find yourself in a very uncomfortable situation. I'll give you these quotes from the *Course*. You can jump up and run out of here because of fear of what I'm telling you. It's very fearful to you. It doesn't seem as though it would be fearful, but it is. I'm not threatening you with your own reality. This is that barrier that you need to pass in the relinquishment of your own perceptual form. Jesus says this is the illusion of the thought forms that you have constructed to keep yourself from seeing the reality of the Light that's all around you. Literally you have done this; you have capped your own perceptual mind. That's fearful for you.

All of the admonitions of the minds about you that you think are minds will say, "Don't do this. Don't decide to make this commitment." You're at your point of fear. Always before, you have turned back from this. This time you're not going to. Why? I'm here to help you at that point. I'll sustain that for you very easily, but I can't do it for you. It's only in your own mind. Nobody can do it for you. You say, "Master, why don't you do this for me?" I can't. I can declare to you that through your own whole mind you can see that I am with you at what you call the portal of reality. Jesus calls it what? The borderland. He says you stand now at the borderland where things are no longer holding in your illusions as much as they used to. This is lovely *Course.* He says now sometimes you go into a little different dream and then you get fearful and you fall back down into this dream. And then, what? You say, "No, I don't want this dream. I'm going to die in this dream." Then what do you do? You relinquish and you go through another experience.

Now what am I teaching you? Holy Instant! Do you feel this? When I begin to teach at a high level you will begin to feel this energy. Why? I am releasing my own conceptual necessity to teach you. If I do that, I will leave here. I'm held together by this momentary necessity to present this to you. These are the direct teachings of Jesus Christ. Just for that moment, I retain an image memory of you in my own memory, although I know it is not real, so I can declare to you: No, this is not real! If you will accept that from me in your mind, you will shorten time immeasurably. You will collapse it. You won't have to continue to experience the pain and frustration of your attempts to hold yourself separate from reality in your own dream.

Finally you have got to understand that it is an experience that you need to undergo. You think I don't know you guys; I know all you guys perfectly. There were only twelve of us to start out. Do you think I don't know you out of time? Don't be absurd. How many do you think there were of us? I'm here to tell you the war is over. Further than that, I'm here to tell you it never happened. Were we all part of the original screw up? Yes! We all share that original moment together. Can you see this?

Now, where are we, finally, in time? We have come back to that original moment. We've made a full circle again. We're back at the time of the actual occurrence. And this is very fearful to you because the momensity of that single happening is so intense that you just defend yourself from it. The necessity now is to look at it without fear. Say, "No, I'm not going to go back out again. I'm east of Eden in the land of Nod. I'm not going to go back out into Nod and sleep again. This time I'm going to hear it."

All consciousnesses who come to me in this relationship are different. Many of you can remember your previous death experience. A lot of you, when you were born into this episode, just went, "Ooohh. What am I doing here again? How did I end up here again? How did I get in this crazy place? How come I'm different than these other consciousnesses around here?" I'll tell you why. You can remember your last intimate death association. And at that time, because of the pain you felt at that termination of bodily function you underwent a bright-light realization and subsequently, because you had not undergone the total exponential experience, had to come back into another association. This is a little occult, I don't know whether you hear it. I'm giving you a fact here.

What am I inducing in the Holy Instant? The death experience. I am literally inducing this light brightness that you felt at your last episode of death. Have you ever seen a bright angel of light around a dying person? Have you been around people that died much? Some of you healers, or so-called healers, that have been around consciousnesses that have died have had the experience — I have, a lot — of actually seeing the release of their own energy and the actual extension from their chakra lovely light and energy that will come around them. And they will many times exalt the Lord. I've heard declarations of New Jerusalems and all of this new bright association as they apparently depart the body. Is this what you are undergoing now? Of course! What did you think you were undergoing? What you're going to do is undergo it with a full realization of all of the memories that you have brought with you into this configuration: Nicodemus, know ye not that ye must be born again? (John 3:3) This is that happening, that death experience that you are afraid of. In order for you to be born again you must undergo the death.

Okay, here's the top teaching: Each moment this is occurring. Each moment time lasts but a moment and you are living within that moment — all of your so-called death experiences. You guys will begin to read the *Course* entirely differently than you've ever read it. These are direct quotes from the *Course In Miracles.* You can stretch that into fifty years or eighty years or a hundred years if you want to, but it was only a moment. And each moment it is available to you to come back into eternity through the relinquishment of time in your associations with yourself. I guarantee you that that's true.

Is it possible for you to come into the Holy Instant and live in it for the remainder of your time? That's what these new minds have done! The light begins to shine out of their reassociations with themselves. Can you get this by judgment of them? Don't try. That's the fallacy, isn't it? "Oh, gee, I can see that he's undergone an experience, I wish that could happen to me." Nonsense. He's a projection of your mind in the denial of the experience that you must undergo. Do not judge your brother in his spiritual acuity, his capacities to undergo what these consciousnesses are doing.

This is a process of individual atonement. Your sole function here is to undergo this experience for yourself, for indeed, you are the world, aren't you? And that's what's happening to you and that's what you are doing. Be grateful that you have a shot at this. You be happy with the idea that it is possible for you to lay down the necessity for you to die and get sick. I understand that the world is going to say, "Stay with us." You have constructed them to do that. I understand that the world is going to declare to you that you shouldn't throw all your eggs into God. "Let's not go off the spiritual deep end. Let's stay grounded here so that you can get sick and die with the rest of us." You do that. Am I an alternative for you in that? Sure! Like Jesus says, will the world despise you and crucify you for teaching this? Exactly. That's what they are.

If I could take this up just a step for you, I would like you to see how really little you've identified yourself here. You insist you are a body. You're just so little. Jesus calls it little. You look up at the stars and you say, "Well, those stars are a thousand trillion trillion miles away from you." That's absurd. The furthest star is right here. The furthest galaxy you can see is this neighbor right here. This is a galaxy. We are establishing intergalactic association.

What did I have to do to do that first? I have to take my microcosm, the distance in my subatomic particle association, which is exactly the same as out there, and establish interstellar drive with my own relationship. I had to do that before I could go intergalactic. Jesus calls you a constellation. That's okay. Perhaps a galaxy is a better word. Until you had interstellar drive, you had to fight the distance of your own chakra, what you call in Revelations your own church. Well it took you ten thousand light years to get from your stomach association to your mind because you tried to do it at the speed of light. But remember, measured subatomically the distance from your stomach to your head is approximately eighteen thousand light years! There's just exactly as much smaller than you as there is bigger. Can you hear any of this?

The whole universe that is contained in you is precisely the universe that is all around you. This is *Katha Upanishad*. I keep falling back into this other stuff. As above, so below. As within, so without. You don't mind that, but your conceptual mind wants to make it symbolic. It's not symbolic. You are the universe! Everything that you do is all that the universe is. The only thoughts there could ever be in the universe are the ones that you are having.

If you say there is no God, there is none. But there is; therefore, you are not real. And by maintaining that there is none, you have separated yourself and made yourself unreal. The consciousness that declares that is not real and it never happened. Ready for the biggie? This never happened! It's impossible. Look around you, for crying out loud! It's like you are standing in a real small place. It's like you fell into a well and we are fishing you out. I'm going to let a little line down. Take a hold of the darn thing and I will pull you out instead of trying to keep turning around within your own dream. You got knocked out. You are hallucinating. You are asleep. You are dreaming. This isn't real. I am right in the middle of your dream telling you to wake up.

There have been some very major shifts in perceptual consciousness here. Do you know what is so lovely? You guys begin to communicate with each other in the Great Rays at another level of association. The more that you release your perceptual associations with yourself, the more that you will accumulate new energy and associate at a new thought form, if you are just being held by your own self in your own bondage of thought. Remember that it is your obligation to undergo this. Don't try to experience it in relationship with your brothers, guys. It won't work. Your relationship is false. You keep trying to identify where he is in his spiritual awakening. That's absurd. He can't be anywhere that you don't posture him.

Are these Holy Instants happening to you now? Sure! Are these stored up in your genetic relationships? Of course! Those of you who are beginning to have these lovely memories will suddenly have a lovely memory of this. This is a memory. You'll go, "Oh, yeah, I can remember being here and sitting here and going through this." And you will be absolutely right. We are reminiscing about this right now. We're actually outside of time talking about it together. Isn't that fun? Is that Jesus with us? Yes! He's the little short guy, He's about five foot four with a hooked nose and pocked face. No. He's a six foot four inch red-headed Irishman. I changed that. He's sitting right here in this chair. There He is right here. Would you like to see that energy? The energy of *A Course In Miracles* is this energy.

Remember that *A Course In Miracles* is an established thought-form association out of time, but still in the congruity of the association with perceptual reality. It's a borderland. The contact that you're feeling, although some of you may transcend it into your own whole light, will be a contact with this final Christ-face. Many of you are undergoing experiences that transcend what you call the rim of fire, and you are actually going into full illuminations. When you do that, you will not long remain here. But certainly we would like to use your revelation to cause vision, which is what I'm doing. Those of you who had these lovely visions last night — some of you had some fear ones — are utilizing my revelatory energy to revision yourself in association with your projections. That's what you are doing with your mind. I am encouraging you to use this light brightness — the Holy Spirit you call it — to undergo the reillusionment of you to a higher framework of harmony and peace within your own mind. This is a dream. Let's dream a true dream together for just a moment, and then we will be out of time together, won't we?

Do you want to stay in a body and walk around a little bit and get real bright? I'll do that for you if you want to. Or do you want to change and have a different one? I repaired this one sufficiently. I wouldn't recommend that you trade this. I wouldn't go through another death experience. There's no need for you to do that. This one works okay. Why not use this one? You've got a real good dream going here. You've got it all together. Why would you want to go through another death? Don't do that. If you are capable of hearing me tell you this, you are capable now — and I know you are early and Jesus says in the *Course* that there are very few consciousnesses in this fold of time who have reached the capacity for full maturation to reality. But you wouldn't be sitting here if you couldn't do it. I just took a look at what you have designed your death to be. Don't do that. I've already been through that. That way won't work. You think this one is going to be real gentle and easy. But you're going to come back and you're going to be sitting right there. And the next time it won't be so gentle and easy. Why? You have to undergo all of the stress and pain that you have subtracted from your mind, and have died rather than experience it. I want to encourage you to go through the experience now — even if it appears to be painful to you. I'll give you all of the sacrifice you want, but make it! Go ahead. What have you got to lose? Make the last useless journey, as Jesus calls it — the journey to the cross.

Some of you are going to begin to have some lovely experiences here now. Remember that what I am teaching you at this level is literally out of time. I am making no provisions for your future at all. A lot of you are going to go out and have a future and die. I'm not offering you that. I am offering you the immediacy of salvation. I am not offering you conceptual associations where you can stay here and have an establishment of a church. The church that we've established makes no allowances for time at all. It simply says, "Now is the time when you don't need the church." Did you need the church for the moment that you needed it? Of course! Then make your whole life this Church of Full Endeavor. Make everything that you do from this moment on a dedication of your determination to come into the new light. That's what the church is. Did I have to build my church on you? Of course, because you needed a church. Is there really such a thing as a church? Of course not. But you think there is. The church is the process of you coming from your separation to your reality. That's why I named you Peter. You denied me thrice. You keep denying me.

Is there someone else I can build my church on? No! Those that don't deny don't need a church. So all you need do is make that simple admission in your own new spiritual identity. Stop wanting to be crucified upside down. Remember that you are the Christ. Can you get that by following? Only by full discipleship! You instructed me to re-identify the certainty of your Christhood. That's what I am doing. You requested from me in your mind that I show you your own brightness, how you really are in super-consciousness. It is impossible that not be so or I would not be doing it. You had to ask me to do this. Somewhere you asked for help. And somewhere the intensity of the necessity for your help identified by your inability to deal with the terrible things that are going on around here have caused you to continue to ask for help in the relinquishment of your necessity to cure the evil.

See how easy it is? We are not all equal in time. Of course not. That's what's called the Circle of Atonement. We need each other with the declaration through forgiveness of where we are in our mind associations. I have no grievances. Why would I hold a grievance? The world is not real. I say to you, give up your self-association. Give. Give yourself away. Give away. Don't possess. Don't hold on. And you'll wake up and be in Heaven. And it will be Heaven that you never left.

Some of you guys are really making some moves here. I'd like to authenticate that for you. Don't pinch yourself down. Get out of yourself for a minute. Drop your practice. Quit it altogether. Come on home. There's no such thing as practice. Everything is real each time you declare it. I know your necessities to serve man. That's why you're with me. I know your compassion of the pain you feel for your brother. I know your need to be a healer. I'm just encouraging you to understand that you are whole, healed, and by that declaration, you become a real healer. I know your passions of need to help the plight of the sick and the dying. I understand it perfectly well. That's why you got me. The frustrations of your inability to do that are now obsessing you. You're searching around for a solution to this, and there isn't any. Be thankful there's no solution here. If something were really sick and you could cure it, you would have a very serious problem. You listen to me now.

I'm going to have a little quiet time now. We started our quiet time at nine o'clock and it's now eleven and we haven't succeeded in being quiet yet.

Listen. The reason that I do this is I want to bring you into a re-conceptual association, utilizing this energy, rather than having you simply have experiences here and not integrate yourself. If I don't do that, you'll take this energy, this shakti, and you'll bring it back down into the practice of your own self, utilizing this power in limitation. That's called magic.

There are consciousnesses that constantly come to me and go out, reformed in their own minds, and they become very successful. Very few people hate me. I'm only teaching love, anyway. They decide they don't want this, but they're very willing to take the part of that that they're willing to hear out into the world. Is that okay with me? What do I care? But don't tell me it's real. And don't tell me you're going to succeed in dying because you're not. But use me.

Will I use your energy out there? Of course. I'll use the energy of your reassociation to the full advantage of the whole universe. You are the one that's made the decision to use your own energy to die. You can do that if you want to. But you won't make yourself real. I'll just be gone. Will you still be here? No. You maintain that you are, but that won't mean anything to reality. You will simply remain asleep in your own constructed dream. Come on, guys! This is a process of the waking up of your mind. Can you get hold of the idea that you have constructed the world and that you're not really communicating at all? It's like I'm punching my way through your shell here. You keep wanting to re-identify with what's out there. That's not out there. There's nothing out there.

An idea never leaves its source. Nothing has ever left you. You're just contained. You're spinning around inside there, and I'm knocking on your thing: "Come on out. Come on out now. Stop dreaming your dream of death." Chapter 21: You're the dreamer of the dream. Don't dream this dream anymore. It's futile. You ought to be able to look around and see that you're doing the same things over and over again.

There is no escape from the world as you have constructed it. Literally. You have designed yourself not to get out. That's okay.

Perhaps we'll have *Field of Dreams*. That would be nice because this is the new dream that you are dreaming. You're all going to go out now. You're going to walk into the corn. Of course, walking into the corn only takes you into sort of an astral space/time association. Perhaps it's better than this. Perhaps Iowa really is Heaven. If Iowa isn't, where is it?

Gently now. We'll leave the tape on through a little of this and let some of this energy get onto this tape. That's a pretty good talk this morning. I never know what I'm going to say, but that isn't too bad.

This is my favorite memory, Doubtful becoming Doubtless. Thank you. Welcome home, teacher. Good to see you again. See me?! You quit fooling around. That's an order I got for you. You start getting into this instead of that. I'm always right when I give specific orders, teacher. So you must have told me to tell you that. It's important that you look at it. You're ready. You've been fooling around. See, you've got too much energy in here and you're fooling around with it, and you don't want to do that. The only one you can hurt is you. Don't do that. This too. This has got to kick it in. It keeps going down into here. That's okay, I mean, if you have to. There's no reason for you to do that. I'm going to take care of something for you just for a second here. There. That'll be fine. See? There.

Just let it hang out. Hey, come on back. I got a job for you. Some of you guys are reaching here. There you go. It's okay. It's all right. It's okay. All right. Come on home. What the heck have you got to lose? You're coming along. You better come see me. Yeah, I know it. Some of you guys are saying, "Is this really happening to me?" Yes, this is really happening to you! You're getting ready, too, teacher. Oh, it's so nice to be with you guys. What a relief! Oh, look at this! One of these days... You're coming up there. You'll be all right. Give it up. You have a little grievance. Look at this. Don't grieve. Quit grieving. You're in your own mind. I need you. Good. Good. I got you. I'm going to take this off for a minute.

What are we going to do here with this? There was a click in time, and everybody's sort of gone out of this. Let me see you guys. Oh-oh. Look out! See, that's very noticeable, teacher. That's called whole-face, we call that. Face on. Jesus calls it face on. It's a new capacity to look, rather than shield. See? You're doing it, too. Face on. It's a form of purgated innocence. You become innocent. You say, "The hell with it! I mean, it's okay." Jesus teaches it as non-guilt, but, boy, when you got it, it's like that. That's okay. Then you learn to be very discreet with it because you become very penetrating. As you look, you'll learn to shield in the supermarkets. We'll show you all this. This is part of your training. This is what they call the Masters Academy, and this is part of what we're doing to show you this.

What you'll notice is that the texture of your consciousness is different. See? It's a different feeling. You have a different association with your thoughts. In the *Course* Jesus describes this. The way you can tell is that it's all new to you. It's a different kind of you. Not in your form associations, but rather simply in the way your mind now activates. It becomes whole. Hi, Teacher, Dear. Nice to see you.

You see? If you persist in this, will you go to light? Yes. Yes! Is it possible at this depth for you to flash out? Jesus calls it "going to brightness." Oh, yes. It's very possible for you to do that. Certainly. If you do that, and when you've done that, except in divine associations, you're just written out of the script. You no longer were. You're just gone. When you come in the manner that you're coming, you're being used as a vehicle of communication. Jesus says in the *Course*, it would be unfair of us to provide you with a mechanism of Atonement without allowing your own teaching devices. You wouldn't be with me if you weren't healers. Listen. Healing and teaching are the same thing.

Your instructions, from the time of your, what you would call "early maturation", were to be healers. I know you guys. You can call that Messianic complex if you want to, but a lot of you have always wanted to be healers. That's why you're with me. You've wanted to save the world. I know you. What's happened to you? You said you wanted to save the world. What's going to happen to you? You're going to save it. Of course! You might have identified it separately when you were twelve years old and formed the disciples around you or felt that you wanted to go to church and look at the stained glass windows and wondered why other people didn't feel how you felt when you went into the icons of the church and how you liked the smell of it and how you thought you might be a nun. Come on. I know you guys. All of those things you've already done. It wasn't necessary for you to do them again. You've tried that. You have tried to withdraw and you've tried to participate. You've climbed mountains and gone down into valleys. You've charged up hills, attacking the enemy, you have defended yourself, you've resigned yourself, you've killed yourself, and you glorified yourself. And still you have been you. And now, suddenly, the whole you is emerging. Be happy about that. Be very happy. Be happy.

If I were you, I would be very grateful for what's happening to you. I would look back and say, "I don't want this." Let Babylon burn, you guys. The line is getting real straight for you now. "Straight the way and narrow the gate." (Matthew 7:14) Don't hide your light under a bushel. (Matthew 5:15) Let it start to show. I'm doing Christian vernacular here. But that way now is straight to you. You can see it. In the *Course* Jesus says the road will get real straight. You've decided. It gets narrower and narrower. It's called "the razor's edge," we used to call it. You find yourself like this. You may glance back very occasionally, but it's getting too straight. Why? You have become one-eyed. (Matthew 6:22) This is what you want to do. This is what you want to do.

You'll be distracted and then you'll come right back onto it. Don't turn around. Let Babylon burn. Some lovely sentences in the spiritual thing. I mean, you've climbed out through the top of the roof. Let your possessions be. Don't go back down into the burning building. Let it alone. Or you will turn to salt, and your salt will have lost its savor. And what good is that going to do you? You are the salt of the earth. This is Lot's wife, isn't it, when she's leaving Sodom and Gomorrah. She looks back and whoppo! (Genesis 19:26)

You built the wall around Babylon (II Kings), and you've been babbling in your attempts to reach God, which, of course, you can't. Now let's let the walls come a'tumbling down. All right? Or Jericho. "Joshua fit the battle of Jericho, Jericho, Jericho-ho-ho-ho, Joshua fit the battle of Jericho, and the walls came a'tumbling down." Ha! You guys are Christians! Who ever thought Christians would get this? Well, how else could they get it except with Christianity, if you stop to think about it? If we're teaching transformation of mind, which is all we ever really taught.

Getting the *Course* in here was really something, wasn't it? You talk about a miracle. That *Course* is coming, intact, into a conveyance, a receptacle, that could put it, that could scribe it without judgment, as it was. That's an incredible accomplishment. And, of course, that's what we needed. We needed a scribe. We didn't need somebody that was going to enter into a perceptual interpretation of it. As soon as Helen enters into interpretations, it falls off. Like her prayers and that, which are not *Course*, obviously. You can tell the difference very decidedly. But imagine being able to actually continue and bring that down into this reality. It's an astonishing thing. There at least then you had the presentation of it. You use that! It started to slip sideways. I don't know how you could slip the *Course* sideways perceptually, but you did it. And it's beginning to go like this (straighten it up) — that's what I'm for, to get you back into what it says. That's why I got the assignment. I'm not connected to the *Course In Miracles.* This is an assignment for me. Can you hear this? I have a whole mind, and the *Course* is beautiful — it's the vernacular of your cellular memories.

Greater things will you do than I have done simply because you're going to do all the things that are in your whole mind in regard to this. I'm a mercenary. I'm here with the total truth to let you see that through this reflection. Can you hear me? I was gutted out on my last death. I'm not from here — I remember here — neither are you. See, that's what you are coming to know through this *Course In Miracles.* The guy that was supposed to be the savior missed it. You know that happens sometimes. You never know up to the end whether the guy is going to make it or not. Your designated one fell off the truth wagon. Did you know that? You had a variety coming up. So you guys are maturating very rapidly now. And you had a consciousness that had evolved to a point, but when you can't get a total light insinuation, this is the other measure — they just grabbed me and threw me into it. If it hadn't been me, you wouldn't be here now. I'm an understudy. But it's a good thing for you that's true because now we're in. We're okay. We're going to be all right. The steps that have been taken today are extraordinary. That little click that you heard about ten o'clock this morning was a whole shift in consciousness. Everything that is in this room now is completely different than it was. You can sense it if you want to. You can sense that it is different. It's later in time. See if you can hear this. Even though it's later in time, it would appear to be in the same association, wouldn't it? Why? The same things are happening but they're at a higher integrated frequency of consciousness response. And you are actually sharing it up in here rather than down in here.

Now that sorting out process will continue. Those of you who are going to slip a little bit back into time will come back down in and then that may evolve and tomorrow you will undergo a dramatic experience and you will be back up into it. The reason it appears chaotic is that when you are this early in what you call the history of time, coming from total chaos, coming from a black hole, coming from compacted thought, back to reality, there is no real stability. There's no way we can hold onto light consciousness and balance it. It's too chaotic. So all of you, individually, are coming from different places in the space/time fabric to enter into this fabric. Some of you are ahead in one regard; some of you are a little behind in one regard. In what? In what Jesus calls the Great Rays. This energy you are experiencing is just what? The twelve Rays. The emanations that became light in fractured consciousness. The twelve notes on the chromatic scale. The twelve tribes of Israel. And on and on. So when you meet a consciousness at this depth, you may match very well with him in some of the centers, but in other centers you are way off. So you love to hate and hate to love, and you think you love him but you keep trying to establish these relationships. Now if you will use this energy, this bright energy — this is later on for all of you in time — you can organize around this if you won't judge it. And don't judge the brother that you are with. Then you will come into this new light. That's what is happening to you.

Oh, I've got to take off my socks. No wonder I'm having a problem. Oh-oh. We have a great Christian tradition of bare-footedness. Did you know that? We do feet. We have a Jesus tradition of doing feet that is real strong in us. Not necessarily body manipulation, but we do do feet. The only part of you that could ever be corrupt would be what touches the earth. At the last supper when Jesus is doing feet, Peter says, "Well, let's do the whole body." Jesus says, "Just do the feet." (John 13) Just take care of the lower energy. The part of you that's connected to the earth is what needs to be recovered. That ceremony has kind of gone away at Easter, hasn't it? Remember the old ceremonies where Christians used to do each other's feet? I see some Episcopal people didn't like the idea. It wasn't sanitary to do each other's feet, so they decided to wash each other's hands instead. I thought that was sort of Pontious Pilate-y. You know, when he washed his hands of the whole thing. (Matthew 27:24) There was a story about it in the paper that it's not hygienic to do the feet, let's get together and wash each other's hands. Typical. That's just typical. They're going to wash their hands of the whole situation.

So here you are in this new Light arrangement. You're looking very lovely. What do you do now? Nothing! The miracle works just by stepping back from it. You have the energy now, if you want to make application of it. But you don't have to go charging out to prove that you have this. There's no necessity to prove you. There's no alternative to what's happening to you. This is simply a maturation of your mind. Let it happen. Will you be confronted by these other consciousnesses out there? Sure! Just keep backing away from them. Hello! Will that be a little chaotic? Perhaps. But what do you care? You've got a little piece of something here, and you're not going to let that go. Jesus in a lot of the *Course* says once you see this, you won't persist in being human. You may not be able to express it. You may find counsel in your own closet. I would admonish you to ponder this in your heart. You go and get alone and you will begin to feel this energy, and you will start to breathe, and the next thing you know you will begin to have spontaneous reactions to this new flow of you. You don't have to get into a big group to demonstrate that. In fact, the less that you attempt to demonstrate it in mutual association, the more rapidly this maturation will occur because this is an individual process.

In the integration of this, I have three lessons I'm going to read you from the Epistle of Jesus Christ in *A Course In Miracles* for two reasons: (1) to show you the incredible certainty of the *Workbook* of the *Course*, that is, so that your new mind can see that it's not hyperbole, that the *Course* says what it means. I don't know what the lessons are, I wrote them down, I was given a couple of numbers. And (2) it will also give you, perhaps, a little more association with the manner in which you may teach the *Workbook* or may teach the *Course* because your minds have a tendency to pass over sentences. Some of you have been doing the *Course* and doing the *Course* and doing the *Course;* you have never actually stopped and looked at what it says. I may help you do that a little bit.

I'll read very quietly. I have a contract to do this. *A Course In Miracles,* from the *Workbook,* by Jesus Christ of Nazareth. Our lessons for today are... That's the Text. I need my *Workbook.* Where's my *Workbook?* Where are my glasses? Where am I? Our lessons are... The three lessons we're supposed to do... The first one is a wonderful lessons. Listen to this, this is Lesson 79, and this is what happened to you this morning.

Let Me Recognize The Problem So It Can Be Solved. Let me recognize what my problem really is, and then I will be able to solve it. It has always seemed to you that out here are all sorts of problems and you keep trying to solve them. They're like brush fires. You rush out and you do that. You rush out and do this. Let's stop, like you did this morning, and take a look at this. Listen:

A problem cannot be solved if you do not know what it is. Even if it is really solved already you will still have the problem, because you will not recognize that it has been solved. The first admission in the *Course In Miracles* is what? First you have to know you have a problem. There are all sorts of consciousnesses that participate in the conflict that won't even admit they have a problem. They just say, "That's the way life is, that's the way the world is, you've got to expect it to be conflictual. You're going to have to go out and fight for everything you've got. That's not a problem to me, that's a demonstration of my own reality. And I'm going to attack and defend and prove myself in that situation." The next step after that is to say, "Hey, I've got a problem here. I'm having problems solving it. I seem to solve it, and it keeps coming back again." That's what this says. A problem cannot be solved if you don't know what it is. You know you have it. You don't know what it is.

This is the situation of the world. The problem of separation (of your mind), *which is really the only problem* (that you could ever have — being separated from God), *has already been solved. Yet the solution is not recognized because the problem is not recognized.* If you don't consider your problem only to be separation, it would be impossible for you to see that the problem has already been solved because the cause and effect are not apart and you are not identifying the problem. Your problem is being separated from God, not in reality but in what you think you are. Now you can see that the problem has already been solved. But first you must what? Delineate the problem. Make the admission that you are separate, and apparently can't solve the problem by your own devices.

Everyone in this world seems to have his own special problems. Yet they are all the same, and must be recognized as one if the one solution that solves them all is to be accepted. Who can see that a problem has been solved if he thinks the problem is something else? Even if he is given the answer, he cannot see its relevance. You keep finding solutions to separation. You keep justifying your existence in solving the immediate problem that presents itself to you within the association of your own concept of what you are. You don't seek the whole problem, but you identify yourself in the limited sickness that you possess, for example. And you take an aspirin for your headache — or all of the results that you bring about in an attempt to satisfy your existence in relationship with the falsity of the separation.

That is the position in which you find yourself now. You have the answer, but you are still uncertain about what the problem is. A long series of different problems seems to confront you, and as one is settled the next one and the next arise. There seems to be no end to them. There is no time in which you feel completely free of problems and at peace.

The temptation to regard problems as many is the temptation to keep the problem of separation unsolved. You literally cannot solve the problem if, in your perceptual association with yourself, you continue to identify separate problems in association with what you are. Are you ready? One problem. One solution. You have one problem. It's you! This will get real nice for you if you are willing to accept it. Then you can move to: "I am the cause of this; nothing outside of me can harm me." Which is really into the teachings of the *Workbook. The world seems to present you with a vast number of problems, each requiring a different answer. This perception places you in a position in which your problem-solving must be inadequate, and failure is inevitable.*

Listen. You know this is true! *No one could solve all the problems the world appears to hold. They seem to be on so many levels, in such varying forms and with such varied content, that they confront you with an impossible situation. Dismay and depression are inevitable as you regard them. Some spring up unexpectedly, just as you think you have resolved the previous ones. Others remain unsolved under a cloud of denial, and rise to haunt you from time to time, only to be hidden again but still unsolved.* They're buried down, like your death that is coming on you now. Holy mackerel. I don't know how you could stand this. Isn't this lovely? Are you ready for this?

All this complexity is but a desperate attempt not to recognize the problem, and therefore not to let it be resolved. Notice it says "not to *let* it be resolved." It doesn't say, "to resolve it." It says, "to let it be resolved." *If you could recognize that your only problem is separation, no matter what form it takes, you could accept the answer because you would see its relevance. Perceiving the underlying constancy in all the problems that seem to confront you, you would understand that you have the means to solve them all.* And this is what I'm trying to give you! The constancy to recognize that all of these problems are only you. And by the admission that you have the problems, you can bring them together in the single solution of the relinquishment of your necessity to solve them at all. The problems of the earth cannot be solved. This is what this is telling you. They cannot be solved! They are constructions of your determination to hold onto yourself in your false perceptual associations. A problem that is not real cannot be solved. Any problem that was real, and that would be your problem of separation, would have to be solved instantly if it were a problem. It could not *not* be solved. Can you hear this? The idea of a problem is the idea of the solution. You could not construct a problem to which there is not a solution. Can you hear this? What you do is you hold it down and say, "This is the problem. This is the solution." You hold it in a limited perceptual association. The fact of the matter is you have one problem and one solution. It would be impossible to have a problem that's not connected to solution; otherwise, how could you have the problem? Not only that, but you must have solved it! Because if there is a problem, there is a solution because cause and effect are not apart. You keep them apart and then go through all this ritual of space/time of attempting to solve the problem separate from its source. You attempt to solve the effects of the problem that you have instigated in your own mind. You can't do it, and it won't work.

If you could recognize that your only problem is separation, no matter what form it takes, you could accept the answer because you would see its relevance. Perceiving the underlying constancy in all the problems that seem to confront you, you would understand that you have the means to solve them all. And you would use the means, because you recognize the problem.

Perhaps you will not succeed in letting all your preconceived notions go, but that is not necessary. All that is necessary is to entertain some doubt about the reality of your version of what your problems are.

Let me recognize the problem so that it can be solved. Let me admit that I am suffering pain and sickness and death and that through my admission of this and the letting go of my associations I can come to know God. One problem. One solution. You be happy that you're the problem. Do you realize the momensity of the weak mind, the self-constructed mind, if you really have a problem outside of yourself and you have to mitigate it in an attempt to be understood? How are you ever going to solve it if it is out there? You then become dependent on a judgment that you have placed separate from yourself to solve your problem. This is the condition of your mind, guys! It's awful! You ask them to solve the problem for you, but they can't possibly know the answer except that you have given them the solution within your own mind. Wow! Then you get into a double bind of guilt because you listen to the answer that that mind is giving you, and that mind is going to share your guilt with you, isn't it? That mind is going to authenticate the problem through the effects rather than you recognizing that you are the cause of this.

This is Lesson 79 of the *Workbook.* This is after Lesson 76 that says that *You are under no laws but God's,* that direct you to simply relinquish everything. The toughest lesson in the *Course.* I'll let you do that by yourself tonight. Is it okay if we do the *Workbook* of the *Course?* That's what salvation is! This is the method that you can use if you choose to — the catechism of reality that you can choose to let this be so.

I have a problem. I have the solution here with me. It is not out there. There is no one on the face of the earth that can solve my problem for me but myself. I am doing this but to myself. No matter how tempted I am to believe that there is something out there that is causing this to happen to me, let me let go and see that I am the cause of this. Because if I am the cause of this, then I can be the solution. And if I am not the cause of this, I'm in a lot of problems. I'm going to have to attempt to sacrifice to something outside of me to arbitrate, to go through *quid pro quo*, to demand reciprocity in association with idolatry thought forms that I have constructed outside of myself to mitigate the impossible problem in which I find myself. (I'm flowing a little bit here.) I want you to try to get a hold of what is the impossibleness of this. That's Lesson 79 of the *Course*.

Lesson 80 is: *Let Me Recognize The Problem Has Been Solved*. Wow! That's nice. We won't do that one though because that's not on our list. But that's coming along. You go to bed, you be real good, and tomorrow we'll do Lesson... No, we must do two more lessons here. This lesson is... I'm anxious to see what this one is. I think it's a good one. Oh, wow! Is this lovely. This is Lesson 158. *Today I Learn To Give As I Receive*. Sometimes the titles to the *Workbook* lessons won't particularly pertain to the lesson, as you may have discovered. Never mind your perceptual observations, listen to what this lesson says because sure enough this is what we've been talking about this morning. It's going to tell you that this is the time that you chose. But you didn't know you chose this time until you chose it. And when you chose it, it had always been chosen. Do you know that's what this lesson says? I'm going to tell you; that way when I read it, you'll hear it a little better. The time has already been set, but you don't know it's been set until you choose to set it and then it's always been set. Everybody got that? Why? Because it's already all over. And you say, "Well, I'm changing it." And I say, no you're not, it's all in the fabric anyway. Isn't that fun?

Now, you have total free will to do what's already been done. And you say, "That's not free will." And I say, oh yes it is. Isn't that funny? This is a great theological discussion — you are caught between your absolute pre-destination, which is your Presbyterian determinism in which everything has already happened, confronted by your determination to be free and assert yourself. I'm going to give you total freedom by the acknowledgment that everything has already been determined, but perceptual mind doesn't like that very well. It's going to attempt to do something within the linear condition of time that it hasn't already done. But it's impossible that it do that. Feel good about that, not bad.

You are tempted to attempt to do something that's never been thought of before. This is *Rosencrantz and Gildenstern Are Dead;* it's a play if you ever want to read it. Rosencrantz is determined he's going to do something that has never been done before, but obviously he can't. He's going to try not to motivate anything. He's going to have a thought that's never been thought of. The quantum physicists are trying to do that. They're trying to set up experiments in what you call wave-particle association and then pretend that they didn't set up the experiment. That way they can step back from the experiment and observe the electronic associations of the wave-particle. But they can't do it; they're caught in their own subjectivity. What they discover is that they are influencing the experiment with their mind, which is, of course, what they are doing, since the experiment is only contained in the retrospect of their previous dramatic demonstrations of experiential unreality. You got that! Good. Because I don't have any idea of what that is! But it sounds good!

All right. It's an amazing thing. It's always: "Will it be there if I don't look at it?" "Was it always there?" And all these sort of things that go on in your mind. Here we go:

First of all: *What has been given you? The knowledge that you are a mind, in Mind and purely mind, sinless forever, wholly unafraid, because you were created out of Love.* Listen: *Nor have you left your Source, remaining as you were created.* Now, listen carefully to this: *This was given you as knowledge which you cannot lose. It was given as well to every living thing, for by that knowledge only does it live.* This is the statement that beingness is singular; that this I AM that you are expressing is singular; that everything is only its own beingness. Try to get ahold of this. That's what this says. That's what creating is. You are as much God as you are God's Son in the sense of your own Being Wholeness. That can't not be. You can't lose that. That's what you are. Now what's happened?

You have received all this. No one who walks the world but has received it. It is not this knowledge which you give, for that is what creation gave. All this cannot be learned. Actually, this is what we would call in space/time the ontological admission that all of come from a common source, that we have a dharma, that we have a spirit of absolute reality that is singular in us. That's not the knowledge you're going to offer. The knowledge you're going to offer is your limited perceptual association coming to that determination. Listen to this:

All this cannot be learned. You can't learn it; that's what you are! *What, then, are you to learn to give today? Our lesson yesterday evoked a theme found early in the text.* The theme found earlier in the Text was "Into His Presence Would I Enter Now." This is the statement of the transformation of the body that you are undergoing now. That was the lesson just before this. No listen: *All this cannot be learned. Our lesson yesterday evoked a theme found early in the text. Experience cannot be shared directly, in the way that vision can. The revelation that the Father and the Son are one will come in time to every mind. Yet is that time determined by the mind itself, not taught.* You can't teach your limited associations what you are. You determine within your own total idea about yourself, contained within the fabric of your reality, when that time was. You can't teach that. Why? It's already happened and you are gone from here. You are teaching only in the limited associations of your perceptual observations of yourself in order to forgive the previous grievances or what you call sequential time associations that keep you from seeing that you are actually whole. That's the relinquishment of your own self, isn't it? Now listen:

Yet is that time determined by the mind itself, not taught. The time is set already. It appears to be quite arbitrary. You're going along, you're going along — why? You can never judge where you are in relationship with yourself. You cannot perceptually be the determiner of your own revelation. You think you can, and you keep trying to identify yourself in association with it, and that's what holds you in your space/time association, doesn't it? Your need to *have* the thought rather than *be* the thought. Your need to *have* the emotion rather than *be* the emotion. The need to justify in your thought forms the anger, rather than being the anger, rather than being the love, rather than being whole unto yourself.

It appears to be quite arbitrary. Yet there is no step along the road that anyone takes but by chance. It has already been taken by him, although he has not yet embarked on it. Because each moment that he embarks on it, it has already been taken. Why? Cause and effect are not apart. As soon as he apparently has the problem, the solution was always there. This is what I tried to say to you at the beginning of this lesson. Do you see? Each time you think the problem isn't solved, it's really solved. This is what's happened to you now. You've accumulated a lot of solutions that didn't work. You've rejected those from your mind and you're just coming into a moment's whole association with yourself. Was this the time that you decided to wake up and become whole and remember you were in Heaven? Yes! "This says it can be some other time." No, it doesn't. It says it can only be this time. This time appears to be arbitrary to you because until the moment

267

that you come into the wholeness of your own atonement and undergo the experience, you can't know that that was the time that you did it. You'll always be caught in this attempt to find it in your limited form associations. This will come to you. Let it sink in a little bit. You'll get it. Ready:

Yet there is no step along the road that anyone takes but by chance. It has already been taken by him, although he has not yet embarked on it. For time but seems to go in one direction. We but undertake a journey that is over. Yet it seems to have a future still unknown to us. Not possible. Any time you justify your present condition based on previous experience, you have literally created the previous experience that did not exist until you justified it in the effect of you. Can anybody hear this? You call that preventative maintenance. An accident never happens until it happens. When it happens, you justify it by the previous associations. Isn't that astonishing? Can everybody hear this? If you're flying in an airplane and suddenly it blows up, they look back to the past associations to determine what caused the accident. They discover it was bad maintenance. But the maintenance was okay until the plane blew up. Can you hear that? There has to be a reason for everything happening, but until it happens... It's terrible, isn't it? You must justify. You literally create a past association to justify your present condition. That's an astonishing thing to do. Isn't that amazing? You had to make the engine defective because the accident occurred. Otherwise the engine was perfect. What made the engine defective? The crash! Actually, they're both going on at the same time, but that's hard for you to see. Really what's happening is every time you think of "crash" you are crashing. What you've really done is create a statistical possibility. With a framework of linear time, if you create a statistical possibility it has to come about.

There's no such thing as "statistic." Everything happens by the thought of it. Can you hear this at all? A million-to-one chance is exactly the same as a one-to-one chance because until it happens it's not. When it happens it becomes a one-to-one. "Wow, there was no chance that could have happened. I don't know. One single little bolt had to come lose..." And on and on and on. It never stops. Yet it did happen. Why? Because there was a thought that it could happen. And if there's a thought that it can happen, it will. All prophecies are self-fulling. That's why you need to die. You contain within you the elements of the certainty of your death. How are you going to keep from dying until you change your mind? You can't. You will just keep on dying.

Yet it seems to have a future still unknown to us. Time is a trick, a sleight of hand, a vast illusion in which figures come and go as if by magic. Yet there is a plan behind appearances that does not change. The script is written. When experience will come to end your doubting has been set. Notice it says "experience." Notice that it says that the doubting that you have about yourself cannot be overcome except by the experience that you are undergoing now and if you think it can, you're going to be around here a long time because *you* are the doubter. And the doubter cannot be real. What is it that he doubts? This is Lesson 139, my favorite lesson in the *Course.* He doubts himself, but what is it that he's doubting? The doubter can't be any more real than what he doubts, really. That's why you have to undergo this experience in order to be real.

The script is written. When experience will come to end your doubting has been set. For we but see the journey from the point at which it ended, looking back on it, imagining we make it once again; reviewing mentally what has gone by. This must be true. Why? Because the atonement or the repair of the apparent schism occurred at the moment that it happened. It was shooo-shooo. You are actually looking from the creative essence of yourself back into the occurrence.

Here's the problem you have with that. You think that your identity is emanating from the bottom of the schism. Let's try this for you; see if you can get this. This will help you. You think that your identity is emanating from what you would call the black hole, from what you would call potentiality; the idea of the activation of the thought from, the earth, the moon, the female, mother earth. "We all came from mother earth. I can see the evolutionary process evolving. My identity is to activate as I evolve from this source." Aahh, but here's the hooker: *Your source is not here!* Your source is here.

Remember what we said: shooo-shooo. This is why there is no gender in the *Course*. I should cover this for you guys that think you ought to be sisters. I don't know what the hell that means, sisters or female. There is no such thing as female because female is potential and is activated by the force of reality. It becomes whole automatically. This has nothing to do with female and male as you engender it, but as Jesus would say, there is no such thing as potential. That creates what? Time! You are saying to me, "I can be a female and I can engender a form of reality based on gathering together in the karma, in the evolutionary process, and reproduce myself in increasing dimensions." Ahhh, but whence comes the power — from soul, from the sun? From God, of course! What happens to a human being is, where you are evolved in the chaotic association, that you are meeting yourself coming and going. This is the only place in the position of space/time where you are nuts. You don't know who you are because you're feeling the insertion of the power emanating from the Source and it is causing conflict with your associations that you emanate from the female, the evil, the Ishtar, what you call the Elohim, seven centers, the Seven Sisters, the Pleiades. "In the beginning God created Heaven and earth." That's seven females, isn't it? The requirement, then, is what? That you activate your female, which is your potential, through the utilization of the power of God, or the light source, shooo-shooo.

Here we go, shooo-shooo; here is your Ida and Pingalla, what you call your yin and your yang. And you are meeting yourself half way, and your mind is split. Why? This appears to be your source. What has to occur to you? You need to activate all of the memories contained in your genetic association. Why? There's no such thing as time. The moment that time was thought of, it was totally fulfilled. It went from what? This black hole, this impacted consciousness association, into the bright Light of your reality. And that's what's happening to you. That's why there is no gender in the *Course*. It has nothing to do with sexual, male/female. That's not what we're talking about.

Need the female become a virgin to be impregnated? That's the whole story of the birth of the Christ. The Holy Spirit impregnates the female who previously was Magdalene the whore, who was out whoring. She now becomes pure by the assertion of her virginity, the truth of her, by bringing her resolve together to become whole, to become innocent, and is immediately impregnated by the Light of God. Is this too esoteric? All awakenings are female. My awakening was very female. Literally. The problem that a male consciousness has in his own relationship is that he's in competition with his father. Did you know that? This is pure *Course* now for a minute. The male actually thinks he has usurped the power of his own Creator. Oedipus Rex, sort of. He's going to marry his mother. That gets into a little stuff. But what we are saying is that the necessity for the awakening of the constabulary of unreality as constituted in the body requires the emergence of the female.

In my awakening, I became very female. Would you like to hear this? My breasts swell up. Why? I am going through, in order to be impregnated, I am taking all of the thought forms that are a part of my genetic association. There are a lot of people who will demonstrate to you the passions, males particularly, who undergo enlightenment will tell you that it was very much the passion of being loved by God. That's what happened to me. Those of you who are female must do what? Stimulate, through the bringing together of your female associations, the recognition of the male in you. I don't care where you are hearing this. I'm giving you fact here. Not in gender, but in the necessity for you to take time, which is the potential, which is the memory of you, which is your *I Ching*, contained within you, and totally activate it to make it whole. That's what's happening to you. And that's what did happen to you. Be happy about that.

As long as you associate with the thought forms of your evil, of your Eve, you will remain in this association and continue to miscreate by your definition of yourself as Adam and Eve. The product of Adam and Eve as separate gender can only be death because it's associated with time. And you left the garden, which was eternity, didn't you, and became that. So that will make you feel real good because a lot of you want to marry God. You feel this thrust of your passion to come up into this new you that's up in here. That's what I want you to do. Let that happen. Understand that your body is undergoing these changes, glandularly; using the glands, the churches, the chakras in your body. Is that all right for you to know that? Did you know that? Sure! Where did the human condition come from? It came from the pancreas, which is the ductless gland which is the Pleiades, which is the Seven Sisters.

All of the esoteric teachings of the physical body associations are to give you a recognition that you are participating in your own awakening. If you can get this, it will be very, very valuable to you. Nothing is separate from you. All of the reality that there is in the whole Universe is right here in this room right now. There is nothing outside of this. I know that may seem startling to you, but you can only have one thought at a time. And when you have that thought, that's all that there is.

It seems as though you are undergoing this for the first time. But actually we've done this before. These *déja vus* that you are experiencing. This recognition, suddenly, that things are getting brighter, that they seem "whole-r" to you. This is the coming together, the fulfillment of your potential, leaving not unresolved the conditions that caused you to die back down into yourself. You are emerging from what? The tomb. You are emerging from the tomb of earth. Your temple is rent by the fire of reality and you are springing forth. How long does it take you to do that? Three days. You have descended into hell. You must remain in hell for one day. And then you return. This is the certainty that there is no such thing as two. You can't come down into hell, the idea of a schism, without having been there. That's why there's no such number as two. Wherever two or more are gathered, I will be there as the resolution to the two. Jesus, when He's crucified, He descends into hell, and the third day He rises up. One day to get there, one day to recognize His plight, and one day to go out. The teaching that I am directing you to is that it occurred instantaneously. Shooo-shooo. And, really, you are just living within that framework of time. And it's actually already all gone. Isn't that nice to know: That this is all over!

What was I doing? Ohhh. Wait a minute. I got off there for a minute. Where was I? Oh, yes, Lesson 158. "That didn't sound very much like Lesson 158." Well, it was. I'm going to finish it.

For we but see the journey from the point at which it ended, looking back on it. And this is what I am encouraging you to do with me. *Imagining that we make it once again. Reviewing mentally what has gone by*. Listen: *A teacher does not give experience, because he did not learn it*. What happened to me wasn't learned. Are you kidding? There is no possibility that what occurred to me could have been learned. I can't give you the experience of my revelation. What can I do: *It revealed itself to him at its appointed time. But vision is his gift. This he can give directly, for Christ's knowledge is not lost, because He has a vision He can give to anyone who asks. The Father's Will and His are joined in knowledge. Yet there is a vision which the Holy Spirit sees because the mind of Christ beholds it too.* This is the same idea as your projections are becoming real to you now through the whole-mindedness that you are coming into.

You might want to look at it this way: Everything that you are seeing about you here is a vision. It's a projection of the light forms of your association. What we are doing now is giving you enhanced vision. You are better able to see because you are not in conflict with your own thought form association. Can we do this from this energy source? That's what's happening to you. Is that what a savior is? That's precisely and exactly what a Master, a Savior, is. What you actually do is you stay in association with him, if you would like to know. I can't teach you, I can only demonstrate my beingness to you. You, then, integrate it into your association with how you have projected me. That's what we are doing. That's what this says. I am then giving you the revision of your own mind — not my mind. I am reflecting back to you your own thought form in the drama that you and I previously played out together. Otherwise why in hell am I here? It must be that this is what you did. And indeed this is what you did. Wow! You can make this be anything that you want it to be. That's the power of your own mind. But I would suggest that you utilize it to the lesson that we previously did to let you have a single problem so that you can re-vision to what? A single solution. And that's what you want to do.

Yet there is a vision which the Holy Spirit sees because the mind of Christ beholds it too. Here is the joining of the world of doubt and shadows made with the intangible. Here is a quiet place within the world made holy by forgiveness and by love. Here are all contradictions reconciled, for here the journey ends. I can't understand how people could have this *Course In Miracles* and not teach this. Somebody is going to have to tell me. *Here the journey ends.* Where? In experience! *Experience - unlearned, untaught, unseen - is merely there.* What you did was remove the obstacles of your own mind, and what do you see? The bright light of reality that's always been around you. It's always been there! You are removing your own obstacles, aren't you? *This is beyond our goal, for it transcends what needs to be accomplished. Our concern is with Christ's vision. This we can attain.*

Christ's vision has one law. It does not look upon a body, and mistake it for the Son whom God created. It beholds a light beyond the body; an idea beyond what can be touched, a purity undimmed by errors, pitiful mistakes, and fearful thoughts of guilt from dreams of sin. It sees no separation. And it looks on everyone, on every circumstance, all happenings and all events, without the slightest fading of the light it sees. You listen to me!

This can be taught; and must be taught by all who would achieve it. It requires but the recognition that the world can not give anything that faintly can compare with this in value; nor set up a goal that does not merely disappear when this has been perceived. And this you give today: See no one as a body. Greet him as the Son of God he is, acknowledging that he is one with you in holiness. Wow!

Thus are his sins forgiven him, for Christ has vision that has power to overlook them all. In His forgiveness are they gone. Unseen by One they merely disappear, because a vision of the holiness that lies beyond them comes to take their place. One consciousness and all of it disappears. One consciousness. One Savior of the world. How many saviors of the world does it take? One. Who is that? YOU! Darn right! *...because a vision of the holiness that lies beyond them comes to take their place.* He sees through them. *It matters not what form they took, nor how enormous they appeared to be, nor who seemed to be hurt by them. They are no*

275

more. And all effects they seemed to have are gone with them, undone and never to be done. And never to be done again. Gone away forever.

Thus do you learn to give as you receive. And thus Christ's vision looks on you as well. This lesson is not difficult to learn, if you remember in your brother you but see yourself. If he be lost in sin, so must you be; if you see light in him, your sins have been forgiven by yourself. Each brother whom you meet today provides another chance to let Christ's vision shine on you, and offer you the peace of God. Wow! Isn't that something!

Boy this Lesson 159, the next lesson here, is really great. But we won't do that now. So what's happening here now to you? A revision. A new emergence of mind brought about by what? The revelatory experience of you that then changes the manner in which you see. You stop attempting to change yourself in the thought form and allow the revelation of your mind, which is real thinking. Any thinking that is not revelatory is not real. All mind does is create. What I am offering you, and some of you will really experience this, the breadth of your creative capacities will be very much expanded by this energy. You will begin to paint, perhaps, sing, begin to dance. You will discover that there are a lot of things in your mind that you can do. Of course. The limitations that you have placed on yourself are extraordinary. This new vision that you have of yourself is the genius of your whole mind creating in the new perception of identity of yourself — all things about you. That's why thinking is revelatory. Anything that any mind can do, you can do. Do the circuits of genius overload? Sure. They can't stand the passion of your creative necessity. They kill themselves. They cut off their ears. They die young. Why? Because this need to create has become so intense in one particular field of their genetic field of their genetic association they literally can't stand it.

They have a vision without the capacity to express it fully. That's why you kill yourself.

I am giving you the capacity through the reassociation of your mind to create. This is what you call liberal art. This is the highest form of mind thinking. Man has slipped pretty much into linear time. He is into a lot of thought form. And one of the reasons we're wrapping up this association is the necessity for you to go vertically rather than horizontally now in your thought forms. That's what we are bringing about in you. We will be wrapping this one up real quick. We're not going to nurture the shallow roots. There's no reason for us to keep spreading computer associations. That will just prolong the time, won't it? We're going to take you out of here, if you would like to go. You can stay here.

This is lovely stuff. I am reading you the *Workbook*, right out of the *Workbook*, out of a mind out of time! This is a very careful plan that was put together by you for your salvation. Did you know that? Who did you think did this? The twelve of us that found the solution! What is the Last Judgment? The Last Judgment will be done by my brothers and I, as Jesus says. The twelve of us, which are all of the consciousness associations, will sit in judgment of our self and find ourselves innocent. Is that what you're doing now? Sure! Is this the Last Judgment? Yep! Is this really over and gone? Yeah! Boy, there is a lot of energy in here, guys. We have to do this last lesson before we can finish. You're kicking this up. Boy is it hot in here! In the Eastern tradition, that's called passion. Earth, air, fire, and water. When you guys crank up your energy, you generate a lot of heat. That's called passion. But you need the passion in association with the earth, which is thought. Earth, earthiness, is thought. Air is breath or spirit, isn't it? Earth, air. Fire is your passion, your red ray association. And water is the elixir of light generated from your reproductive associations that are causing you to flow freely to God. Those are lovely comparisons for you.

Is the awakening physical? Sure! This Christ Child has been born in you, hasn't He? In the *Course,* Jesus says you nurture this little nomad, this little baby that's born in you because He has to cross, in the lunar cycle, from Bethlehem, which is your association, to Jerusalem, which is your crown, your head, or crown chakra. He has to get past the Pharaoh, which is the desert. The Pharaoh obviously will attempt to kill Him because this is your human associations in here. You protect Him in the Passover, or the parting of the Red Sea, which is the passion, so that you can come from the wilderness up into Jerusalem where you can what? Undergo in Golgotha, which is the place of the skull, your apparent crucifixion and resurrection. That's what's occurring in your body! These are lovely esoteric teachings of the passion of Jesus Christ. You meet now in the upper room and are joining together to bring this about. Isn't that lovely! Happy Easter!

That being said, we have one more lesson to do here, and it is Lesson 184, see how this connects. *The Name Of God Is My Inheritance.* Isn't that a strange idea? There is a warehouse of love that is waiting for you that is your name. I'm going to try "name" for you just for a second. Since you have named yourself, you must have one perfect name. In that regard, you are absolutely and totally unique. That's why the place in Heaven, at the gate, has been prepared precisely for you. Because you are bringing together all of your own memories of yourself into that perfect image of Christhood, aren't you? So you are named by God in that moment of disillusionment to the wholeness of you. That's who you are. That's completely individual, isn't it? Jesus in the *Course* says that has been carefully prepared for you and awaits you as the totalness of you.

You live by symbols. You have made up names for everything you see. Each one becomes a separate entity... Isn't that interesting, He calls it an entity *...identified by its* *own name. By this you carve it out of unity.* Adam named the animals and carved them out of unity. Obviously the second you named anything you would have to go on naming forever. Do you see that? If you name something separate, you are caught forever in naming something else. Wow! What a thing to do. *By this you carve it out of unity. By this you designate its special attributes, and set it off from other things by emphasizing space surrounding it. This space you lay between all things to which you give a different name; all happenings in terms of place and time; all bodies which are greeted by a name.*

This space you see as setting off all things from one another is the means by which the world's perception is achieved. It's the distance between you and the objects that you have projected from your own mind. Holy mackerel! *You see something where nothing is, and see as well nothing where there is unity...* Because once you see unity, you will see it as whole. You see something where it literally isn't. You project your own thought form and make it a whole body outside of you. It's actually not there. It's only in your memory. And you keep changing your own memory about it each moment and attempt to identify it in your own projected association. Isn't that something? *...a space between all things, between all things and you. Thus do you think that you have given life in separation. By this split you think you are established as a unity which functions with an independent will.* This is the definition of a human being. A mis-creator. Do you have the power in your mind to do this? That's exactly what you are doing right now. You are creating this condition of illusions by the projections of your own mind. Holy mackerel!

What are these names by which the world becomes a series of discrete events, of things ununified, of bodies kept apart and holding bits of mind as separate awarenesses?

You gave these names to them, establishing perception as you wished to have perception be. The nameless things were given names, and thus reality was given them as well. Because if you name it, you make it real in your mind. *For what is named is given meaning and will then be seen as meaningful; a cause of* (apparent) *true effect, with consequence inherent in itself.* You literally let the thought form out there be responsible for you. Boy is that crazy. Why? You've named it separately from you. Do you see that? You've given it a name and let it act on its own. Boy is that crazy. That was all only in your own mind, wasn't it?

This is the way reality is made by partial vision, purposefully set against the given truth. Its enemy is wholeness. It conceives of little things and looks upon them. And a lack of space, a sense of unity or vision that sees differently, become the threats which it must overcome, conflict with and deny. In order to hold its own reality.

Yet does this other vision still remain a natural direction for the mind to channel its perception. It is hard to teach the mind a thousand alien names, and thousands more. Yet you believe this is what learning means; its one essential goal by which communication is achieved, and concepts can be meaningfully shared. This is what you do with your children, isn't it? You construct them and you teach them then to tell the difference in things in the forms of your own mind. "That's a stove, you'll burn yourself." "Look out for that." "Lock your door." "Don't associate with that." "Practice this." "Do that." Out of your own memory, you have constructed, you have created another memory form which you call an offspring. And an offspring of your thoughts he becomes. Remember that you have created him separate from you because you are separate from everything. You then teach him the autonomy of existence. You teach him to protect himself in association with your false shared thought forms.

Now, is this a necessary part of your learning mechanism device? Of course! You are in that conflict. That conflict must be brought into a form of associate reality so you can identify your ego — who you are, and utilize that power of your mind to overcome yourself.

This is the sum of the inheritance the world bestows. And everyone who learns to think that it is so accepts the signs and symbols that assert the world is real. It is for this they stand. They leave no doubt that what is named is there. It can be seen, as is anticipated. What do you do? You see it as you have constructed it in your mind to see it, don't you? That's what we did with the chair this morning. Each moment you can see differently, if you choose to, rather than allowing that form that's created in your mind to come back to you. *They leave no doubt that what is named is there. It can be seen, as is anticipated. What denies that it is true is but illusion, for it is the ultimate reality. To question it is madness; to accept its presence is the proof of sanity.* When I tell you that you don't know who you are, that that chair isn't real, that this isn't real, that there is no such thing as this, you tell me I'm nuts. Your reasoning process, separate from wholeness, has assumed a projected consciousness that defends you in association with yourself. One of us is wrong.

Such is the teaching of the world. It is a phase of learning everyone who comes must go through. But the sooner he perceives on what it rests, how questionable are its premises, how doubtful its results, the sooner does he question its effects. Learning that stops with what the world would teach stops short of meaning. It has no meaning at all. *In its proper place, it serves but as a starting point from which another kind of learning can begin, a new perception can be gained, and all the arbitrary names the world bestows can be withdrawn as they are raised to doubt.* And this is what we are teaching you to do. This is the expansion of your mind, isn't it?

Think not you made the world. Illusions, yes! But what is true in earth and Heaven is beyond your naming. When you call upon a brother, it is to his body that you make appeal. His true Identity is hidden from you by what you believe he really is. His body makes response to what you call him, for his mind consents to take the name you give him as his own. And thus his unity is twice denied, for you perceive him separate from you, and he accepts this separate name as his. Holy mackerel. Now you are caught. Now there is no escape for you. Boy, a lot of you have decided not to name anything here, haven't you? Holy mackerel. We will be having a quiet time in just a moment. I want you to really think what your mind has been doing so that you can see that you have been the dreamer of this dream, and that now you are having the experience of changing your own mind. And this is extraordinary.

It would indeed be strange if you were asked to go beyond all symbols of the world, forgetting them forever; yet were asked to take a teaching function. This is what I just said to you. *You have need to use the symbols of the world a while. But be you not deceived by them as well. They do not stand for anything at all, and in your practicing it is this thought that will release you from them. They become but means by which you can communicate in ways the world can understand, but which you recognize is not the unity where true communication can be found.* And this is what you are doing.

Thus what you need are intervals each day in which the learning of the world becomes a transitory phase; a prison house from which you go into the sunlight and forget the darkness. Here you understand the Word, the Name Which God has given you; the one Identity Which all things share; the one acknowledgment of what is true. And then step back to darkness, not because you think it real, but only to proclaim its unreality in terms which still have meaning in the world that darkness rules. This is the definition of the Savior.

Use all the little names and symbols which delineate the world of darkness. Yet accept them not as your reality. I'm using all of them. *The Holy Spirit uses all of them, but He does not forget creation has one Name, one Meaning, and a single Source Which unifies all things within Itself. Use all the names the world bestows on them but for convenience, yet do not forget they share the Name of God along with you.*

God has no name. And yet His Name becomes the final lesson that all things are one, and at this lesson does all learning end. All names are unified; all space is filled with truth's reflection. Notice it says reflection. *Every gap is closed, and separation healed. The Name of God is the inheritance He gave to those who chose the teaching of the world to take the place of Heaven. In our practicing, our purpose is to let our minds accept what God has given as the answer to the pitiful inheritance you made as fitting tribute to the Son He loves.*

No one can fail who seeks the meaning of the Name of God. Experience must come to supplement the Word. But first you must accept the Name for all reality, and realize the many names you gave its aspects have distorted what you see, but have not interfered with truth at all. One Name we bring into our practicing. One Name we use to unify our sight.

And though we use a different name for each awareness of an aspect of God's Son, we understand that they have but one Name, Which He has given them. It is this Name we use in practicing. And through Its use, all foolish separations disappear which kept us blind. And we are given strength to see beyond them. Now our sight is blessed with blessings we can give as we receive.

Father, our Name is Yours. In It we are united with all living things, and You Who are their one Creator. What we made and call by many different names is but a shadow we have tried to cast across Your Own Reality. And we are glad and thankful we were wrong. All our mistakes we give to You, that we may be absolved from all effects our errors seemed to have. And we accept the truth You give, in place of every one of them. Your Name is our salvation and escape from what we made. Your Name unites us in the oneness which is our inheritance and peace. Amen. Isn't that lovely? That's Lesson 184. Lesson 185 is *I Want The Peace Of God*, which is really all I have to say to get out of here. Try it. All: I want the peace of God! Good-bye.

That's a nice lesson, 185, it says that everyone says it, but very few have ever meant it. That's what it says. Well, is the only necessity to mean it? Sure! All you have to do is mean you want it. But to say you want it and not be willing to do the things that are necessary is an example of a poor learner. If you want the peace of God you have to be willing to do the instructions in order to know that you are the peace of God, don't you? That's what you are doing now. There is no sense in coming to me and telling me you want to do this and want the peace of God without being willing to do the things that you have to do. That makes you an unhappy learner. It's kind of silly, really. You just contradict your own reality. That time is about over for you. Was it necessary that you come into this split mind in order to know that you could come to the truth? Of course! How else would you know you had a problem? That's you meeting yourself coming home, isn't it?

I'm going to review in energy what's going on. Be real quiet with me for a minute. Still your minds. You are so lovely. Hi, sweetheart. The reason I did this lesson is I want you to take this lesson into your heart and mind so you can see that this is an out-of-time reference. This reference is not even in body form. Use this one, and use this body form and this will help you because I am you leaving here. I have assumed this identity in association with your thought forms to get you out of here. You know me perfectly well, don't you?

Breathe. Everything has changed here. This is a happening that has taken place in this room, in this time, in this place. You've got a good mental association with this, teacher. A little too comfortable. I'm going to run you through one more episode there. Otherwise you're going to sit with that, and you won't get out of here doing that. You have an understanding at a particular level that's going to cause you a lot of problems. Sometimes you can get into this clairvoyant association where you are in high service to yourself, and you have to get dislodged from that. Otherwise there is some sort of gratification in the mind association at this new level. Jesus describes this under "Occult" in the *Teachers Manual*. It's a form of reassociation that is not particularly hard to see, but given the circumstances, that's a direct quote from the *Course*. It can be kind of insidious because it appears to you that you are only giving. And what you are doing is serving. But you are serving man rather than God. You are serving your own illusion. And you can do that a long time as a Sister Theresa, or as a fortune teller, or a witch, or anything that would hold you into your own. I won't let you do that with me. You'll go away from me because I'll keep offering you the truth and you'll keep wanting to demonstrate your capacity to levitate. And it doesn't mean anything to me. The least you can do is levitate. The least you can do is move mountains. For goodness sake. Don't use your power in the limited association with yourself. You will be here a long time doing that. I don't need your demonstrations of bodily prowess. I understand that you can do telekinesis and projections and astral. What the hell is that? Nothing! All that is is the retention of your own body association.

A couple of you have been doing OBE's, which are your out-of-body experiences. They can be very valuable to you. But remember, the idea of out-of-body is body! Can you hear that? "Oh, I had a lovely out-of-body experience, and I met you at the San Francisco Bay Bridge." I remember it very well. Didn't we have fun? "Oh yes, it was wonderful." Where did that get you? Where are you? You are still associated with your body. You have what they call the Golden Cord. If I snip that cord, you'll be dead. I want the integration of your astral, of your wholeness coming down into this, and then you will be everywhere at one time rather than having to go somewhere. Stop thinking that you can go somewhere that you can't. Will I use this vision of you? Yes. I'm appearing to a lot of you guys all over the world. Everybody tells me how I'm coming in on them. I understand I'm doing that. I want you to see, then, that this new perceptual association with yourself will give you the direction of this teaching. Because I am teaching right at your source. I am teaching from source here. I know that. So do you. We are standing together right at that spot, aren't we?

Boy, some of you guys have really undergone some changes here, haven't you. You are about a thousand years later than you were! That's a nice energy, teacher. Let me see that. I used to call that Amelia Earhart energy. It's kind of nice. It's got a good male sense to it. But it's still female. You guys, when I talk male and female, I'm not addressing gender. I just want you to be whole. I want you to be a whole consciousness. It has nothing to do with gender. About seventy-one percent of this engendering will be of an apparent female association. Why? We're on the way back. We're activating the female. The necessity is to teach to that potential of return. So that's okay. We lost the male, the left brain association, and it's spreading this way now. So we need to stimulate the female to bring it up. That's what we're doing.

Be whole. Never mind your gender. It has nothing to do with it. The emergence of a whole female mind is very beautiful to behold. I look at some of you guys who are coming into your own without the necessity to assert your masculinity. It's lovely because you are being who you are. I don't know where you are hearing this, but boy I love to see it. This has nothing to do with women's lib at all. Throw that out. It doesn't have to do with that. It has to do with *you* as a whole mind.

It has to do with my femininity. I do the ballet. What's that got to do with it? I'm just creating! A lot of the males get embarrassed by my ballet. I think it's beautiful! How else do I do this? Boy you should have seen me in my awakening. I didn't know what was going on in me. I suddenly began to do weird naked ballets in my own bedroom. I had no control over what has happening to me. I was doing this, and I was still wearing wingtip shoes, you know. I couldn't understand why I was undergoing this spontaneous thing. I was told by a lot of eastern traditionalists that what happened to me was impossible; that I could actually undergo a full-blown awakening without any association here at all. It came, obviously, from outside of time. I did, though.

Some day I'll tell my story, a little more of my awakening. Remember that I was in high service. I was doing a lot of giving and extending and teaching and all of that when I entered into it. But my physical awakening was very demonstrative. I should talk about it for a minute, I guess, because when I start to talk about it, it means you have to hear this. Because of this new energy association, you may very well begin to experience changes in your physical body, and some of it may appear to be distressful, particularly in this new head energy. You have a tendency at first to get disoriented and then, if you have blocks coming into the energy, you may feel a lot of pressure in your head because of your inability to illuminate because there is a lot of high energy here.

I'll tell you this one story. During my awakening, this was some years ago now, one afternoon, and I was living in the suburbs of Chicago, I began to get a headache. And I was practicing the principles of the Twelve-Step Program. I was serving and doing it to the best of my ability. I was functioning in the world. I was feeling the frustration of success that still didn't mean anything to me. None of it ever meant anything to me, and I had asked for some additional help somewhere. And I began to get this headache. And it began to get worse. And it began to get worse. And it began to get worse. And not having had headaches except hangovers, and not too many of those finally because I never had to have one. But this was like the worst that you could ever have. And no matter what you did, it was there. It wasn't in association with shaking my head, it was just there. And I stopped by this G.P. (this was in Downers Grove), who is a good friend. I went in and I said that I have this terrible headache. And he said, "Let me see you." And he opened my eye, and looked in my eye, and he said, "You're going into the hospital." He said, "You have a pressure building in your head. I don't know what it is, but I want you there." They took me in an ambulance, and by the time I got in the ambulance, I was banging my head against the side of the ambulance. One of those kind. They sedated me and began to run tests on me, and my EEG was wild. I was in a brain storm. Literally. It was just off the scale. I was going through all of this. And the pain was very intense. The CAT scan showed something that they thought, after the second day, was a tumor. A pressure. And they were going to do some exploratory things.

In the meantime, I was in Hinsdale Hospital, I've got this incredible pain. About one o'clock on a Thursday morning I was lying there saying, what is going on here, and as though by accident something passed over me, as though they looked down, and said, "Oohhh, don't pay any attention to that. You're undergoing a transformation. You're undergoing an adjustment of your own mind. A transformation." And I went, Oohhhh. It went just like this: Shaaaa-Shooo. And it was gone.

It was just gone. I guess they forgot somehow to tell me that I was going through this. Everything is accidental. They really don't pay much attention to you. I guess, sometimes I feel they just would have let me have that. "Oh, didn't somebody tell you, you're undergoing a process." You see, my process was not connected to spiritualness at all. My process was totally physical. There were no images. There was no Jesus Christ. There was no doctrine. None of that was in my awakening. That's why I am able to do what I do. I wasn't connected to my own awakening. Of course it was one o'clock in the morning and I felt very good, and I simply got up and demanded of the nurse my clothes. She said, "You're not going anywhere." I said, I'm fine, I'm going home. I prevailed. In those days, I prevailed. I did pretty much what I wanted to do. And that was it.

But I began to have some very strange, bizarre experiences. I mean strange. I identified it as a kundalini awakening. I had no frame of reference for it. And there is no real tradition in Christianity for my bodily awakening. It's just not there. I found it later on. I can see, of course, the Christian mystic, and all of that. But what I needed at that time was the acknowledgment that I was undergoing a body transformation. And whatever happened only then became a verification. I lost my fear. I wasn't afraid of it at that point. I passed through my portal. At least I thought I had. Little did I know.

But all of this energy began to pour into me, and I didn't know what to do with it, so I turned it into creative purposes, like a lot of you guys have been doing. And that's okay, but where is it going to end? I didn't know what to do. I couldn't sleep. First of all, I didn't sleep for at least two months. I literally didn't sleep. I just would lie there. I didn't need to sleep. I needed to write or create or do something or formulate something with this mind. A lot of you may begin to have experiences like this. I encourage you to do so. Now they may not be as intense as this simply because you are willing to integrate them more immediately, if you will accept that you are actually undergoing a process here.

I want to encourage you that it is physical and that it is happening to you and that it is also mystical. It's a mystical occurrence. I'll give you one mystical story if you don't know it.

I had a tremendous amount of energy and it's suddenly about five o'clock one morning I got up out of bed — I had never done anything like that before — and went out and started to walk two miles a day. I had no reason. I had to justify it, so I bought a pair of shoes and took my pulse and said, "Well, I'm going to get myself into shape." Everything that occurred to me spontaneously I had to justify in my own mind. And I had a family at this time. And nobody could believe that I would get up at five o'clock in the morning and begin to walk. My body was being prepared for the ordeal. I was smoking at that time. I wasn't sedating, of course, and this is what was causing this to come about. I remember very distinctly when I stopped smoking. I was crossing the pasture. I had a couple of acres out in Naperville. I had horses. And I was walking back, and I had a package of Winston's up in my pocket, and a voice — a voice — "You don't smoke any more." "Oh!" Listen. I not only didn't smoke any more, but I had no need to smoke. It would never occur to me to smoke. It wasn't abhorrent to me, just any recognition that I had of being a smoker was simply relieved. Those of you recovered alkies, a lot of you have had that final dramatic experience.

But this began to happen to me more and more frequently. So I didn't know what to do with the energy. So in my mind I thought, well, if everybody would come together in communication and love and energy; if everybody would start to walk, they would run into each other and they would communicate. I had an idea that they should share. I just didn't know how to express it. A vision came to me that I would form a walking stick company. Can you imagine this? It was going to be called the Peerless Walking Stick Company. It was like a bright association because I discovered that when I walked I picked up a stick. So I did all the research on walking sticks. Can you imagine? And I flew out to San Francisco and I became a cane importer. This was about a year before my final awakening, in the sense that I arranged some Ting Ling cane, which was real lovely and the finial and the heads and that. And I went out to San Francisco to arrange to buy cane. And I was up in the, I think it was the St. Francis. It was one of the hotels downtown. And I was undergoing these dramatic experiences. I was literally running a kundalini awakening. The energy would come up my side and cross over my head. And I was lying down there, going, "Ohhh," like this, and I suddenly decided to get up and walk down on to Post Street in San Francisco.

And I walked into a book store. I know that nobody is going to believe me. I'm walking around the book store and a book... I might as well tell you. I'm never going to tell the story. It fell off the shelf onto my head. And it was a book on kundalini — psychosis. A lovely little book by one doctor at that time that was going to explain to me. And I didn't really have to read the book. All I had to know was that it was a process. I looked at it and I said, "Kundalini? Oh, that's what's happening. That's what's happening to me." And then I found another book.

Those are the kind of things that happened to me. Otherwise, I'm not in the Eastern tradition. I had no idea what kundalini is. That didn't sound like a very nice word to me. I thought it must be something that consenting couples did in private. Kundalini? What a strange word! So that when I speak in those words, it's just a manner in which I'm attempting to express what happened to me physically/spiritually.

Now listen. I understand — and was told this in one of the few direct statements made to me — that the idea of spiritual physicalness is very difficult. The actual idea that you're undergoing a physical process that is spiritual is the antithesis of what you're being taught. You're taught that the flesh is evil. Somewhere you're taught that the body is corrupt and that it's spirit that you're searching for. This is not so. There is no real difference between the body and the spirit. The difference would only be in your compacted association with yourself.

So I want to verify, totally, the transformations that you will undergo by the certainty, as Jesus would teach it in the *Course*, that you only have one function here on earth, and that's to allow this maturation of your mind to occur. Let everything that happens to you now be a demonstration of that, regardless of what it is. Then you will be miracle-minded. Like I just read you, every association that you have can become a demonstration of this awakening that you're undergoing.

Need you undergo that last moments that I had, when I was devastated? You are going to have face your fear if it's there. You're going to have to come to that portal that Jesus talks about, that we all finally undergo. And certainly, you're not the judge of your own Gethsemane. Are you the judge of finally being deserted or the energies that demand recognition from you in association with yourself, or the fears that are engendered in your own cellular memories? No!

So many times in the *Course* Jesus keeps saying, "Don't be afraid. Don't be afraid. It will be okay. These are just your own images." But when you're suddenly confronted by a horrible face or association — Jesus describes this in the *Course* — it's a very real thing to you. It seems as though it's separate from you. Why? You have projected that outside of you as a protection for the Christ face that lies directly behind that. This is in the *Course*. It's really beautiful. It says, don't be afraid to look at this face, although it drips with blood. Why? It's a projection of your own mind, and it has no reality. But it can seem very fearful to you.

It's impossible for you to reach this too early. A lot of people like to say, "Well, we wouldn't dare present the consciousness with a real awakening. He has to prepare himself for that. He has to be isolated. He has to go into a temple. He has to be directed by a master. He has to undergo certain rituals of initiation." Okay. That's what's happening to you. The readiness is always determined by your own mind. Isn't it? Of course! This is what we just read. Yet the time is already set when you do it, so stop pretending that there's some sort of ritual that you have to go through. I understand the process of initiation very well. We taught it. We taught it as the secret wisdom, as the *Philosophia Perennis*, as the hidden doctrine of truth that we don't dare reveal, as the esoteric aspects of Rosicrucianism and Masonry and the Egyptian death rites of Hermes Trismegistus and all of the other demonstrations of limited mind becoming whole, and the ritual involved in that.

The Masonic associations are lovely. I'm teaching you to undergo the third degree, followed by the fourth degree, which is called the Royal Arch, which is your union with God, dear Masons. You then become what? Through the degrees of Master Mason, after you complete your union with God, I'm teaching you to be a Master, a Master Mason, so that you can extend from you in your own temple, the temple that you have built in your whole mind, to be able to be a master communicator, to be able to do these things that you're hearing and seeing now.

What are the necessities for this? The simple admission of you. Your function is fulfilled intrinsically in your definition of yourself, which is what we just called God's naming you. He has a perfect name for you, which is your re-entrance into this new energy association. It's impossible that that not be so, since you are the only one separate in reality.

After my awakening, I had to go through a period of integration. I was extremely sensitive to pain, as well as during my awakening. But following the enlightenment, I couldn't even listen to music. I had to be re-educated. The only music I could listen to was a flute. I could listen to a reed flute and it would sound pleasant. Then, after a couple of months, I moved into symphonic. I could listen to Beethoven, which was really my next big step. Then, over a period of a couple of years, I got so I could listen to music as that became part of me. I really went through a whole historic reassociation. I had at that time no intention of becoming a teacher. I had no idea what a teacher would do. My presumption was that everybody would understand this. There was no way in my mind that it would occur to me that you wouldn't know what this is. When I walked out into the living room the day after my awakening and I said, "Well, everybody knows this isn't real. Of course, you understand that." It came up in the conversation. "Well, I know, but we all know this isn't real." And there was this absolute moment of silence. There was no way that I could associate anyone who didn't immediately understand that there was no reality to this. I mean that literally.

In Brother Sun, Sister Moon, when Saint Francis throws all of his goods away — have you seen that movie? — he thought that his father would love him for throwing all of his goods away. "Just think, Father, I'm getting rid of all of this stuff that has held you in possession. Now you can be free like I'm free." He meant that in his mind. He didn't mean that as a demonstration of how a mind ought to be. I mean that as a demonstration of how I really thought about this. All enlightened minds are like this.

I thought that there would be other consciousnesses that would know this. I thought there was an Aquarian Conspiracy and that I would run into you somewhere and that we would immediately look at each other and we would understand perfectly what had happened to me. It took me a considerable length of time, and I kept searching around. I never told this before. How did I get into this? I began to look around for somebody. I thought I would go into K-Mart or something and suddenly go, "Ha!" That somehow we would immediately know each other. I didn't understand that was a little bit later on in time. That's what's happening now. This is indeed an Aquarian Conspiracy, if you want to look at it as that. Why? Because you recognize each other in an out-of-perceptual association. There's no judgment of how you're together. You simply know that that's the way it is. This is a very lovely happening. That's the emergence of a new species. Do you sort of culture it and defend it a little bit? Perhaps.

I took it literally. When somebody said, "You undergo this experience," I said, "Yes, I underwent that." I went to the Theosophical Society, and I simply began to read everything that was there. And I said, "Yeah, that's right. That's right."

One more, and then I'll stop. The second day I went to the Theosophical Society — I think I was into something like Dionysus, the Aereopagite, some sort of Christian mysticism — and the librarian there, her name is Mary Jo Schneider. She's moved to Ojai, a lovely theosophical consciousness. I have a lot of associations with Madame Blavatsky and all of that early energy, all of the, what you call "early Krishnamurti energy". See, Krishnamurti was to fulfill his Christ obligations and slipped. He never quite made it, as you know. But I have a lot of associations with that energy from 1880 to 1885. That's that century-end energy. All of you do, too, incidentally, if you would like to look at that.

I had no idea of how to describe what had happened to me. She gave me a book — I forget what it was — and I went home and I read it. And I got all excited because I knew what I was. And I remember, I walked back in to the library, and there were a lot of people in the library, and I said, "Mary Jo! Mary Jo! I've discovered what I am." And she said, "What?" And I said, "I'm an avatar." She went, "Shhhh!" I didn't think that was such a big deal. What was the big deal about being an avatar? Obviously, everything I read about that was the association. She said, "You mustn't go around saying you're an avatar." I said, "Oh, okay."

Are you ready? You're avatars! You are coming into your own real associations. Jesus calls you Saviors of the world, Christs. Right? Sure. You're allowed to talk about it now. At least around me you're allowed to. I don't know if you want to otherwise.

It isn't very difficult to say that you're the only savior of the world if you're not going to take any credit. Why wouldn't you want to admit that you're the savior of this place? Why would that be considered to be something? You created it. To save it would be only to change your mind about the things that you've done here. You give it some sort of grandiosity, but that's not what it is. It's a very humbling experience.

Amazing! We still haven't heard how the *Course* showed up. And you probably never will, either. How did the *Course* show up, he wants to know. Oh, everybody's got so much energy, I can't formulate it here.

It doesn't hurt you to hear this. The main message that you get out of this is, while my preparations had been in my own inability to deal with my pain and all of that — the necessity for me to serve and all, whatever that was — the awakening was spontaneous. And I direct that to your attention because I'm teaching you if you'll get out of your way of your own judgment of this, it will happen to you spontaneously because it's what you are. And all the miracles that happen along the way, if you won't tie yourself into them, they will be very natural.

I had no idea what the *Course In Miracles* was. I had no intention of teaching and I, for some reason or other, went into Unity in Chicago. And I walked into the Unity minister, and he said, "How do you do? How are you?" And I said fine. And I was with another couple. And he said, "I wonder if you would be willing to give the service on Sunday." Strange. I had never given a service. I had no idea. I have no idea why he would ask me. And this was at the Ambassador West in Gold Coast, Chicago, a real nice Unity Church. Mike Matoy, nice consciousness. And I said, "Yes, I'll give it." So I went and stood up just like this in front of all these people and said basically what I'm saying now. Well, maybe a little different. And at that time the *Course* was mentioned, but it wasn't anything. And I came home about a week later and the Parcel Post had delivered *A Course In Miracles* to me, and it was sitting in my living room. I remember, I picked it up and opened it up, and I started to read it. And I said, what is this?

And I had the habit, of all the books I would look at, I would write in the margin, "Nah, nah, nah." I was looking for some truth. And my book is still marked. I began to look at the *Text*, and I began to go, what? And I put, "Okay." And then I turned the page, and I put, "Okay." And then I began to skim through it, and I said, what? And at that time I thought perhaps there would be *Course In Miracles* people. And I said, "Well, gee, this is going to be easier than I thought." There will be *Course In Miracles* people that will see immediately that this is coming from Light Source. Well, no, not quite. That was not the case. Now, of course, it is. But it turned out that that was the job.

The *Course* was delivered to me. The frame of reference with the Jesus Christ energy has always been intense in me. My karma is Christian, of course. I went through the Crusades with you guys. We were Knights Templars together. We were put on the rack together. And we were Troubadors together. And we were Cathars together. We all have that heretic nature in us that was always persecuted by the established church. Now we're back in. This is the return of the heretics.

Boy, that makes Him happy. That makes Master Jesus really happy about this. He's very happy about this, guys. He is a shared memory that we have.

So this awakening... Let this happen to you. I've never really told my awakening story. That's okay, you guys hear that. Who will you be as you undergo the final processes? Who are you going to be? You're going to be you. You'll be you! I'm me. You'll be you. How could you be someone else? You keep trying to be somebody else. You won't be. You will just be all you — all new you, but it will seem very natural for you to be that way because that's the way that you are.

All right. It's been a very, very extraordinary day. I'm going to do a review with energy now for you, if you would like. You guys are real up high here. You hold your council with this. There's a lot of happenings going on. If you go back out into the world with this, you be real gentle with it. Remember, some of you newer people, you don't have to prove anything about this. Just let the miracle happen. It will happen to you. Just keep stepping back. You are in the flow. Don't analyze it. Utilize it. It's sitting right there for you.

The need for you to teach it and declare it will come about in you, but there's no need for you to give dramatic demonstrations. I know perfectly well who I am, and I know perfectly well who you are. I have no need for this. We're not ready for this kind of exposure. What I want, what we want, is what's happening with these lovely awakened minds now, who will go out and give us some citadels of brighter light. As one consciousness hears this, obviously it's a contagion. It's a catching on of energy, isn't it? It's actually caught, and that's what's happened here. That suddenly is what's happened in San Jose. That will happen around the world. It's a little bit slow in coming, but remember that this has never happened. As Jesus says, there has never been a broad awakening at this level.

So you get in on this and then hold your council. You come back and see me if you can. You stay with this, what's happening here in Denver. You sign up to get into this light and it will work perfectly. Decide you're going to do this, and nothing in Heaven and earth could ever stop you from doing it immediately. Nothing except your own determination to give it qualifications and not get it. This is a required course. You have no alternative in this. You may still want to present to me the idea that there is something else you will do besides this, but there isn't. You never left God. Let that be the truth of you. Let that be real, rather than this. There is no need for you to verify this.

The demands that will be made on you now are to come back into secularism, come back into time, "Share death with us." And one of the lovely consciousnesses you formerly knew is going to open up their mouth and say something, and it will sound crazy to you. They will say something like, "Well, we know that it's terrible, these things are happening." You're going to go, "Oh, no, that's not how it is." And they'll say, "What do you mean, 'That's not how it is?'" What has happened to you is your mind has changed. What originally made sense to you has become senseless. And what formerly didn't make any sense to you at all, the things that I'm saying, will suddenly make perfect sense. You will pick up the *Course* and read a sentence, "This world is not real, and that's what everybody must come to know, and that's the reason for the *Course*," and you'll go, "Well, of course. What other reason would there be?" It doesn't have to do with relationships. It doesn't have to do with solving your problems. It has to do with this. It's what it says it is. You have become what you think, rather than what you think you are. You've become what you are, rather than conforming to your own associate thought forms. What is that? That's the opening of the Holy Spirit. That's the coming together in your mind. And that's what's happening to you. Stick around me. You're doing beautifully like that.

Don't try to measure it. Don't judge it. Just let it happen to you. You are absolutely unique in that regard. There is only one of you! No one else shares completely this association. This is what I just read you. You have a specific name in the

Atonement Principle. You look lovely, teachers. I'm going to be seeing you all real soon. We're not going anywhere. These lovely demonstrations that you are going to undergo, some of these newer ones in the next few days, can be verified very well by the awakened minds that are at the Endeavor Church. You come there and get into this declaration, and then it will expand more and more in your mind.

What have you got to lose? Wouldn't you rather that this be right than what you're doing? And that's really what I'm trying to get you to look at. Why not take a chance at it? What have you got to lose? I'm not going to let you die, anyway. I don't care what you tell me. It will make no difference to me. It's not real. Why would I allow anything here to be true?

Thank you for a lovely day. We're going to have some quiet time. Some of you may disappear here, and all I wanted to say was I'll see you at the rendezvous point. Can you tell me where it is again? I'm sort of mixed up. Have you got any late word? It's right here? Oh, I'm glad. This is the point of departure! Wow! You've speeded up some time here, guys. It's very lovely. Look at this. There's a lot of celebrating going on. They celebrate up in here. You don't realize how valuable you really are. It's not that big a deal, especially those that have got the projects. It's lovely. It's working perfectly.

So now we will have some quiet time. Should we play some music? I'm going to take this mike off. We're glad you joined us today, those of you who will be listening to these tapes. We're here in lovely new realizations of our associate love, and we're making declarations now of our mutual forgiveness with the positive identity that we come from a common Source which we call God. And coming from a perfect, whole Source, we are perfect and whole. And we can come together now in our minds and share that. That's what we are doing. We hope we see you soon.

That Friday Night
In Boston

It's important to remember that this is a course in the redirection of your perceptual associations. The first requirement would be to release yourself from the bondage of the previous self-identity so that the miracle can happen. This is *A Course In Miracles* from whole mind consciousness out of time — eternity — directed specifically to you to bring about the miracle reassociation of your attack-and-defense modality, and by that manner awaken you from the apparent separation from wholeness and love; that is, the certainty of your constituted reality.

It is a required course, and I mean that in the literal sense, not in the figurative possibility perceptual sense. Obviously, if you are in sickness, pain and death and you have established that as a manner in which you consider yourself to be an association that is life, you are going to have to undergo a reassociation, or a discovery of your own reality. And that's the miracle.

The purpose of this gathering is to present to you the *Course In Miracles* from the perspective of the certainty that God is and this isn't in any manner. The problem that you have had with the *Course In Miracles* heretofore has been that somehow the manner in which you have transcribed yourself, that is, in a perceptual relationship or in a concept of self-association or ideas, can lead you to a miracle experience. And it can't. *A Course In Miracles* is a course in the relinquishment or the loss of your perceptual associations, much as the Eastern tradition of detachment from your self. It's an imperative if you will look at your associations with yourself as being figures of projected illusions within a time framework.

Everything I'm going to say to you is in the *Text* of the *Course In Miracles* or in the *Workbook*. I will say nothing but that. I will direct you to nothing but that. If the vernacular appears to be subtly different, tolerate that, please, because it's important at this point to subtract you from your previous perceptual concepts, first of all, of what *A Course In Miracles* is. *A Course In Miracles* is a course in enlightenment, or your awakening from your own concepts, your own associations. That's the requirement.

The technique of doing that is to give you a provision of reassociation that is beyond your perceptual association, literally a miracle, a happening that transcends your previous identity with yourself. Until that occurs, how would it be *A Course In Miracles* if you are the miracle? And you are the miracle! You are not making miracles. You are not comparing yourself in your own ideas about yourself. You are a miracle. You are God creating. I can't show you what love is because that's what you are. I can show you what the obstacle is and that's you in your perceptual association. How simple, then, is salvation! But how difficult, since the constitution of your makeup depends on your identity in your previous form associations as you're sitting here, as you are. And you are in a position of defense of your mind, as constituted in what you term objective reality.

This is a message to you that this is not real. The easiest way to look at it is to see with certainty that objective reality is not true. There are not separate source emanations. God Mind, Universal Mind, is singular, and you must be that. Now, if you'll start with that premise, it will help you a whole lot because obviously you are in a dualistic association with what constitutes your reality and are holding yourself in the bondage of your own self identity.

Everything that I'm going to say to you will now appear very reasonable to you because it is reasonable. If the conflict is only in your mind, the solution is: Don't defend yourself; forgive your associations your previously constructed images. Are we all okay so far, miracle workers? Is this what we do? We're going to forgive.

At the time that it's necessary to forgive, you have obviously taken on a bondage of self-identity, rejected it or cast it out from yourself, and literally believe that someone is doing something to you outside of your control, that is not under your direction. This is not true if you're going to teach *A Course In Miracles*. *A Course In Miracles* is a course in absolute, positive, unequivocal, subjective reality. There's a lovely sentence in the *Course* where Jesus says that the preoccupation of conceptual mind of self-identity of the earth is the problem that you're experiencing here. We're not interested — and this is the key to you advanced teachers, you listen to this — we have no concern about what your concepts are. It makes absolutely no difference what your concepts are if none of them are true. And this is the core of the curriculum. There is no sense in comparing one association with the other. Neither are so. And this is in the Text.

The next sentence says that what we are interested in is that you can think; that the mind thinks and can then choose and make decisions based on its frame of reference. Here is the problem. If your frame of reference is constituted by past associations, you will rely on them, and must rely on them, to direct you into the correlation of the situation in which you find yourself. And you do that. This is the time when Jesus begins to use the word *insanity*, or *insane*. I'll give you the sentences: There's no such thing as a past. No matter how tempted you are to believe that time as you have invented it in your mind is sequential, it is not. And this can be a real big step for you. Why? When you come in here and sit down, you will be more willing to release yourself in your association from the previous constitution that brought you here. These are the first fifteen lessons of the *Workbook* of the *Course In Miracles*.

Lesson Number 1: Nothing in this room, in this world, in this place ever means anything or ever will or ever did. You have a fear of releasing your sequential mind because if you did, you would wake up in Heaven. Can you see? Remember that the distance between the conceptual thoughts that you are having is what space/time is. But the most you can say about a thought that you had, or are having now, is that what? It's gone! Here's the key. Yet your perceptual mind is holding it in the tolerance of your own genetic association and presenting yourself objectively in time, in association with your own projected thoughts.

Lesson Number 2: No matter how tempted you are to believe it, there is no communication going on here at all. None. None! I'll give you the sentence: Communication, to be real, must be whole. Partial communication is no communication. You have struggled in your own perceptions to communicate with each other, based on a previous frame of reference. It would be literally impossible for you to know everything about that association. Yet you demand the attention and attempt to justify yourself in the association with the condition in which you find yourself. That's crazy.

The problem is not solvable. Why? Because the relationship is based on duality, or the idea that somehow you are separate from each other. All you really end up doing is correlating previous thought associations in group context and maintaining a distance between yourself in association with what you think the other projection is. Can you see that? At no single moment is the body real at all. All you did was bring it in, in your own past associations, and projected from it other past associations that are always gone. You're always gone. You're gone!

Listen. This old world was over a long time ago. You're gone. You're going to struggle with that, and you say, "No, I can remember last week." Well, last week is gone, isn't it? "Yeah, but I'm going to stir it up and bring it back into my memory and hold it now, based on the previous associations, and project that association into the future." And what? What's going to happen to you? You'll get old and die. You can't get old and you can't die. It's impossible. There isn't any such thing as death. If there's no such thing as a body, how would there be such a thing as death? There's no such thing as a body.

The skeletal frame that you identify as a body is less than a a hundred days old, all of it. There's not a cell in you, there's not an atom in you that was there a year ago. Ninety-nine percent new. I mean literally new. Look what you're doing with your mind. You're holding yourself in a static relationship with previous thought forms, constituting yourself in a form of reality, so that as you produce new cells you can command them from your own genetic association to be sick. Otherwise how the hell would you have cancer? You can't have cancer if you're producing new cells, unless you're producing cancerous cells. Why do you want to do that? The whole premise is that if there is a single universal consciousness, every single cell is all universal consciousness. Do we have some sort of agreement on that — sort of a quantum leap — that it's all finally all the same stuff, which is God, which is God extending or creating whole, and that's what you are?

Remember this: Every time you glitch creation, you form a static relationship in your own memory. This is called the schism. This is what happened. This is what you would call in Newtonian physics a particle. Quantum physics will lead you directly to Jesus in the *Course In Miracles*. Quantum, or quanta, is the relationship of a particle and a wave. One of the great original physicists, Neils Bohr, made a great discovery that it was a wave until you looked at it or began the experiment and then it became a particle — that it was impossible that the experimenters did not influence the experiment. A lot of you are familiar with this. So he saw very clearly that it was a wave until what? Until you tried to observe it, and then it became a particle. At that point, he says, why don't you just stop observing it? That was not acceptable to the physicists, obviously. That's a great mind. He could see immediately that it was the self-observation that was causing the particle, or the lumpiness, in what? In the wave. That's *A Course In Miracles*.

You are in a condition of lumpy thinking or projecting from you a particle through the identification of your own particleness. But at any moment you can be a complete wave by not interacting with your own lumpy associations. That is, not demanding a reflection back in a material sense from what you have projected from your own mind. Here is the key to this: An idea never leaves its source. Whatever you are is all there is. There is not another thinking going on outside of you. I'll give you the sentences from the *Course*, if you'd like. You are the only living Son of God. God only has one Son and that's you, creating fully with your divine mind. You can not *not* be that.

There appears to be conflict here. Now, here's the direction we must take. And this is fundamental, psychological, basic teaching. You are the cause of your own pain. That's the first determination. The whole teaching of the *Course In Miracles* is that you are the cause of this. You are doing this but to yourself. No matter how tempted you are to believe that there is an objective reality out there that you are discovering, you are wrong. Do you understand that? I know you're tempted to do it, and you will cast around in these split minds, determined that you're going to grab all of these things and fit them together in some sort of a computer of knowledge. That's crap. It's nothing but your own projected mind in your own thought form.

Key: There's no communication going on at all, and if you think there is, you're wrong. You might just as well look at it. The reason that wholeness knows not of this is simply because it is whole. Obviously God doesn't know anything about conflict, sickness and death. Now, if you believe that the Master Divine Creator knows of conflict, sickness and death, there's no sense in your sitting here. Because you're determined that somehow He is the cause of your problems. And that's been your problem. But most of you are past that, I think. But you do need somebody to blame. Somebody's got to be responsible for this place.

Course: You really think that when you came here the world was waiting for you to act with it and to interact. (Lesson 132) Wrong. You brought this world with you when you came. Salvation: Change your mind.

Is it within your power to miscreate in associations with yourself in your own self-identity? That's what you're doing. Are you capable of experiencing a miracle? Pretty near. If I can get you to begin to have experiences, my problems are over. Your problem is you resist the experience. I'll demonstrate to you what miracles are. Miracles are nothing but the reassociation of your own thought form in regard to what you think you are. You can use any and all means or devices, but I would suggest that you begin to stop trying to exchange with the apparent reality that's outside of you. It's obviously not going to do you any good because you have constituted directly to share and relieve yourself of the responsibility of the condition in which you find yourself. And it can only respond to you in the manner in which you wish to have the response. Is there a question on this? Somewhere you may want to question that. You try to get away with the idea that you're not responsible for it, but that's impossible.

I know that's tough. It's difficult for you to believe that you have chosen death, but you wouldn't be here if you hadn't. Listen. You wouldn't be here if you hadn't chosen death. There's not one single thing that you do here, in this so-called time association, from beginning to the end, that is not a protective device against your apparent annihilation. Yet the key is: If I defend myself I am attacked. Now what the hell are you going to do? I'm offering you an impossible solution to an impossible situation. As long as you defend yourself from what appears to be objective reality, you cannot see that you are the cause of the problem. Listen to me. This is the teaching of Jesus Christ of Nazareth, pure and simple. *Don't resist evil.* Do you see? Regardless of what you're presented with, don't resist it. Ever. Never. That's *A Course In Miracles.* See how simple it is? Why? When you don't resist it, the miracle occurs immediately because projected thought form, or objective reality, is a resistance to your own creative purpose, and you have set it up specifically to limit your own self-identity and share that limitation with the projected unreality. Do you see? And you will never be happy doing it because you're a creator. You are as God created you. Your mind is creating right now. It's what you're doing. There's no question about that.

The question is: What is the result of your creation? The result of what you are doing with your mind is the earth as you see it. As long as that's okay with you, you won't let it go. And when it's not okay, you will let it go. But remember that, as Jesus says in the *Course*, no one can stand pain indefinitely. Somewhere, sometime you're going to have to look at the impasse, the impossible situation that you're in. There is no solution to your problem. There is no solution to this problem as you have constituted it in your own perceptual mind. It is not real! There can be no solution to it. Jesus in the *Course*: We are dealing with an impossible situation. You will now trap me in my contraptual associations with you and demand recognition for your contraption, what you call your spiritual quest. If you're looking for God, why don't you just find Him?

You want it from the *Course*? You're very much afraid of finding Him. You'll lose your identity if you find Him. You've got an authority problem. You think you made yourself. Well, you do. You're standing here somehow, defending and protecting yourself in your own associations, aren't you? And you're absolutely right. You have to be or you wouldn't do it. There's no sense in arguing with yourself. You have a tendency to kick that out into perceptions and pretend you're not doing it. You're doing exactly what you want to do.

Many of you have an idea that you could actually die. I know you think that. But what the hell kind of a life is it that's based on annihilation? Did you ever really look at that? What's it like to be dead? To be annihilated? Are you telling me that in all the universe, here you are caught in this little place in space/time, and that life is based on not being annihilated? It doesn't make any sense. It's senseless. I know you're determined to obliviate yourself, very simply because you can't stand the conflict of your own perceptual relationships with yourself. You use up all of your time memories. Don't you? You are in a specie of genetic association that demands a correspondence of time association and will literally be used up in the karma-drama of your own mind at any moment. Jesus says you tread your pitiful little way through a world that's absolutely in your own dream, constructed by you in your own mind, and it has absolutely no reality at all. None. This is *A Course In Miracles*. Obviously this is all it says.

But somebody had to tell you that it's okay to believe that. Because you have to start somewhere with the assumption that this is not Heaven. That this is hell. That somewhere in your own mind you're caught in this and can't find a way out. That the solution is not here because the solution is not here. If you have never found the solution before, what in the hell gives you the idea you're ever going to find it? You're not really looking for it. What you do is satisfy yourself in a temporary association with what you think you are and get cancer and get old and die. That's crazy. It's nuts. It's senseless. Don't do it anymore.

How do you get old again? Help me. Think with me. How do you get old? Your mind doesn't get old, does it? How would it get old? It's all new, anyway. Never mind that. But what do you do? So you remember old thoughts? And you identify them with the thoughts of your body. You give your body control over you. Jesus says that's just crazier than hell. There's nothing crazier than that. You let your body, in your association, tell you how you are. You actually let this pump, this beautiful pump that's going on in here suddenly stop and you're going to die. That's crazy. Why don't you tell it what it is? Tell it it's a whole, beautiful thing, working perfectly in coordination with your mind. Will it work? How the hell wouldn't it work? It could not *not* work. What are you? The proof that it doesn't work.

If you get into the Christian vernacular, the idea of the resurrection will lead you to the same thing. Jesus rose and everything went with Him, and this is not so. Period. This is my whole teaching. This is the whole teaching of the *Course In Miracles*. This is over and done. One man did it; it was done. Who was that man? You. Positively. It's over and done. How could you be the residual to the resurrection and be real? You couldn't be. It wasn't real in the first place.

"Well, I'd certainly like to believe you, but it sure seems to me that I'm stuck." You are, too. You need a miracle. But you keep trying to identify it. You insist that somehow you can correlate it in your own mind. Somewhere you're going to give it an identification like you do God. No concepts are ever so. Form has nothing to do with content at all. You'll use a million devices to give identity to that form. You'll build giant computers, monstrous things, always separate forms that will correlate with each other that literally have nothing to do with thinking at all. There is no thinking connected with it. It is one form in association with another form, neither of which is real. You see it? Can you see it?

If it was never true, if this was never true, the result of this could not be true. It's the same idea as, if you'll admit to me that this is past, that your mind is past, the result of the mind that you're bringing here to formulate a future couldn't possibly mean anything. Isn't that so? What could it mean? It's already gone. Here's the key: If you won't destroy, by your perceptual associations, the continuity of time-thought — if you won't destroy it by taking pieces and hunks of it and projecting it — if you'll simply stand still and release that, you will experience what we call in the *Course* a holy instant. Quite literally, if you will stop associating with your projections, an instant of wholeness of your own mind associations will occur. And hell, you guys are doing this all the time. That's what you're doing. I know that you then reassociate it and demand further evidence of yourself in your association. If you'll take the *Workbook* of the *Course* tomorrow and start with Lesson 1, I would be very surprised if you could get to Lesson 7 without transforming and being in Heaven. I don't know why you wouldn't if it's over and done, anyway. Start with Lesson 7 — this is all past, and that's why your thoughts don't mean anything, and all the things that it says — that's why you're frightened of this, that's why this doesn't mean anything, because it's already gone. Unless you don't want it to be.

Now, for some of you the necessity to associate Love, which is wholeness and God creating you perfectly, timelessly forever, with sickness and pain and death and anger and greed is a requirement. And until that begins to get intolerable to you, you will not hear this. You might just as well look right at it. You look at this: You can't hear it. Because why? You're always solving the problem. Is that so? Each moment, you're solving the problem. I'm not interested in the concepts of it. Listen. I don't care how you're solving it. I don't care whether you're solving it in love, in hate, in anger, in pity. That has nothing to do with what I'm talking about. You think you can tell the difference. "That's sick." "That's too bad." You think you can tell the difference between pain and pleasure. We're not concerned about that. What we're saying to you is that the perceptual mind is continually solving its problem because it must in order to exist. It has to defend itself from its own associations. It's not real. And you say, "Well, how did I get into this?" What the hell difference does it make if you're in it and you want to get out? When you say, "How did I get into this?" it simply means you don't want to get out. You are just defending yourself in your own association.

So this is a course for people that are sick and tired. It would have to be if you look at it. It has to be a course for people that are looking at this and saying, "Well, this is futile." Most of you, when you were fourteen, when you went through your adolescent schizophrenia, demanded an answer to the problem, and everybody said, "Shut up. That's the way it is." And you looked right at it and you said, "Well, this doesn't make any sense. No matter what I do, I'm still just going to fend off death and I'm going to die and I'm never going to know what's happened and I'm caught in it." And they say, "That's the way it is." So what did you do? I don't know. Slit your wrists, I suppose. You couldn't stand it. Right? You just said, "No, I don't want this. Then I don't want to be here." "Oh, come on. You can do it. Stick with us." So now you've stuck with them. And here you are, in exactly the same dilemma you've always had — an attempt to correlate the perfection of your own mind with the obvious sickness and death that you're seeing here. There cannot be adjudication because there's no adjudication necessary. There is no conflict.

"Well, I certainly wish I could believe you." Well, it doesn't make any difference whether you believe it or not. What's the key to it? Salvation is beyond belief. What are you going to do, tell me what God is like and how you are in that relationship? That's just silliness. Let God be God. Many of you have used a mechanism of: "I can't do this." A lot of you have used the mechanism of unmanageability: "I'm powerless. I can't do this anymore. There must be some other way out of it. And I'll turn my will over to that." And the problem was solved for you. That's *A Course In Miracles*, isn't it, those of you who are familiar with the Twelve-Step Program?

The steps of the Twelve-Step Program are what the *Course In Miracles* is. "I'm powerless over this, I'm addicted to it, I can't stand it and everything I do doesn't do me any good. There must be another way out of this. It's not constituted in here. I'll turn it over and go free." And the miracle happened. Those of you who have overcome what you term addictions in that manner will understand that it was a miracle that brought that about. All I'm directing you to is, the more determined you will be to see that you had nothing to do with the recovery, the quicker you'll get out of here. And Jesus really teaches this. He says, "Don't help us. Don't bring the solution that you think is the answer to your problem into it." And those of you who have had the miracle, when you knew everything was impossible and it was the worst it could possibly be (I'm speaking from deep experience here), simply said, "I can't do this," and the problem was solved for you. You experienced a miracle. And you're very willing to let it be a miracle until somebody in your past demands that you take credit for the association and get into some sort of therapy that can help you hold on to the resentment that held you in the bondage of your own associations in the first place.

It's exactly what you're doing with the *Course In Miracles*. You're seeking to hold on to the identity to bring about the miracle. But the miracle is your inability to solve the problem, or the loss of your conceptual association. Isn't it? That's how the miracle works. How else is it going to work? Isn't it okay if it's a miracle? I'm giving you the reason for it. If you've projected the thought form and are protecting yourself from it, if you don't do that, you'll undergo the harmony of the reassociation of your own mind. What's wrong with doing that? That's nice to do that.

This is your world. The shadowy figures that you have brought with you here, that you have named in your own mind, that are products of your own mind, are here for a moment in time to verify your association with being here. They are not real. There's no reason why you advanced teachers of the *Course* can't teach this. I'm teaching this right out of the book. These are the exact sentences out of the book. You must start from that premise. There's no requirement that you believe it. Do you see? But there is a requirement that you say, as you're constituted, "I can't solve the problem within this framework. There's got to be another way."

Will the miracle really happen? I don't understand the question. You are whole and perfect. This is the miracle because that's all there is. There is nothing but this miracle. Everything and everyone in the universe knows this except you. Come on. The sleeping mind doesn't know that, but remember that it's not communicating. It can set up all of these things and attempt to communicate and then feel the frustration of objective reality. You demand a response from the association, and when you don't get what you think is proper, you have the conflict of your own mind. Boy, that's a hell of a way to be, isn't it? You're the cause of this!

For a lot of you this is much too uncompromising. Somehow you say, "I know, but I'm here, and I'm doing this." And that's true. And you have the power to stay here, and you have the power to do the things you're doing. And you listen: There's nothing in the universe that can stop you. Nothing. Nothing! God obviously doesn't know anything about it. Yet the power of your mind, which is God creating, can bind you in that time association if you want that to be so, if you want that to be that way.

There is nothing, sensibly, in the universe that could possibly stop you from communicating with God right now. As a matter of fact, it's the most natural thing that you could do because you are as you were created. The problem you have is you look for confirmation of what I told you in your associations and it's not there. The associations are designed to keep you from communicating. You want the sentence? The associations of perceptual mind are designed specifically to keep you in time and from communicating with God. They have been set up as a protection, as a veil, Jesus calls it. He says whole cities will arise in your projected mind, and you'll see this, and it's not so. None of it is so. None of this is so! You can reach your hand, here, right now, right through the veil, and be in Heaven. It's right here. All the separate ones stand in one little tiny spot, and they call that time. Not so!

Now look at your situation. I'm presenting you with an alternative that is not of the earth. Now you can choose. This is the *Course In Miracles*. Why? Because each time you direct yourself to the limited association, you can say to yourself, "What am I doing? Why am I doing this?" And don't try and con yourself if you're getting the satisfaction of your own association. The release of that will give you the miracle and then you can move from time to eternity. Curiously, if you will allow the *Course In Miracles*, or me as I am directing you now, to be a product of your own mind, the solution will be very simple. It is impossible that I am telling you this without you having instructed me to tell you this. That's literally true. Are you okay with that? You can deny it. And you will give me any credence that you want. But I am teaching an impossible message here. Everyone must come to know that the world is not real. But why wouldn't that make you feel good? It does!

Good. And the better it makes you feel, the less you'll participate in your own death. But each time you attempt to do, it Jesus says, suddenly all of the things around you will say, "Don't look up. Don't leave us. We demand that you stay in this association." Isn't that true? That's what's happening to all you guys now. All of your previous frames of reference were based on death. So you have plenty of associations that are going to say, "What are you doing? You're abandoning your previous dedication to death and sickness and pain and cancer." You're saying, "No. I'm not going to do that." And there's a certain dedication to fear. There's a need for you to sacrifice somewhere. You feel the satisfaction of the exchange, don't you? You like the idea that you're giving something to get something back. You can take credit, then, in the association of your own mind. And you do. And that's okay. But it's pretty small.

Key: You can't get back more than you ask for. And if you ask to be in Heaven, it's impossible that you're not there. But you've got to want it. And the only manner this can be taught is to teach, "You don't want this." Because there is no connection between the two. Got it? There is no connection between this association in perception and reality. None! Except the momentary time when you release your own perceptual association. At that moment, at that holy instant, you're whole, aren't you?

If we can get you, starting now, to relieve yourself of the necessity for preconception and really start to do the *Workbook*, then when you come into a situation like this you won't immediately demand a reciprocal identity with what constitutes your reality. Because you're dead wrong. All you're doing is saying to me, "My reality, as I sit here, is going to be based on the things that I brought in here from my other experience." Right? And they're gone.

How do you do that? How can you stand that? What's Lesson 5? It says you've got a resentment about that because it's already gone and you can't go back and change it. And I'm telling you that you can change it very simply.

See if you can hear this. One of the miracle principles, one of the beginning statements of what a miracle is (I think it's 13) shows you that a miracle is the alteration of temporal order. If you come into a situation and release the past, the past will change in the present and change the future. Can you see that? That's a miracle. Are you actually changing what happened previously? Of course. If you think it's there, why not change it? Remember that you are bringing the resentment, the need to get even, what you call the balance of the perceptual mind, what you call the First Covenant, *an eye for an eye*, the wrathfulness of the need to associate with the projection.

If you get to the teaching of Jesus Christ, it is nothing but love. "Give up and don't resist your own inclinations to defend yourself. Just let that go." Then the miracle happens.

And it's happening right here and now, very extensively. This world is over any minute. This is going to be gone. I didn't want to tell you that until you came in here. That's kind of scary, isn't it. This is over. We came to tell you that this segment is over.

What a terrible idea. It was just a dream. We're striking the set. It's going. Look at it. You know this is not so. You know this is a dream. If you guys that are here, if you got this far, you ought to be able to really look at this. How the hell could this be real? You can't go anywhere. You can't do anything. You're a little film of a poison-breather in some sort of constitution of a body. You can't go a mile down. You can't go two miles up — outside there are a thousand trillion trillion stars that you know about. And here you sit in this little thing. Why would you want to hold on to that? Because you're afraid you will die if you let it go. Why don't you just let it go and see what happens?

The problem can't be solved by annihilation, can it? That's terrible. The teachings of the *Course* are directly this. Since an idea never leaves its source, every idea that has ever been had by any perceptual mind in all of space/time is what you are. You can drag up all sorts of ones, you can reject other ones and say, "That is not me," you can project them onto the other association and deny that it's you if you want to, but it is you. Not only is it you, but if you're causing pain, you're getting the pain that's happening to you. And I don't mean it's reciprocal. I mean the pain is happening to you right now. Those of you who have felt your brother's pain have become teachers of God simply because you've tried to alleviate the pain that you feel for yourself and your brother. You reached a point finally where you discovered the pain could not be alleviated. At most, you can die to get out of it. Isn't that so?

The healers are gone. It's going back some, but I used to work with impaired physicians, real healers. And they had a very high suicide rate because they discovered no matter what they healed, it always died. No matter what they did with it. They want to heal, they want to bring it about, but they couldn't. They always failed. That's very frustrating because you guys are fundamental miracle workers. You really want to heal the world. You couldn't have gotten this far. You are all saviors of the world. That's why you're here. You wanted the job.

Stay with me. It's impossible that you didn't want the job, or why are you here, doing it? You really, really have in your mind that you can bring about a change in the civilization of the world that will help it. Otherwise you couldn't be here with me. And I'm telling you, yeah, that's true, that you can do that. But it requires what? An experience of the transformation of your mind; an enlightenment, a resurrection, a forgiveness.

Can it be okay now that knowledge or love or truth could be gained by an actual transformation of mind, where you wouldn't be too threatened by that? That's kind of hard, isn't it? If I sit here with you, somewhere in your perceptions you want to know how this came about, "What did you do?" "Who are you?" "What's your background?" "What's your identification?" "What did you do in order to bring this about?" And if I tell you, positively, absolutely, in the certainty of my whole mind, that I had nothing to do with it, you will not let me do that. You will not let me. You will demand an association in order to either credit me with something or deny something to me. That's called an idol. This is all pure *Course* now. You need to have an idol that you can share an apparent reality with and subsequently deny because if you made the admission just for a moment that what I'm telling you is true, you would spring into Heaven.

Your association with authority, or total authority, what you call totalitarianism, is one of protective attack and defense. Do you see? "Power corrupts and absolute power corrupts absolutely." Crap. Absolute power is God. It has nothing to do with corruption at all. Yet you are threatened by the authority of a non-judgmental reality. You demand an association in your mind that will verify an authority that says nothing to you except, "You're the only living Son of God and you never left home. And you're home with God. Wake up and come on home." Why do I have to say something else to you? You are so deep in your reflected association, in your own chaotic forms, that what? You can't hear it. You have no frame of reference for this message. It's not light enough for you to see. It keeps running into what? Your previously-constructed thought forms. Now you look through a mirror darkly. If you're looking at me, are you giving me identity or are you evolving the miracle-ist's capacity to release our apparent exchange of identity. *Course In Miracles*, isn't it? Certainly. It's not kicking the sin out there and then trying to forgive it. That's crazy. You will never do it. You are totally justified in defending yourself if you are actually being attacked. And if you try to teach the *Course* that way, you're going to be here a long time.

Practicing forgiveness makes absolutely no sense. You've got to start with the fundamental premise of subjective reality; that you're the cause of it. Then you can come to know there's nothing to forgive. Otherwise, there is something to forgive. And you have every right to demand it. And you do. And then, bless your heart, you try to practice, "I've got to forgive it even though..." You'll never do it. You can't. It's not forgivable. You understand? It's not forgivable. If it's real, it's not forgivable. Right? If God really had anything to do with this world, I don't want anything to do with Him. I knew that forty years ago, fifty years ago.

Somebody said, "Well, that's God's will and He does whatever He wants to." That's crap. No, I have a right to know what my qualifications to be in Heaven are, and nobody would ever tell me. See how simple this is? What are your qualifications to be with God in Heaven? Answer, anyone? None! You have none. No. The qualifications are none. That's not tolerable to you. Because you have qualifications in your condition of mind. In the Eastern traditions there's a lovely guy that teaches this to the point where you can't get it. Who is that, the sweet guy? Krishnamurti. He's undergoing all of his experiences but he's holding on to a self-identity. Any reasonable mind can see that God is not perceptual, that He doesn't have moving parts, that you can't compare the wholeness of God with something else, that He's just singularly whole. That's not hard to do. Why would it be? It's an abstraction. The problem is not that. If you stay with the idea of transcendentalism, you cannot know God, but you can then go to "I can be God." You have to make that step. That's what the *Course In Miracles* does through Christianity. It teaches existentialism. Can you get this? It teaches *cogito ergo sum*, "I think, therefore I am." The question is what the hell am I, and what am I thinking? The *Course* answers, "You are nothing, and you're thinking nothing." That's the first ten lessons of the Workbook.

You just keep batting your head up against it. Why? You have previous associations in your mind that are going to protect you and guarantee your heart attack. And you feel very resentful if I tell you that you can't die. And the manner in which you will prove that I am wrong is by killing me. Can you hear this? I'm teaching pure *Course* now. Face it, you crucify the Christ each moment. If anything dies, everything dies. Can you see this? You're going to prove I'm wrong about this by saying, "Look at all the things dying around you. How dare you teach that, when all of these lovely souls are going to have to go out and die?" I'm teaching the *Course*. Somebody accused me, saying, "How dare you teach this — that this is the moment of salvation and we're all going to be in Heaven — when you know very well that they're going to have to go out and get sick and get old and die?" No. No! You're not going to do that. No. There's no such thing as a future. Everything that you can ever do, you're doing right now. There isn't anything else. You're going to prove I'm wrong about this. How? You're going to get up and run out into the world and do all sorts of things and get cancer and die. You're going to prove I'm wrong, but you will be dead. What the hell good does that do you?

When you really get into the *Text,* when you begin to let your mind think this way, you'll be astonished how much of this is in there. This is nothing but the *Text.* Life based on death is absolutely meaningless. Everybody walks around here and says, "I'm not dead yet." It doesn't really make any sense. "How are you doing?" "Well, uh..." "How good are you at keeping God from being totally here? How much are you able to defend yourself from reality?" And you say, "Well, you're exaggerating." Wrong. I'm not exaggerating. If anything, I'm trying to hold it down to give you some sort of perspective in this.

This is not a real place. You got it? I just stopped by to tell you this is not a real place. You don't have to know what the other place is like. You can't know what the other place is like. But this place is not real, and it is at your command to change your mind about this because this world is your mind. Now, I don't care whether you believe this, but you pick up the book and start teaching it and it'll happen. Why? This world is your mind. And there is a God. And that is real. And there is a Heaven. And you are there. And it's going on right now.

This is Lesson 130. The two worlds do not know each other. But that does not mean that the other world is not going on now. And what you're actually experiencing are glimpses of Heaven. And you are bringing your constitutional unreality with it because it's a thought form in time that you have perfected in a whole relationship with your own mind. And you will actually set up quadrants in time of what Jesus calls a Borderland, where your minds together will share this new reality that has nothing at all to do with this dimensional association in time.

Can you hear me at all? This is a hologram. I'll do it that way. This is nothing but a hologram, an association of nine dimensions — Father, Son and Spirit; Father, Son and Spirit; Father, Son and Spirit — nine dimensional association plus the tenth dimension, which is time. All of it is going on all the time and is changing each moment. Tomorrow we'll do some quantum so you can actually get an idea that this is not solid, that there's just as much distance in your microcosm as there is in fifty thousand light years. Do you see? And that they're the same thing. And then, when you read the sentence, "The body's not real; you are not a body," you begin to say, "No, I'm not. I'm a mind." What will the body do? It will be perfect. What is there to stop it if you were the conflict? That's how the miracle works.

There was just an occurrence of a spontaneous remission here. Do you know that I'm allowed to tell you that? And you might view that as magic, but that's perfectly okay. What happened is the association just suddenly said, "I don't need to do that anymore." You see, sickness is a need. Listen. Feel it? Sickness is a need. You need to be sick to verify your association. How else could you get well? Can you hear me? What better describes the sickness than the remedy? The sickness and the remedy are the same thing. If you didn't have a remedy, you would never get sick. You couldn't. You had to have the remedy before you could get sick.

Cause and effect are not apart. I'm going to reverse temporal order for you. See if you can get this: The plane crashed. They discovered that a part in the engine had failed. Therefore the plane crashed because the part in the engine failed. Wrong. The crash of the plane caused the part to be defective. Do you see? Where did you find the cause? In the past. Now you're going to set up preventive maintenance based on past associations. Yet the idea of it happening is the assurance that it already happened, and it's impossible that that not be so. I don't know how many of you are hearing me. I'm going to tell you anyway. A trillion-trillion-trillion-to-one shot in statistical possibility is exactly the same as a one-to-one shot because until it happens, it's not a possibility. It doesn't make any difference when it happens. Boom-bo! "Oh, that was a million-to-one that that would happen." Crap. What's the difference between being one-to-one and a million-to-one?

These are the teachings of a whole mind to you. The cause and the effect are not apart. You can reverse the temporal order and by not bringing your previous effects into the present, you can change them. The key, the real key to it, if you would like to know is that there's no reason for this at all. If you never verify your association in perception you will wake up and be in Heaven. That's the *Workbook* of *A Course In Miracles.*

Boy, I don't know how you can stand it, being gone. People die all around you and then you just what? You cry, and you actually think you've lost them. It's crazy, guys. You can't lose anything. You can't lose. Where did it go? How do you do that? You are sharing associations that are dying now. I don't understand that, unless you intend to die. But if they're going to die, then everything is going to die. What's the sense in life if everything dies? Sentence: Either everything dies or nothing dies. See? That isn't hard. The idea that the body would die and there would be something going on later on is just senseless. That's just your defense of your own self. "Well, where will I be when I die?" Right here. "What will I be doing?" This. Unless you choose to do something else to try to solve your problem.

What am I trying to get you to do? Die. Class? Class?! Know ye not ye must be born again. Obviously you have to lose the form of your association. To you that's death. To a whole mind that's life. What you think is death and undergo is actually life. I'm encouraging you to speed up the time of your misconceptions so that you don't go through long periods of slow time. Listen. Listen to me. Just try to get this. I got to bring in some reserves here. What the hell's the difference between a hundred thousand years, and ten years if it's over? Come on. If They have come, what the hell's the difference if it's time for you to wake up and go home? This is right out of the *Course*. Somehow you want to keep a longevity. But remember, if you keep a longevity you will project it into a future association and prolong your own projected timeline. Time is not sequential. What page is that on, everybody? 234. Chapter Thirteen. Chapter Thirteen of the *Course*. Time is not sequential. You may make it sequential in your own mind but then do not believe it is true because it is delusionary, and you are basing your reality on a past, and there is no such thing as a past. Some of you are starting to hear me. I'll do it with energy in a minute. You'll hear it.

You can hear this if you want to. You will relinquish the past. You will stand here and say, "No, I'm not going to do that." Whoppo! Holy instant! Suddenly all of the grievances of your past, of your own karma, have been converted through forgiveness, if you want to use that word, to lovely associations. The association remains exactly as it was, but you have no grievance about it. You brought it into yourself in a whole new love association. That's the way you can tell an awakening mind. It doesn't get together and form groups to retain hate, sickness and death. They're forming groups for everything, aren't they? Groups for those who were molested. Everything. I'm not even going to get into it. Why? It's a defense of the previous association in an identity with the resentment. How sick. How sick!

Listen. One cause; one solution. One problem; one solution. I used to teach the alkies this. Your problem is that; your solution is that. No other problems. So you undergo a miracle and you no longer feel the need (I keep coming back to Twelve-Step a little bit) to feel the addiction. And now you think you need counseling in order to re-establish yourself in your own resentments. But the reason you were sniffing in the first place was because you couldn't stand the world. It was just too painful for you. You literally couldn't deal with it. Now you have to go back into the conflict in order to justify the miracle that occurred, that has relieved you of this. And this is exactly what you're doing each moment when you don't let the miracle happen. Listen. I promise you that you are as God created you and that it's going on right now. It has nothing to do with what you think it is.

Those of you who have had light experiences, and everybody has had them. You couldn't get this far without having had them. And you're going to tell me you had them last year or in 1978 or whenever. But you had a lot of them. And a lot of you had them when you were real young. And they were reassociations in your mind of connections with reality. You call them religious experiences of wholeness of your mind. Those are holy instants. But you can't have a holy instant, you can only *be* it. Don't you see? Having or remembering the experience is not what the experience is. I can't teach you that. I don't think you can hear this.

See if you can hear this. This would be important: Let's say that when you were eight years old and you got something for Christmas, you were underneath the tree and the lights were shining and you felt a great deal of contentment and there was a fire in the fireplace. And suddenly you felt this beautiful feeling of reality, as though someone were watching you. You felt whole for just that moment, almost as though you were standing and being observed doing that. That was a joyous holy instant for you. When you have these holy instant experiences now, that is when you had them then. Those are simultaneous. I can't teach that. You are directing yourself in your own previous experiences. The associations that are directing you now or when you were a child or wherever you were in time are nothing but your own mind in a later state of time — nothing but you and I sharing together, out of time. Jesus uses the word *reminisce* only once in the *Course*, and he uses it in this context: We are remembering this together. And you can go into your own individual past and experience that moment of networking, of enlightenment, that you felt. That's what the *Course In Miracles* is for, to keep you in a continuing condition of revelation, of awakening from your own projections in your own mind.

I need some help with this. What else would it be for if it's *A Course In Miracles?* Isn't it a course to wake up and remember that you're with God? That's what it says. It's not a course in the continuation of the repair of your associations. You can do that, but finally they're just going to fall apart anyway, aren't they? Don't make predictions about the miracle. I know a lot of you are facing the dilemma of the need to relinquish with the demand from the associations that are around you that you hold on. But you remember this: Finally you're the cause of all of it. In a very real sense the *Course In Miracles* is not a detachment from reality. It's an inclusion through forgiveness. And the necessity for the miracle that will literally change the perceptual thought form association that's going on. And this is a tough step for you. It's very difficult for you to see that if all time lines — you call these *sutras*, a *sutra*, the time line — if all time lines are going on all the time, there have been dramatic changes in the relationship of your mind and these projected minds since you've been in this room. And if you will allow those changes to be real, we can speed up time to the time when you simply sprang into Heaven because obviously you've already done it, and when you do it, that will be the time that you did it. And this is the time that you're going to do it. What other time do you have to do it? Won't some other time be this time? Why do you keep putting it off? You would rather die than hear this.

And you will succeed. But you won't die. You will suffer the pain. Or you'll give the pain to someone else. And you'll be here. And you'll suffer the pain. And you'll give the pain to someone else. And you'll struggle. And you'll be here. Do you want the sentence? Nothing can be solved by conflict. Can you hear me at all? Nothing can be solved by conflict because neither side of the conflict is real. This is the whole teaching. Neither side is real. You don't mind the idea that somehow you're a Holy Spirit in conflict with the ego. Not so. That's literally not so. Wholeness is not in conflict with anything. If you can't take that step, don't try to teach the *Course*, for goodness sake. You must somewhere go with the assumption that the cause and the effect of this association are not so. And by not judging them, or forgiving them in your own association and mind, you will remove the obstacle to love. These are the first sentences of the *Text* — I can't show you what love is, but I can show you that the perceptual mind is the obstacle to God creating. And you are that.

The *Course* is about to expand very, very rapidly, all around the world. It's going to be challenged. But we want it challenged at the level of God, wholeness, versus the conflict of perceptual mind, not in the perceptual conflict level. We don't need that. If you're going to teach it, you're going to have to teach, "No, this is not true." Now, the more you teach it, the more you'll come to know it is so. You must teach it because you have the power of your own mind to determine the result that you want it to be. There's no sense in giving that to someone else. This is a lovely sentence in the *Course*. Jesus says subjective reality, that is, the acknowledgment that you are the cause of this, places the burden on you but it also relieves you of the possibility that somebody else is causing your pain. If you are willing to accept the burden, this burden is actually light. *My burden is light.* What do you do? Turn it over to God and the problem is solved automatically.

So here you sit. And here I sit, telling you this. One of us is wrong. If I pick up the book — I'll be the book. I am the book. So are you. Try to do this with me, will you? This will really help you teachers of the *Course*. Don't attempt in your mind to separate the source of the *Course* from the *Course*. Will you please do that? Studying the source is a denial of the material. It's a determination to judge it in relationship with what you think Jesus Christ is. Let me see if I can do it. The whole basis of the teaching is that this is Jesus Christ, here. There is no separation between the object and the result. The thought and the result are the same thing. If you break it up, you are faced with the necessity to question the source, like you're doing with me right now. "How did you come to know that?" Now somewhere that might be an acceptance, isn't it?

I don't know how you could pick up this book and look at it and believe that it came from earth. Yet if you don't believe that it came from earth, you're going to have to admit that it came from somewhere else. Then you begin to look at it from that association. But if you divide up the cause and the effect (this is in Chapter 9 in the *Course*) you're caught with trying to determine and judge the association with a previous experience you've had in your mind that will verify what I'm telling you. Quite literally you're saying to me, "How do you know that?" All perception on earth falls short of knowledge. There is no knowledge here. You see? It's just an association of your own mind in time.

Now, tomorrow, if you would like to pick up the *Course* with me, we'll pick up the *Course* and you should immediately, after the experiences you're going to have tonight — this is a transition night for a lot of you — you'll have an experience, and tomorrow you will pick it up and all you'll say is "Well, for crying out loud!" You will actually look at it and say, "Yeah, that's what that says. That's what that means." You'll hear it. Or not. But remember, if you don't hear it, you are no-thing.

See if you can get this: All awakened consciousnesses that are going to be demonstrated are the cadre. All of you are in this association — everybody in this room. Everyone is what they call teachers of God, or advanced associations in time. All I'm doing is what? Speeding up your death association. A lot of you have gone through death, life, death, life, death. And I just keep shortening it down. I digress from that. Remember what I said about eighty years not being any different than five minutes if it's gone? Can you understand that some time is faster than other time? Is that okay with you, that you'll be contained within your own segment of relative association of time and cause and effect? Can you get that? Can you hear me?

Can you get the idea of potential? Starting from impactedness and returning to light, at the very instant the speed of light accelerates, time will be slower as it comes out of a black hole until it reaches a quasar. Can you factor that, that each galaxy has a black hole, which is nothing but your black hole, here? This is your constituted potential reality, impacted into what you call particle. Jesus directs His attention to this when He says your problem is potential. You have the idea of objective reality, that you can take thought form that's been impacted and utilize it in a limited association with yourself. And you do it. But you never activate it wholly. Yet each moment, if the schism occurred, it went to total impactedness and immediately became whole again. And you're somewhere in between. This is the old Hindu teaching. You are somewhere in between that — the emanation, to the black hole and the return to your natural condition, to remembering that you're God.

Now, nature worshipers or Moon, so-called Moon children, obviously are doing an identification of the potential of their minds as the source of their reality. Not so. The source of your reality is out here, and you are returning to the source of your reality by activating the thought forms contained within your configuration. Can you hear this? The Yin and the Yang. You're always meeting yourself, coming and going. Split mind, what you call human-condition mind, is the equal distance between God — which is an acknowledgment now in your mind that there's something outside of you — and the earth mind that constituted your previous reality. Do you see that? Male/female. Does that help you? You're activating your potential through the utilization of the energy. Jesus calls these "Great Rays." And this is lovely to look at.

Now, where are you as a human being? Obviously you see you're not completely from the earth because your mind has expanded to the stars, yet you don't know what's out there. For just that moment that's called ego, that's the split mind. But remember that it only lasted for a moment. You could only ask the question once: "Is there a God?" without being God. Can you hear me? A hippopotamus doesn't say, "Is there a God?" You could only construct time or death once in your mind without trying to find a way to overcome it, which would be eternity. Then death and eternity are the same thing and they are in your mind. If you continue to ask the one thing in all the universe that doesn't know — this is *Course* — what it is, you can't possibly get an answer because you're asking your own form, and that potential does not know the answer because it's forgotten that it came from here. Yet it cannot be so that it is not. Jesus uses a lovely term, He calls it "the great reversal." He says when it goes out so far, then the return journey begins and if you want to look at it as time, it's going on all the time. This is it. And you're somewhere, contained within that. And we can shorten your time associations if you won't move laterally on us.

Remember, once you find a schism, you begin to go off into devious associations, and it can take you another million years to get out of here. What's my answer to that? That million years just passed. Now you can go. This is speeding up time.

I'm trying to speed it up for you. If you are determined to go through another death experience, who in hell is going to stop you? And by hell I mean here. Who in hell, here, is going to stop you from going through another death? They're designed to verify that you can get old and sick and die. I hate this. I hate it. Stop doing it. Somewhere you're going to have to accept the idea that God is whole and that you are in Heaven. I'm telling you that's so. If you try to look for a verification for that here, it won't be here, will it? Of course not. How would it be here? It isn't here. This isn't here.

Do you know what I'm telling you perfectly well? Of course. How else could I be telling you? You can deny it. But the craziness of constructing a whole beautiful God in your own mind — remember God's an idea — and subsequently denying it is the height of insanity. I keep doing the *Course* because it's so beautiful. Face it, you actually believe that you have usurped the power of God, as though somehow you can do that. But you can't. You are going to be God's Son, whole, creating, whether you like it or not. At this point you don't like it, but that's not going to make it not so. And don't tell me you do like it because if you did, you wouldn't be here. Something about death still attracts you. Do you see? There's no sense in denying it. As soon as it doesn't, you'll be gone. That's a fact.

I'm surprised some of you don't start to remember me. I know all you guys. You ought to be able to hear some of this. How the hell would you meet a stranger? Come on. Let's do the *Course In Miracles* for just a minute. If these are projections of your mind — can I get that far? Is that okay? Can I get you to admit you're the cause of this? How would you possibly meet something that's not constituted in your own state of condition unless you don't want to know him? And you don't want to know him. You don't like the things that they've done in your own mind, and you have rejected them from your mind. But they are your mind. You lust in your heart and you lust everywhere. That's one of Jesus' famous sayings. The thought is the same as the deed. There is no distance between the cause and effect. You are getting back a reflection of your own mind that you don't want to acknowledge. And when you won't acknowledge it, you cloud your mirror, if you'll look at light as consciousness. Then all you see are the projections of associations that you are in conflict with in your own mind. You guys ought to be able to start teaching this.

Don't do that. Forgive them. Let them go. Step back. "Well, they'll keep on attacking me when I do that." Of course. "Well, now what am I supposed to do?" Step back. "But they keep on attacking me." Yes, they do. There's no sense in me telling you you're not being attacked. Your defense is what the attack is. You will believe the *Course* totally or you won't believe it at all. The *Course* is either totally true or there's no truth in it at all. What a terrible problem that leaves you with. You know what it leaves you with? Faith. Because it's teaching, you can't know it perceptually. The happiness that you're experiencing, that you're seeing in some of these associations, is nothing but a determination that this is not real — not that there's something else that they're going to be in. Can you hear this?

God is not an alternative. Who can hear that? God is not an alternative. This is the whole *Course* now. All of your alternatives are wrong. Got it? You can't choose Heaven. If you could, you would have. You can always tell an advanced teacher of the *Course In Miracles.* Why? He teaches no choice. The whole basis of the *Course In Miracles* is that you have no choice, that this is a required course. You say, "Yes, but I can choose the time." That's nonsense. You wouldn't choose to stay in sickness, pain and death if you knew you could get out of it. You believe somewhere that you're choosing to do this. Somewhere you believe that there's a separation or you wouldn't be here. But it's not true. You have no choice in this.

And you say, "Well, how come you're offering me a choice?" I'm faced with an impossible situation. That's a sentence directly out of the *Course*. When we say to you *an impossible situation*, we don't mean, "Oh, it's just so difficult." We mean it's *impossible!*

This is not a doing, is it? This is an un-doing. It has nothing to do with doing at all. What is it? Transformation of your mind. Maturation of the species man to a new range of thought form, *homo superior*. You want that? I'll give it to you. But what are you waiting for? You're going to tell me it's going to happen a million years from now, as man gradually pulls himself out of the mud? Crap. How does that solve my problem? The *Course In Miracles* solves the problem very succinctly by telling you that you are the cause and the effect, that if there is a problem you are the problem, that if there is an Anti-Christ you are that. But if there's an Anti-Christ, there must be a Christ, and you are that. Key: There is no such thing as conflict in the whole universe. The universe is only loving and whole and real.

If you're going to teach subjective reality, teacher, you teach that's all there is. There aren't separate thoughts. Don't try to do it. It won't work. You will just conceptualize God or something outside of you. It's not possible. I promise and guarantee you that any stricture of mind that occurs with you is all that there is at that moment. There is not more.

Now, you can string those moments together and call it time, but that original moment of your limitation was not real. There is nothing outside of you. I'll do it again. There's nothing outside of you! See? If you conceptualize it as being outside of you, you must create it in the image of your own limited associations. You ought to start hearing this. This is the *Course*. And you'll get back the exact result that you asked for. By asking for no result at all, you commend your spirit to God. Now, that may be a point when you say, "Father, why hast Thou forsaken me?" I'd be very surprised if it wasn't. Because this problem's not solvable. And the more that you bring into the problem, the more you're going to demand a solution to it. Jesus calls that sacrifice. And you actually believe that you are going to contribute something to reality — that something separate from reality has something to bring to reality. Not so. Not so! The moment that it had anything to bring, it brought it and became whole. Do you see? That's what salvation is, the admission that this is not so and bringing it to God.

How does this come about? It's an experience, a change of your mind. You know what I'm curious about? See if you can help me with this. How would you teach this as not physical if you're physical? Jesus handles it very beautifully. He says the body will become a vehicle of communication. But the idea that you can subtract the body from the mind is just crazier than hell. The body and the mind are the same thing. There's no difference between the hardware and the software. You are what you think, and you create it in what you call thought form and make it real. This is what we call physical resurrection — the teachings that at any moment your body can be made whole and sanctified in pure light. That's Christianity, as pure as it can get. Can you get a feel for this? Resurrection? That you are the resurrection and the light? Now. Now! Here! That was a resurrection. This is gone.

Stay with me. Phenomena will not solve your problem. You are already the residual of the nomenon. I guarantee you this is true. I just disappeared in Light. And it wouldn't have made any difference whether I did or not. Some of you would have simply said, "Well, he was sitting here one minute, and the next minute he was gone." And you will go back out into the world and say, "We don't know what happened to him, but let's put a shrine up because anybody who can do that deserves a shrine." Isn't that funny? And then you're stuck with what? Your associations with the phenomenon that occurred. No! When Jesus goes, everything went with him. There was nothing left. A lot more went out than you think, incidentally. In fact, I'll show you on the master map how much went out with Jesus of Nazareth after three years of teaching.

You think that that was two thousand years ago. It was last week. Some of you really start to hear me. I just told you, it's not two thousand years ago. It's last Sunday. He's right here.

Question: How about now?

That's another curious thing. No, we'll let it be past. Why? It's a past association. I can look at it and be with that. That will bring that into the now. Then He's sitting here. Where did you think He was? He's right here. He would have to be. He could not be anywhere but here. He says He's here in the *Course*, obviously. He says, "If you'll look on me as always being with you, I assure you it'll be very true because I am." Where is He? Right there. Can you hear that? Could you hear that's him. He's around here somewhere. Where's Josh? Oh, there. He really thinks he is. And he is. You guys, for some of you, it's real hard for you to hear this.

See if I can do it for you so you'll hear it. This is *Course In Miracles*, pure *Course In Miracles* now. One savior is the same as any other savior if none of it is true. Anybody hear that? In other words, it wouldn't matter what you brought into it. It's all going to be not true, anyway. It's not like there are separate saviors. There's only one. Why? Because none of the saviorship is really real. Saviorship is just a sleight of hand. It's not real. There's nothing to save. You see how simple salvation is? Shall I show you how really simple it is? You're my savior. I'm home. Anybody? How would it not be so if that's a projection of my mind? Forgive your brother! How would it not be so? Somebody answer me. How would it not be so? It has nothing to do with the characteristics of what he is. That's what holds me in the bondage of the judgment. He's either my perfect whole savior or he's what? Nothing, and I am nothing with him. If I give him an identity separate from myself, neither of us is anything. We are just the distance between our thoughts, and we kick them out there and we study them and we do everything we can to keep from getting any closer than that and we call it a relationship.

Boy, the *Course* handles this so beautifully. Finally you end up calling it a good relationship where you don't put anything into it except your own agreed forms that somehow you've agreed not to be conflictual about, until they fall apart and you get conflictual. Astonishing. And if we get too close to you, you get scared. You're very much afraid of love. It scares you to death. It's the release of your own passion. You will start to create. And you're afraid of your own mind. You're very much afraid of your own creative mind. You're afraid you will kill somebody. You'll turn on yourself and kill. You won't. You won't. You'll be fine. You're not going to be flung out of here. Ha ha ha ha! We won't suddenly cast you into Heaven. Ha ha ha ha! Just trying to get you to get up a little closer. You're coming to the spot where you always chickened out.

It's lovely in the *Course*, just lovely, where He describes this place where you always come to. You must come to the place. And then you choose either life or death. And you're doing it all the time. Now you've got yourself crowded up against it. You've used up your alternatives. Literally. Don't you see? Straight the way and narrow the gate. This is a vertical access now and you're looking straight at it, and you don't have any more foundation to hold yourself, to keep yourself distracted. And if you stay there just for a moment you'll undergo an experience. And that's what happening here now. But you've got to stay there long enough to undergo it. And you have to have faith that it's going to happen. And you will. Because you did. My faith in you is absolutely total and complete. It's impossible that you did not do this. There's no such thing as failure. You can't fail.

You can't fail, doing this. You are what failure is. You see? You can't fail any more than you've failed. You keep trying to recover from your bottom. Don't recover. Some of you guys recover from the bottom, and you'll end up white-knuckling it all over the place. When I used to teach this, I'd say, "Bottom out all the time." Then you'll feel good all the time, won't you? "I can't. He will if I'll let Him." Of course. How would He not? Plus it will happen today, not last week or not last year. It's going to happen now! Are you going to spring into Heaven? Yes. Yes! Did you? Yes. Is this world gone? Yes. Yes. How else do I have this book?

Now the alternative is in your mind. Now you can say, "No, I doubt that very much." Now I can say, well, look at your situation. See? Look what you're doing. You say, "Yeah, but I'm not the cause of it." Yes, you are! See, you have to be willing to accept that. Swear not to die, you Holy Son of God. You made a bargain which you can't keep. The bargain cannot be kept because it's with two unreal things. You can't die. You can't obliviate yourself.

You can't meet a stranger. It's impossible. Just don't try to understand him under the circumstances you're presenting, and the miracle will work. You ought to start teaching this. I'm doing it right now with you. You keep fighting back, but what I'm saying is, don't come to me for answers. Come to me if you want to know there aren't any. Don't bring me your answers to the problem and ask me for a solution. You are the problem and the solution. I can't answer the problem for you, but I can tell you that it's not real. And I can give you the reflection of my mind that is certain of that. All right? It is not real. And if you will let me do that — this is the definition of what you would call a later-time teacher — I can only be later in your own time associations. Do you see? That later time is going on just exactly as much as this time is going on at this time now. And if you change your mind, all of the associations of your mind will change. You may not recognize them as changing, but who the hell cares? They're changing all the time.

The miracles that are going on from your divine whole mind are so much greater than anything; you couldn't possibly know. There's no such thing as an idle thought. You have absolutely no idea of the power of your own mind, except what? You restrict it by your own limited self identity, and it cannot exceed the source, and you demand recognition in your own limitation. What do you get? Recognition in your own limitation. And you send out these thoughts to bring you back the result that you want to hear. Now when you read that in the *Course*, you'll say, "Hey, that's what I'm doing. I'm not going to do that anymore. I'm going to come into a situation and shut up. I'm not going to pre-judge it."

I used to teach this, as a human. And when it started to work with me, it really started to work. Don't come in there with a predisposition. Don't come in there with a limited goal. Sit down in a board meeting and shut up. And let it mature. Why? Minds communicate. Bodies don't communicate. If everybody comes in there with a body thought, they'll throw it onto a table and the units will be so small that you can't make anything out of the solution. If everybody steps back, they'll fall into a harmony of a reassociation of their minds. This is *A Course In Miracles*; that's exactly what it teaches you to do.

But if you're going to form your groups and come in and jabber, "Blah-de-blah-blah," about your other associations with each other, all you're doing is condemning each other to your past death associations. You've got to release them from the judgment of your identity. Is your mind blabbing? Oh, it blabs. "Blah-blah-blah-blah-blah-blah-blah-blah." And it compares the blabs. And it gives them a reality. And it's got all different kinds of blabs. This is in the *Course* And you sort them out and you go through them and all that. Jesus handles speech as an attempt not to communicate; that you want to set it up separate so that you can keep your own self-identity.

All right. Now we'll see where this is. That's coming along. Tomorrow I'll teach you how to look through. I won't teach you, but I'll show you a little brighter association of yourself if you want to hear it. If you don't want to hear it, you won't hear it. If you want to hear it, you will hear it. If you go home tonight, and suddenly about two o'clock you'll have this lovely vision and you'll wake up and you'll pick up the *Course* and wow! That's all I want to do. We want to begin to give you the visions of your own new reality to break you out of the veil that you have placed over your own conceptual mind so that it can expand to the reality of you. That's all we're trying to do. It would be very helpful if you didn't attack us for this and demand recognition in your own associations.

I want you to attack it on the very fundamental grounds of the personal observation of your own pain. You must accept Atonement for yourself. And this is the way that it really works because there really is only your own mind. Sometimes you don't think you're making much progress, but I'll guarantee you, you are, and I will remain constant in this. I'm in perception but it will be absolutely constant. Remember that with two false things, there's no such thing as honesty. There's no truth here at all. But there is what? Constancy. It's impossible that you direct your mind to being with God and it not happen. I guarantee you. Why? Separate goals are impossible. If you can have any goal, it can only be to be perfectly happy and perfect in your own mind. That's God. It could not *not* be. But you have constructed Him in your own limited association, and you are getting back the idea that you want. That's an idol. And that will crumble. And you will serve it. And it will fail you because you are failing yourself. All doubt is self-doubt.

I don't doubt you. There's nothing to doubt. It is a comparison with whether you are or not. You are either whole and perfect and with God or you are no-thing. Now, you can say to me, "No, I am not no-thing, and I can prove it." And I'll say to you, "How are you going to prove it?" And you will say, "I'm going to fight off sickness, pain and death to prove my reality." And you do. Jesus says you sell your soul to the devil, yet you always lose. He demands an extraordinarily high price from you — in fact, he demands death from you. And you're willing to sell it to him in exchange for some camel dung (Pardon me) — for nothing. And you grab these little pieces and you hold onto them in your own mind. And then you what? You die. But only at your own hands, teachers of God.

Now, find these things in the *Course* — these are all sentences in the *Course* — and begin to look at them. All you have to say right now is, "I have no need of sickness, pain and death," and you'll be healed perfectly. And I guarantee you, you will never be sick again. And you can't die because you can't be sick and you can't die. *He that believeth unto me will never die but will have eternal life.* (John 14:12) It doesn't say anything about dying or having experiences of death and then being somewhere else. It's a present condition of reality.

This is physiological, for those of you who are beginning to have a few experiences, and I can show you that, too. I just don't want you to get caught up in the mechanism. The key to this is that it's happening despite everything you're doing. Stay with me. The key to the *Course In Miracles* is that it's happening despite everything that you're doing, not because of anything that you're doing, and that everything you're doing is what's keeping it from being there. You are in a process of awakening. It is inevitable. This is a required course. It's an inevitable process because it is constructed in your mind to be that. You can pretend to choose the time, and I can offer that to you. You will then choose the associations of the demand from yourself from that other association. But the quicker you decide that you don't want to do that, the quicker you'll get out of here because this is a dream.

I'll give you the sentence. And you ought to be able to hear now. This is a dream of death. That's true. This is not what life is. Try it that way. This is not life. This is death. Not being dead and death are the same thing. Do you see? Each moment you say, "I'm not dead." Compared to what? Being dead. Doesn't that get painful? See, all you are doing is protecting yourself. You're saying, "I'm not dead yet." Now you're going to get old and wrinkled and go to a nursing home and drool and stare at the wall and get old-timers disease. The hell with that! Don't do it. I'm telling you that it's not true. You're really afraid to take this step. Now watch your fear come in. "I'm getting out of here. This guy's crazy!" Nothing is crazier than this!

The more expressions of insanity you show, the closer you're getting to this, incidentally. Some of you may begin to do very bizarre reassociations. You've always taken a pill for it before, which is an addiction to retain your identity. And when you can't take a pill, you begin to undergo this agoraphobia. And that's what you're afraid of, isn't it? Sure. There's no question you have schizophrenia. We just want to complete the process rather than reducing it to continued schiz. But if you complete the process, you'll lose your split mind and you'll have nothing to compare yourself with. You will be as God created you. Isn't that funny?

Paranoia is worse, isn't it? You've have all these figures all around you. You're afraid of them. What causes that? There are figures all around you. Don't you understand? You had an expansion of your form associations. And everybody is saying, "Don't pay any attention to them." And when you were a kid, you said, "What the hell was that?" They're all around you and that's actually all going on. But you're taught to what? Reduce it to your own conception. And it's called paranoia and it's very fearful to you. Why? You're being threatened by reality, by other forms that you've constructed in your mind, and you want to sort out the ones that you want to have and hold. You guys that go into astral associations remember that all thought form is only your own mind. If you have previously constructed that to attack you, it may begin to appear to attack you. Just step back and say, "Hey, how you doing? You're looking good. I love you." Don't defend yourself from it. You're a little deep. Can you understand? This is still a little chaotic. You're a little early in time.

But it's impossible to be too early. I'm going to give you the other sentence: It's too late. You already know about it. You say, "Well, I'm not ready to do that" Oh, yeah, you are. You must be ready or you wouldn't know you're not ready. You understand? It's the same thing as "not knowing is a decision." You say, "I don't know." Of course you know. Otherwise how would you know that you don't know? You can make a decision not to know, but don't kid me. You know, or you wouldn't know that you don't know. This is Lesson 139. You go home tonight and you read Lesson 139 and it'll excite you. It's the greatest Socratic mind that ever resurrected. Why? It's a combination of all of our minds.

The reason the *Course* is chosen for you is because it's the way that you really think, and I want to encourage you to understand that love is reasonable. Otherwise you'll try to get it with the passion of your own denial. I'll give you all the passion you need, but I want this to be reasonable to you, darn it. There's no way that I would have gotten this with my passion. I had plenty of that. But I also saw that it was leading me to death and derangement and terrible pain. This is a course in reason. The idea of whole mind is very reasonable if you'll let it be. And I'll sit with you for as long as it takes and show you that we're choosing sides and that you're choosing to die; and I'm offering you eternal life that you must know about or you couldn't choose. And if you know about it, you must have chosen it.

Expressions are contained in the *Course In Miracles* from the idea of the hologram, the idea of quantum physics and the idea of temporal thought form reassociations; there's nothing on earth that has ever compared with the *Course*. Nothing. Nothing! That has nothing to do with Jesus Christ being resurrected from the cross, except that it has everything to do with it. Same thing.

So this is a process going on in your mind. And the ecstasy and joy you're beginning to feel, hopefully, about this is the relief or freedom from what constituted your idea of reality, which was bondage to yourself, or bondage to death. You have associated, and all perception associates, freedom with bondage. When you have felt the most free is when you have been the most secure in the protection of your association. That's not freedom. That's bondage. And you bound yourself to that previous association and called it happiness, even knowing that it was going to go. We are teaching you to give all of your possessions (thoughts) away to know that you are free and have them as a creator. You can't do it any other way. It's called for-giving, or giving before, or not holding the thought form in your mind. *You cannot have thoughts.* What would have them? God does not have thoughts. He is thought. When you try to have thoughts you are possessed by the thoughts that you have. You then attempt to hold onto them in your own mind and then they fall apart and you die. But you can't do that anymore.

Who is speaking to you? I am. "Who are you?" I'm in your mind, telling you the world is over. "Oh, I've heard a lot of that before. There's always some guy coming along." I bet you can't hear this. See if any of you can hear this. "Oh, there was a guy that came along here a few months ago, and he got a bunch of followers together. Must have been about a thousand of them. They all went up on the hill over here, Old Breed's Hill, up over in there, on the night the world was going to end. And I remember it happening. And there was great thunder and lightning. And, jeez, it was strange. We felt all of this strange thing. But sure enough, the next morning, there they were, trudging down, all wet, disheveled. Nothing happened." The hell it didn't. They're in Heaven! I don't know if you can really hear me. What marched down the hill was your denial of their salvation. You want to hear this? And that's all you're doing all the time. Obviously the Christ is here every moment, and you're associating with the sacrifice and the death rather than the Life. Not only that, but you're verifying it. You're going to write about this. "Strange man comes here and directs..." That's all crap. It's nothing but your determination to stay in your own identity of your failure to be with God. That's all it could possibly be because you are the Christ. Here's the miracle: it's changing all the time. That's the fun part about it. If you won't hold it, it will change, and you'll begin to like your own creative mind, won't you? So you're going to have a little conflict with it. That's all you are is conflict, anyway. At least you've got conflict with the possibility of a solution. And the more determined you are not to sort out the result of that, the closer and quicker you will wake up and be in Heaven. It's called acceptance, incidentally.

Am I aware that you can't hear this completely? Sure. I'm aware that you can't hear. Otherwise I wouldn't have to teach you, would I? You're insisting that you're sharing this with me, but you're not. You are not sharing it in any regard. You're starting to experience it, I hope, because any attempt for you to share this is what the falsity is. It would have to be. Because you're judging me in association with the construct of your mind, aren't you? You keep waiting for the Christ to come. He can't come. He will never come. Yet He's right next to you. And you attempt to judge Him in association with yourself. You do a projection, and then you can find Him guilty. Now you can find each other guilty; but you're not guilty. You're not guilty of anything. And that's very, very difficult for you.

You want there to be a retribution. The problem I have with that is if I absolve you from sin you won't forgive me. Can you hear me? You'll want to know why I caused you the problem in the first place. Can you get it? There's nothing to forgive. There's nothing more sinful than a forgiving God. Bet you can't hear that sentence. You got it? There couldn't be. You want to know why the hell He caused it in the first place and what the hell was the criteria so that you could be okay. That's all I ever wanted to know as a kid: What did I have to do to be in Heaven? And nobody would ever answer me. "Be a good boy. Don't kill anybody." So I killed a lot of people. When I was very young I killed a lot of people. I was a murderer. I'm a murderer. So are you. But I mean, I murdered directly. I killed people. Now, they told me that was okay, and my mind said, "Well, why is some murder okay and some others not okay?" I'm not going to get into it. But obviously you're a murderer. Because what isn't love is murder. Can you hear it? You're a consumer. You have to kill in order to live. And you say, "Well, I do as little killing as possible." What's that got to do with it? You're in a condition of existence. And you'll protect that, too. Yet it's only your own thoughts. Isn't that fun? Now you don't have to do it anymore.

I'll verify your inability to stand this place. If you tell me you can't stand this anymore, I'll say, "Amen." This is the whole *Course In Miracles.* It says, what has this world finally ever given you? Why would you want it? Why not at least allow for the alternative, that there is something beside this? What the hell have you got to lose? Finally the teaching is, what have you got to lose? As soon as you discover you don't have anything to lose, you will wake up. I'm telling you, you have nothing to lose by doing this.

Are you getting pretty afraid of me now? Some of you get pretty afraid of me. I'm crazier than hell. I'm telling you, you can't lose. You know what you'll write about me tomorrow? "You're asking me to give up all my stuff and my family and come to God." Crap. I'm not asking you to do anything of the kind. I'm not asking you to give up anything. I'm asking you to give up everything, including yourself. You want to specify. Jesus says, you want to choose particular things that you want to give up and hold on to others. That's crazy. Those other things are going to attack you just as much. It's just a matter of time. They'll get you. What a place.

Sometime go through the *Course* in the *Text,* and pick out all the places Jesus describes this place. Oh! And split minds wonder how we can love so much and hate this place so much. That's what a savior of the world is. He knows this isn't real. This is not a real place. Yet he shares it for a moment. And this is your assignment, if you choose to accept it. And you have no choice, since you already chose to. I am offering you a mission impossible. There's no way that you can succeed at this and there's no way that you can fail. This is the statement of being-ness. Just be here in love and the rest will be taken care of. So now you can do it because the way has been shown to you. And I'll be here as long as it takes.

It's important that you remember this: When you're dealing with the principle of Atonement, the manner in which you come to Light has nothing to do with the Light. Can you hear it? Everybody hear it? John in the Bible says, the Atonement was before Jesus. Obviously the configuration, or that memory of your own thoughts coming to that Light, is what the principle of Atonement is, which is what you are each moment. If you choose this segment of your own association with me, I am a principle of Atonement in your mind.

Let's see if I can tell you this. This is all that I do. I don't do anything but this. No matter when you come to me or what the time is, this is what you and I will be doing. Could you hear that? Almost. This is the time that you did it. Now, you can get up and walk out of here and go anywhere you want and be gone from this and it will affect me not in the slightest.

It has no effect on me. You're not real to me. You have come to me and demanded an association with your own reality outside of time. And I can give you that if you'll let me do it. Now, that may require an acknowledgment that you listen to this *Course*, stop trying to identify yourself, and undergo the experience of the holy instant. But that's what the *Course In Miracles* is, isn't it? That's what it is. Otherwise you're doing nothing. You just come and sit around and study the concepts of the association. That hasn't got anything to do with the *Course*. The *Course In Miracles* is you, extending the love or the certainty of your own wholeness in your own conflictual dream of death. It has nothing to do with anyone else at all, including me. And I'll tell you it has nothing to do with me, except the moment that you and I, together, understood for that moment that we were whole.

It's also impossible that you did not instruct me to do this. That is literally true. It doesn't make any difference where you put it in that association. You have asked for this or you couldn't be getting it. You asked for *A Course In Miracles*. That's what you got. Many of you can remember asking for this. You didn't ask for it explicitly because that was impossible. You asked for any solution to an impossible situation and you asked with a great deal of fervency. And when you asked for it, immediately you began to feel the release from it. But remember, it had nothing to do with the problem, only to do with the fervency of the prayer and your need to get out of it. And the more determined you were that the problem could not be solved, the more help you asked for and the more help you got. A lot of you, I can remember your "Helps" real well, where you said, "I can't do this. Help me." And you underwent experiences. You couldn't have got this far without having them. It's impossible that you didn't ask for help.

And a lot of you have suffered; your dues are paid, dummies. I promise you, you paid your dues. There's no need for you to go out and continue to have another experience where the problem is not solvable. And you'll say, "Father, into Thy hands I commend my spirit." The last useless journey. "Why have You finally forsaken me, God? I've done everything You asked me to do. I'm a good guy." This is Jesus. Every time I tell this story, He smiles. And many of you are reliving this, aren't you? He's got all this lovely energy. He's doing all the healing. He's got all His problems solved. His disciples desert him. He goes off. He's in His Gethsemane and He's taken out and hung. And somewhere in Himself He is saying, "This is what I get for doing all this." That's why He's your savior. Not because He knew the answer before He did it. It was because He didn't know the answer and underwent the experience. Do you see? Otherwise, what the hell good is a savior? A savior that knows the answer? We don't need those. We need someone who's coming to it. Do you see? That's the savior of the world. And he saves the world. Why? The world is his thoughts. And as he progresses in it, everything around him must progress. All I'm trying to do is pick up your time a little bit here.

I can snip a thousand-year segments out of your time associations if you'll let me. You'll just go like this, "Brrrrrrrrrrrrrrr!" And you'll stand above them. And you won't use them. Anybody got a *Text?* Who's got a *Text?* Principles of Miracles. Read 13. No *Texts* in here at all? Oh, crap. We got a problem. Read 13 out real loud real quick. I know you want to go home but we put down about twelve hundred years here now. Just read 12 real loud for me. 13? I was afraid of 13 for some reason; 12 is as high as we go. We'll start with 13 loud:

Miracles involve beginnings and endings and so they alter the temporal order. They are always affirmations of rebirth which seem to go back but really go forward.

That's exactly what I just said. They reverse the temporal order. You change the past, which is what you brought into the association, and it changes the future. And you're in a whole new association of space/time. We have changed the temporal order. There is no order to temporalness. Do you see? The associate of 13 is 47. Loudly. Listen. This is all the further you're going to get. You're going to spring into Heaven. Maybe you didn't get past the preamble. It says that anything that's fearful doesn't exist. That's in the beginning, the first thing. That's what it says. 47. Listen:

The miracle is a learning device that lessens the need for time.

Ah! Lessens the need for time. Why?

It establishes an out-of-pattern time interval, not under the usual laws of time. In this sense it is timeless.

Oh, yeah. We are undergoing intervals where all the time, eighty years, a hundred years, a thousand years are passing. It's just like it got snipped out of the time fabric. That's what that says. I'm in charge of it, if you'll let me be. 37. I wrote this. We had a big discussion about what ones to leave in and what ones to take out. You know who I discussed it with? You. Some of you guys start to hear me. This has to be a carefully conceived plan because it's a form of conception, and it's impossible that we didn't do it together. Listen. I'm in charge of this. Listen to what this says now. 37.

A miracle is a correction introduced into false thinking by me. It acts as a catalyst... Catalyst!

...breaking up erroneous perception and reorganizing it properly. This places you under the Atonement Principle, where perception is healed. Until this has occurred, knowledge of the Divine Order is impossible.

Literally. Now, if you'll recognize that this is a catalyst of Light, I'll break up your old previous perceptions and you'll reassociate them at a higher range of your own self-identity. That's what that says. That's all I'm doing. You say, "Well, how do you do that?" The hell with how I do it! I'm reflecting back to you your own thoughts. 12?

24. Yeah, I agree. 24. Why not? 24 is the whole *Course In Miracles*. Listen to it, and if you can see that it's true, it'll be great. Read.

Miracles enable you to heal the sick and raise the dead because...

Wow! Now wait. Stop. You can heal the sick and you can raise the dead. This is dead now, isn't it? This is dead. You're going to raise the dead. I'm not talking about dead body. That's a dead body. That's what this is. We're going to raise the dead. Why?

...because you made sickness and death yourself and can therefore abolish both. You are a miracle, capable of creating in the likeness of your Creator. Everything else is your own nightmare and does not exist.

That's *A Course In Miracles*! All right? Come on. I understand that you're in conflict with this. I don't care about that. I just want you to say, "Yeah, that's what it says." That's all you have to do. We'll do the rest. Just get out of the way of it. Why? This is a plan that we have to do it. And you know it.

It's impossible we're not out of time together. Now, the problem we have is — you don't really call it a problem — there are very few associations (this is in the *Course*) who are willing to stick around long enough in this piece of crap, after they go through their own enlightenment. Do you understand? Can you get this? Why would you want to stay in hell? The time will come when you won't remember this at all and did. But while you can still remember it, we can use it. You got that? And now comes a little tough part: you agreed to help with this. Got it? It's called a covenant. You signed on for this hitch. Can you hear me? I'm telling you. This is in the *Course*. I expect you to live up to your agreement. If you're a savior of the world, I expect you to fulfill it. And you will. You will do it. You can not *not*.

We made a little mistake, right? Well, actually I didn't have much to do with it. One of you guys was the navigator. I don't know. And there was a little fly speck that got onto the map, and the next thing you know, bammo! We missed it. That's okay. I want to tell you: we didn't desert you. You missed the rendezvous point, but you were never deserted. You've just been out a long time. To hear you guys, it was sort of like tapping on a pipe, about two miles down. It's real hard to get a good reflection at this depth. We sealed off this section a long time ago. We thought all you guys were out. I don't know where you're hearing me. I'm just giving you a little allegory. Everything I'm telling you is absolutely true.

Should I tell them really what it is? Would you really like to know what this is? Are you ready? Some of you can really hear this. You're at the Space Academy, at the Masters' Academy, what you call the Saviors' Academy, and you're in a simulator. This is a simulator. There's a bubble over this. Listen. You can see it. Look at that. What the hell do you think that is out there? Nothing. You can't go anywhere. Don't you notice how confined you are? It's a simulator and there was a glitch in the computer. And you're caught inside of that. You're in there, just re-enacting all of this. But it's not true. I promise you, you can say, "Computer Open," and you can walk right out of here. In the *Course* Jesus keeps saying, "The door's always right there." And you know the password.

God didn't desert you, and you didn't desert God. And nothing really happened. Ready? Once more. Nothing really happened. This didn't happen! And boy, you're going to be walking down the streets of Boston about tomorrow morning, and you'll say, "Oh, wow! That's it. I'm getting out of here."

You will. That's nice. We'll dream a true dream here, just for a moment. Just for a moment we'll see if we could dream a true dream. Could you actually dream out of here and have this gone? Sure. Is that too good to be true? You bet. Absolutely too good. It's a miracle. It's pie in the sky. It's impossible. It couldn't possibly be true that there's really a God and that's He's perfect and loving and that He created you perfectly and all you do in your divine mind is create. That's impossible. Yet it's true. And because it is impossible, you can do it immediately.

Listen. Once more: Because it is impossible, you can do it immediately. If it is possible for you to do it, it can take a very, very long time. Can you hear me? The impossible you can always do immediately because it's impossible. Yet it's in your mind that it's possible. Therefore it must have happened. By not trying to do it, or un-doing it, it's accomplished. If you believe you can do it in your own associations, you'll just keep sorting out methods of doing it and you'll make this very difficult. Nothing is simpler to do than something that is impossible to do. Isn't that funny? Because that's the final denial of the possibility. How simple is salvation. It's just a happy dream, where you take all the things that formerly threatened you and you begin to dream the truth.

Some of you have energy. Better make a comment about energy. The highest traditions of teaching in what you call the physiological awakening involve the crown, or the union with God in a mystical association. The highest demonstrations of that, whether in a yoga technique or in a technique of mystical revelation or a determination to seek God, is the experience of union with God, or reality. The miracle is that experience, or the revelation or the revealing of your mind. And that will involve the release of yourself in your perceptual associations. The key to that, when this begins to happen to you, is stop giving the associate identity to someone else in the demonstration of his phenomena. However you are judging that is not so. The idea that you suddenly say, "I found it," and run naked through the streets is no more beneficent than if you simply sat there and said, "Hi, God. I'm home." They're the same thing. Your judgment of that occurrence is false. But your judgment of the love that then emanates from that association is not false and is a holy relationship. And a holy relationship is nothing but your *individual* dedication to seek this and find God. It is not a mutual sharing of your attempts to do it. That is the fallacy of it.

The specialness will not solve the problem. The relationship is formed by your *individual* dedication to it, which causes a reassociation of your previous projections in their individual determination, and you meet with God. Here it is for you, one time only: This is a special relationship. There is no communication here. From this point to this point. Let's do it as a triangle. At either side of thumbs are the two separate associations. There is no communication going on between them. I know you think there is, but you're wrong. The communication can only occur by the individual dedication to it, and then they meet and must meet because their goal is common. You find associations and formulate limited goals. "Let's get married, go to college, be a lawyer, have a family, keep from getting cancer, and finally die and let our children carry on." And you get together and you do that successfully. All I'm saying to you is, why not make an individual dedication to God, not in association with your previous necessity to move in lateral time and then find other associations who are also doing that, who inevitably will formulate with you in later-time associations. They can not *not*. And if they don't, you won't care. You won't care. Why would you care? You're going to God.

You cannot serve God and mammon, guys. This is real gentle talk, but you can't serve man and God. You will love one and hate the other. That's a statement of fact. And each moment, you're doing one or the other, aren't you? I am saying take this holy mind of yours, dedicate it to this *Course*, dedicate it to this association, and the miracle will happen. It must happen because the miracle is all around you and you are the obstruction to it.

Now, I know we're deep. Some of you guys in your later runs will have what we used to call milk runs in the Second World War, where you will appear with a *Course* and boom! You appear in a segment of time. You open the *Course* and you say, "Nothing here is real. I'm come from God to take you home with me. This was never real to begin with. There is no sickness, pain or death, and we're all going home." And you all immediately jump up and say, "Heeeyyy!" And you're gone. That's you a little later on in time. This is you in kind of deep poop yet, isn't it? I mean, you're inherently suspicious of this message. Why? You've got it all sorted out. Jesus says, you don't have a decent frame of reference. You don't have enough Light in your thought-form associations. That's what we're giving you. Why? What will that do? Give you a later-time association. A greater Great Ray, isn't it?

Let's do the twelve tribes. Here come the Great Rays. There are twelve of them. They're going down. They're all chaotic down in here. But as they come into harmony, each one of the Rays contains the whole reference. Then you begin to harmonize with your other Ray associations, don't you? You sing songs. You write poetry. You do music. You love each other. You begin to create with your mind. That's what God is: your mind creating. And you will never be happy until you express yourself totally because creating *is* self-expressing. Creating is nothing but God expressing Himself. And you are not the result of that; you are the extension of that. You are God creating. If you try to create your own formulations, they'll always be limited. You may derive satisfaction from them, you may be happy with them, but they're going to crumble, and they're going to turn to death, and you're going to die because they are products of your own mind.

No more! We're giving you a new bright association. Well, where is the lump when it becomes a wave? Where is the particle when it becomes a wave? Nowhere. The particle is gone because it was a conflict in your own mind that established the distance between lumps. And they're not real. Do you see it? They are not real. And you can look at that lump that you've established right there and if you won't exchange with it and hold it lumpy, it will literally dissolve. Jesus calls this flowing across. You begin to have the experience of one-eyedness if you won't look with split brain, which is what the eyes do. The potential is pulled out of this brain, magnified by this, and you see a dualistic association of yourself, which literally cancels you out. None of you is real! You emerge with what we call the *ajna*, or the one-eyedness, the depiction of the center eye — if your eye offends you, pluck it out. Don't worry about the splinter in your brother's eye. Look at the beam in your eye. You will begin to bring together the extension of your whole mind and you'll see a better reflection of yourself coming back to yourself. That's all it is.

Once you begin to experience it, you begin to love the people that are around you because you won't hold them in the intolerance of your own mind. That's a miracle. That's what we're doing. If you want to do that, come and do it. We're doing it. That's what's happening here now. This is *A Course In Miracles*. It's not explainable. Be glad. It's an experience! It's a maturation. Do you see? And it's happening to you.

You say, "Do I have to use up the other possibilities?" Yes. Are you ashamed that somehow you can't solve this problem? Don't be. Be happy that you can't. All of your efforts of self-identity have been based on the fact of the conflict. I'll give you the sentence from the *Course*: Your reality is your complete dependence on God. Nothing else is real. And you consider that to be a weakness. You only go to God as a last resort. I'm teaching you only always go to God as a first resort and have no other resort and you can't fail.

There's a lot of changes going on in here now. There's no demand on this except your own personal mind. This is between you and God. It doesn't have to do with this. We're not cloistering you this time, are we? You may have a feeling you want to go off and you want to meditate and all that. And that's okay. But this is not an escape. This is an integration. It's a little different way to do this. We're asking you each moment to come into this center so that you can see the miracle that's going on around you.

We'll see where some of you are. I'll lead you through some experiences tomorrow. There's too much chaos in here. See, this is the pressure of the release of you. I'll show you. If you will let that go. Just play just a little soft music. I'll do about a ten-minute meditation. Not that first song, though. Anything after that. Sometimes we use a little music because if you'll let go, you'll begin to have a nice experience. What's occurring here that's hard for you to see is that you are beginning to manifest a lot of electromagnetic energy, what you call Holy Spirit. And it begins to emanate from you. And some of you may get fearful of it. See, it's real thick. It's sitting right in here.

Try to look at it this way. You are not a body. You are not a body! And your minds will blend together. Just be quiet for a moment. That's it. Here it is. It's way up here. If you begin to have this experience, that will verify the miracle or the holy instant, and you'll say, "I want to do that." Remember that until you have it, you don't know what it is. The *Course* is an experience. It doesn't have anything to do with the definition. That's better. That's better!

What do you do? Sit with your mind and keep examining it? You're examining nothing. Nothing! You release that. You are not accustomed to this kind of meditation; my meditation is very demanding. It is very active. I won't let you fall into your *Om.* I don't want that. I'm offering you a lot more energy than that. I'm offering you a release from your conflictual, perceptual association. It's what we call integration of spirit rather than transcendental association, which is about in here. That's better. But you'd want to try to be happy about it!

You guys ought to remember me. Don't you remember me? We've been together for ten thousand years, for crying out loud. You keep saying, "Where? Where? Where?" all the time. Some of you, I have an immediate frame of reference. A lot of you guys were killed in the Second World War. And usually your quick comebacks will reassociate in seven to ten years. See, that's between 1948, '55, and up to '60. A lot of you are right in there. Some of you are what they call religious fullbacks that are back a little further in time. But these are nothing but memories. This is really a very small group. All of the schism occupies a real small space in time. I'm going to take you home. You enter into this dream. I'll take you home. How could I fail? There's no such thing as failure. Do you have to believe me? No, you don't have to believe me. But hang around a little bit. I'll sort you out. You won't be able to stand it. The teaching is to get you to D.O.R. — it's called Discharge On Request. If you decide you want to hear this, what you will do to me — I'm teaching at the highest level I can teach you — you'll say to me, "I have no alternative but this." Then it becomes very simple.

Can you hear me at all? You say there's an alternative to what I'm doing and you're a liar. There's no alternative to this, and this is what you've been avoiding. It doesn't make any difference what it is. You keep saying, "There's another way that I can do this." Wrong. The only way you can do it is through the *Course In Miracles.* Period. The *Course In Miracles* is a required course of the transformation of your mind. It has nothing to do with the manner. Every time you choose another manner, you are denying what's happening. Period! Now, obviously if you don't want to hear that, you'll just go away. But it still remains the truth. This world is not real and you are waking up from a dream. Period.

And those of you who ask me not to let you off the hook, I won't let you off the hook. Can you hear what I'm saying at all? That I'm here at your instruction? Some of you guys, in your high associations, will say, "Go back and give me another try." Don't you understand? You are real deep in your own minds. But it's impossible we're not together out of time. Come on. You give me all sorts of reasons for saying this. I don't have any reason for telling you this. None. That's tough. Why? This is already over and we're gone. If there's any reason, it's in your mind and it only lasted a second. Got it? And you're gone. And you say, "But I'm still here." And I'll say, "No, you're not."

Here we go. "...of romance could be so cool..." That's better. Gently now. Breathe through your nose, please. Never breathe through your mouth again. Never. Some of you will begin to undergo experiences. Boy, is this thick. God came down from Heaven to tell you to come on home. This is the most beautiful thing that could ever happen to you. There is nothing more beautiful or sacred than when an ancient animosity is turned to love. Nothing! In the whole universe. And that'll happen to you if you'll let it happen.

I don't know how much I should open this up. What do you say? Got a lot of resistance here. You guys are doing all sorts of studying. I don't want to scare you. I'll heal you, though. How will that be? You had a little problem. I'll make you healed. Is that okay? You don't have that anymore, teacher. Feel that? Oh, did you really? Yes! I do that. That's easy to do. The healing is real simple. Your believing that you're healing is a little more difficult. Nothing's easier than healing. And you'll say, "Well, heal me again. I didn't get it that time." You got it perfectly. Good! You got it! That's it! We'll notch it up for him. Gently. Afraid to have that experience? That isn't going to hurt you. What do you say, old man? Phew, I don't know if you could feel that. I know you guys. I didn't know you were going to do it this trip. In fact, I didn't even know you were here. Some of you guys can hear this. I know you guys, all out of time. I could not *not* know you. This is a project.

I'll get you to the Borderland here. You better start to see a little bit. You haven't seen. You're blind, deaf and dumb. You're just, just beginning to peek. It's like little kids coming out from under the covers. The whole world, the whole universe is waiting for you, and you're going, "Hm hm hmmm," like that. Come on out. It's like hatching out. Think of it as hatching out. You've been incubated and you're ready to hatch out of this place. That's all it is. It is that simple. I don't know about you. A little suspicious there? "Something's happening to me." That's better!

We've got some Sauls here. Know what a Saul is? Saul becomes Paul in just a second. He just goes "Whoppo!" (Acts 9) Can you hear that? The higher the resistance, if I can get it into focus, the more rapid will be the conversion. Can you hear that? Oh, yeah. The more intense the denial, the closer you are to the truth. A total negative becomes totally positive instantly. It's the mish-mosh in between that's tough. I want you to confront it. There's no question about that. That's what I'm doing. But you keep hedging off of it because you don't want to take one look at it because you'll fall off your horse and a voice will speak to you. Next thing you know, you'll be off, teaching this. Saul to Paul.

That's a nice association. I can tell the guys that have been with me. Thank you, Father. Wish I could teach you a little gratitude, you would get this real quick. Boy, if I were where you were, I'd start to get so happy, I couldn't stand it. You are right on the edge of it. But it involves being grateful. You say, "Holy cripe! I'm getting out of here." Never mind how. You don't have to go telling anybody. Just be glad. God doesn't need your praise, but you sure as hell need to praise Him. This is the communicative link. It's a prayer. "I can't. You can." That's what this is. I reduced it again in perception for just a moment because you're starting to link. I can feel you linking here. That's nice. My job's done then, isn't it? I'm going to go home. I've got some time coming.

I'll show you how that happened. The original savior for this section fell off the wagon; he fell off the truth wagon. I'm an insert. You be glad because, boy, we really went down to get this. If this can get it, you can get it. It was an Eastern tradition. It wasn't even connected to this. This wasn't due for another twenty-four hundred years. You know him, too. He's right here. He's in this room. But see, you guys think I'm talking about personalities and I'm not. I am talking about energy associations. You see? Wholeness, whole reflections of light. There's always a designated association. That's inevitable. It's got nothing to do with good or bad, nothing to do with perception at all. It has to do with brightness of mind or extension of your mind.

So we threw in another one. He's very close to you. This is your way out. Look at your choice, look what you've been doing, and say, "No, instead I'll be *A Course In Miracles.*" And start being one. And you will be out. But don't interpret it because you're dead wrong because you're dead wrong about everything. And be glad. And then you're out. See? It's that simple. If you don't have to be right about anything, it's easy. If you have to defend yourself in any regard, it's tough. I'm teaching surrender but you just don't like the unqualifying nature of it. Somewhere you're saying, "No." So you will go through another death experience and then you will be here, doing this. And finally you'll just give up and come home. That's a nice thing to do. I promise you, you won't die. And the reason I know that is so is because there isn't any such thing as death. You have no choice in that matter. You can not *not* be whole and you. It's impossible. The condition of reality, if you want to call it that, is knowing what you are. And you know perfectly well what you are. And if you will stop trying to give yourself an identification, you will have no problem with this.

I'll take care of that for you, too. Breathe through your nose. Some of you guys are planning on termination. You actually construct your own heart attacks. It's hard to teach, isn't it? That's better. Stay in attention. If you're going to go to Light, just go to it.

All About
A *Course In Miracles*

To many of you now in this accelerated program of awakening, the continuing observation that not a single human being on earth really knows what it is, where it is, where it came from, or where it is going and nothing at all about itself in relationship to the universe that is apparently all around it, is becoming more and more intolerable.

As a transformative imperative, *A Course in Miracles* will perfectly assist and accelerate the necessary confrontation of your objective self-identify and the whole subjective universe that surrounds you, so that you may undergo your inevitable experience of resurrection and enlightenment.

What you are afraid of, and deny through your own possessive fear, is your own illumination; you're returning to God-mind or the memory of your transverse from temporal being to the reality of eternal life. So, it is your transition from death to life, from your old meaningless self-existence that is, in reality, long over and gone. It is a teaching of initiation or the determination of an individual mind to come to its own whole Universal Self.

It is the rite of your passage from time to eternity, from the apparent occurrence of separation to the remembrance that you are perfect as God created you. It is accomplished through a bright reassociation of your individual perceptual self-identity. It is an awakening. This unearthly catechism is directing you to the confrontation of the necessity of parting the veil. Every obstacle that peace must flow across is surmounted in the exact same way. The fear that raised it yields to the love beyond, and so the fear is gone.

FOR MORE INFORMATION VISIT: WWW.THEMASTERTEACHER.TV

DISCOURSES WITH
THE MASTER TEACHER OF A *COURSE IN MIRACLES*:
OTHER BOOKS IN PRINT

———◆◆◆———

These are anthologies of transcripts of profoundly transformative talks given through the revelatory mind of the Master Teacher of A *Course In Miracles*. They are ideas about the means and method of the recognition of the transformation of our minds and bodies, as we freely escape together far beyond the boundless Universe that is all about us.

Master Teacher's discourses always ignite intensely emotional responses in participants as they begin to undergo their individual mental reassociation and transfiguration. You may have highly charged enthusiastic responses to this wholly dedicated, totally simple, lovingly communicated message of truth. Indeed, this outpouring of freedom-to-create that occurs through the release of your former necessity to retain self-inflicted loneliness, pain, aging and death, is the bright contagion of whole mind.

These talks will act as a catalyst for you, the reader, in your own self identity of space/time, to undergo the experience of enlightenment necessary to fulfill your inevitable purpose for living: to remember you are whole and perfect as God created you.

The following books are currently in print:

- ILLUMINATION: *Discourses with Master Teacher*
- HOW SIMPLE THE SOLUTION: *Discourses with Master Teacher*
- THE PARADOX OF ETERNAL LIFE: *Discourses with Master Teacher*
- TIMELESS VOICE OF RESURRECTED MIND: *Bible Talks*
- GETHSEMANE TO GALILEE: *Bible Talks*

FOR MORE INFORMATION VISIT: WWW.THEMASTERTEACHER.TV

www.ingramcontent.com/pod-product-compliance
Lightning Source LLC
Chambersburg PA
CBHW072032090426
42733CB00032B/1228